Stories of Success:

The Young Adventurer
And
The Young Miner
(Illustrated)

Stories of Success:

The Young Adventurer
And The Young Miner
(Illustrated)

Horatio Alger, Jr.

Sumner Books
Hermosa Beach, CA

TABLE OF CONTENTS

BOOK I: THE YOUNG ADVENTURER

BOOK II: THE YOUNG MINER

A NOTE FROM THE PUBLISHER

Once crowned "America's most influential writer," Horatio Alger is hardly known today. Those who are familiar with him think "rags to riches," and that's about it. Most young people have never heard of him.

What an opportunity!

More than a hundred years before our contemporary self-help movement, Horatio Alger paved the way with his vivid illustrations of the keys to success and happiness. Today, Sumner Books is excited to introduce a new generation of Americans to some of the most inspirational stories ever written. Regardless of your age, you simply cannot read a Horatio Alger book without coming away with a good feeling.

Alger's books initially sold in the millions and then the tens of millions and finally the hundreds of millions. In fact, the Chicago Daily News once called Horatio Alger "America's best selling author of all time." Sumner Books is committed to bringing to life this best selling collection in the form of audiobooks read by professional actors and recorded with audio engineers in our studio. Our revised e-books, each with a detailed table of contents and colored illustrations, are professionally edited, including the occasional updating of phrases to make the books as easy to read today as they were when they were first published between 1865 and 1900.

Long after his death in 1899, the magazine Publishers Weekly wrote: "To call Horatio Alger Jr. America's most influential writer may seem like an overstatement ... but ... only Benjamin Franklin meant as much to the formation of the American popular mind."

Our goal is to bring back some of the influence that Alger exerted on millions of young people in America. Yes, it's retro; it's counterintuitive and totally contrary to the cynicism that has become a part of American culture. But we are proud to be leading a movement that is as positive and uplifting as the last pages of a Horatio Alger story.

Rick Newcombe
President
Sumner Books

Stories of Success:

The Young Adventurer
(Illustrated)

Stories of Success

"Lucky can often mean simply taking advantage of a situation at the right moment. It is possible to 'make' your luck by being always prepared."
Michael Korda

CHAPTER I

MARK NELSON'S FAMILY

"I wish I could pay off the mortgage on my farm," said Mark Nelson soberly, taking his seat on the left of the fireplace, in the room where his wife and family were assembled.

"Have you paid the interest, Mark?" asked his wife.

"Yes. I paid it this afternoon, and it has stripped me of money completely. I have less than five dollars in my pocket toward buying you and the children clothes for the winter."

"Never mind me," said his wife cheerfully. "I am pretty well provided for."

"Why, mother," said Sarah, the oldest daughter, a girl of fourteen, "you haven't had a new dress for a year."

"I have enough to last me till spring, at any rate," said the mother.

"You never buy anything for yourself."

"I don't go in rags, do I?" asked Mrs. Nelson, with a smile.

Mrs. Nelson had a happy disposition, which led her to accept uncomplainingly, and even cheerfully, the sacrifices which, as the wife of a farmer in poor circumstances, she was compelled to make.

"You are right, Sarah," said Mark Nelson. "Your mother never seems to think of herself. She might have been much better off if she had not married me."

The children did not understand this allusion. They had never been told that their mother had received an offer from Squire Hudson, the wealthiest man in the village, but had chosen instead to marry Mark Nelson, whose only property was a small farm, mortgaged for half its value. Her rejected admirer took the refusal hard, for, as much as it was possible for him, he loved the prettiest girl in the village, as Mary Dale was generally regarded. But Mary knew him to be cold and selfish and could not make up her mind to marry him. If she had done so, she would now be living in the finest house in the village, with the chance of spending the winter in New York or Boston, instead of drudging in a humble home, where there was indeed enough to eat but little money for even necessary purposes. She had never regretted her decision. Her husband, though poor, was generally respected and liked, while the squire, though his money procured him a certain degree of consideration, had no near or attached friends.

To Squire Hudson many in the village paid tribute, for he held mortgages on twenty farms and buildings, and he was strict in exacting prompt payment of the interest semi-annually. It was he to whom Mark Nelson's farm was mortgaged for two thousand dollars. The mortgage had originally been for fifteen hundred dollars, but five years before it had been increased to two thousand, which represented more than half the sum which it would have fetched, if put up for sale. The interest on this sum amounted to a hundred and twenty dollars a year, which Mark Nelson always found it hard to raise. Could he have retained it in his hands and devoted it to the use of his family, it would have helped them wonderfully, with Mrs. Nelson's good management. Tom, the oldest boy, now approaching his sixteenth birthday, looked up from a book he was reading. He was a bright-looking boy, with brown hair, a ruddy complexion and dark-blue eyes, who looked, and was, frank and manly.

"What is the amount of your interest?" he asked.

"Sixty dollars every half-year, Tom. That is what I paid to Squire Hudson this afternoon. It would have made us very comfortable, if I only could have kept it."

"It would have done you more good than the squire," said Sarah.

"He has more money than he knows what to do with," said her father, almost complainingly. "It seems hard that money should be so unevenly distributed."

"Money is not happiness," said Mrs. Nelson quietly.

"No, but it helps to buy happiness."

"I don't think Squire Hudson is as happy a man as you, Mark."

Mark Nelson's face softened as he surveyed his wife and children.

"I am happy at home," he said, "and I don't think the squire is."

"I am sure he isn't," said Tom. "Mrs. Hudson is sour and ill-tempered, and Sinclair -- the only child -- is a second edition of his mother. He is the most unpopular boy in the village."

"Still," said the farmer, not quite convinced, "money is an important element of happiness, and a farmer stands a very poor chance of acquiring it. Tom, I advise you not to be a farmer."

"I don't mean to be if I can help it," said Tom. "I am ready for any opening that offers. I hope some day to pay off the mortgage on the farm and make you a free man, father."

"Thank you for your good intentions, Tom, but two thousand dollars is a large sum of money."

"I know it, father, but I was reading in a daily paper, not long ago, of a boy, as poor as myself, who was worth twenty-five thousand dollars by the time he was thirty. Why shouldn't this happen to me?"

"Don't build castles in the air, Tom," said his mother sensibly.

"At least, mother, I may hope for good luck. I have been wanting to talk to you both about my future prospects. I shall be sixteen next week, and it is time I did something."

"You are doing something -- working on the farm now, Tom."

"That don't count. Father advises me not to be a farmer, and I agree with him. I think I am capable of making my way in the world in some other way, where I can earn more money. There is Walter, who likes the country, to stay with you."

Walter, the third child, was now twelve years of age, with decided country tastes.

"I would like to be a farmer as well as anything," said Walter. "I like the fresh air. I shouldn't like to be cooped up in a store, or to live in the city. Let Tom go if he likes."

"I have no objection," said Mr. Nelson, "but I have neither money nor influence to help him. He will have to make his own way."

"I am not afraid to try," said Tom courageously. "From this day I will look out for a chance, if you and mother are willing."

"I shall not oppose your wishes, Tom," said Mrs. Nelson gravely, "though it will be a sad day for me when you leave your home."

"That isn't the way to look at it, mother," said Tom. "If gold pieces grew on currant bushes, it wouldn't be necessary for me to leave home to make a living."

"I wish they did," said Harry, a boy nine years of age.

"What would you do then, Harry?" asked his brother, smiling.

"I would buy a bicycle and a pair of skates."

"I heard of a boy once who found a penny in the field, right under a potato vine," said Walter.

"I don't believe it," said Harry.

"It's true, for I was the boy."

"Where did it come from?"

"Tom put it there to fool me."

"Won't you put one there to fool me, Tom?" asked Harry.

"You are too smart, Harry," said Tom, laughing. "My pennies are too few to try such experiments. I hope, by the time you are as old as Walter, to give you something better."

The conversation drifted to other topics, with which we are not concerned. Tom, however, did not forget it. He felt that an important question had that evening been decided for him. He had only thought of making a start for himself hitherto. Now he had broached the subject and received the permission of his father and mother. The world was all before him, wherever he chose. His available capital was small, it is true, amounting only to thirty-seven cents and a jack-knife, but he had, besides, a stout heart, a pair of strong hands, an honest face, and plenty of perseverance -- not bad equipment for a young adventurer.

CHAPTER II

TOM FINDS A WALLET

Since the time of which I am writing, over sixty years have passed, for it was in the year 1850 that Tom made up his mind to leave home and seek a fortune. The papers were full of the new gold discoveries in the new country which had recently been added to the great republic. Thousands were hurrying to the land of gold; men who had been unfortunate at home, or, though moderately well situated, were seized by the spirit of adventure. At considerable sacrifice many raised the means of reaching the new El Dorado, while others borrowed or appropriated the necessary sum. Some, able to do neither, set out on a venture, determined to get there in some way.

In the weekly paper, to which Mr. Nelson had for years been a subscriber, Tom had read a good deal about California. His youthful fancy had been wrought upon by the brilliant pictures of a land where a penniless man might, if favored by fortune, have financial security within twelve months, and he ardently wished that he, too, might have the chance of going there. It was a wish, but not an expectation. It would cost at least two hundred dollars to reach the Pacific coast, and there was no hope of getting a tenth of that sum.

An advertisement for sailing to California during the Gold Rush, 1850s.

"If I could only go to California," thought Tom, "I would make my way somehow; I would cheerfully work twelve hours a day. I don't see why a boy can't dig gold as well as a man. If somebody would lend me money enough to get there, I could afford to pay high interest."

There was one man in Wilton who might lend him the money if he would. That man was Squire Hudson. He always had money on hand in considerable quantities, and two hundred dollars would be nothing to him. Tom would not have dreamed of applying to him, however, but for a service which just at this time he was able to render the squire.

Tom had been in search of huckleberries -- for this was the season -- when, in a narrow country road, not much frequented, his attention was drawn to an object lying in the road. His heart pounded with excitement when he saw that it was a well-filled pocketbook. He was not long in securing it.

Opening the wallet, he found it was absolutely stuffed with bank bills, some of large denominations. There were, besides, several papers to which he paid little attention. They assured him, however, as he had already surmised, that the wallet was the property of Squire Hudson.

"I wonder how much money there is here," thought Tom, with natural curiosity.

He stepped into the woods to avoid notice and carefully counted the bills. There were two hundred-dollar bills, and three fifties, and so many of smaller denominations that Tom found the whole to amount to five hundred and sixty-seven dollars.

"Almost six hundred dollars!" exclaimed Tom, in excitement, for he had never seen so much money before. "How happy should I be if I had as much money! How rich the squire is! He ought to be a happy man."

Then the thought stole into our hero's mind that the wallet contained nearly three times as much as he would need to take him to California.

"If it were only mine!" he thought to himself.

Perhaps Tom ought to have been above temptation, but he was not. For one little instant he was tempted to take out two hundred dollar and then drop the wallet where he had picked it up. No one would probably find out where the missing money was. But Tom had been too well brought up to yield to this temptation. Not even the thought that he might, perhaps within a year, return the money with interest, prevailed upon him.

"It wouldn't be honest," he decided, "and if I began in that way I could not expect that God would prosper me. If that is the only way by which I can go to California, I must make up my mind to stay at home."

So the question was settled in Tom's mind. The money must be returned to the owner.

His pail was nearly full of huckleberries, but he postponed going home, for he felt that Squire Hudson would be feeling anxious about his loss, and he thought it his duty to go and return the money first of all. Accordingly he made his way directly to the imposing residence of the rich man.

Passing up the walk which led to the front door, Tom rang the bell. This was answered by a cross-looking servant. She glanced at the pail of berries and said quickly, "We don't want any berries, and if we did you ought to go round to the side door."

"I haven't asked you to buy any berries, have I?" said Tom, rather provoked by the rudeness of the girl, when he had come to do the squire a favor.

"No, but that's what you're after. We have bought all we want."

"I tell you I didn't come here to sell berries," said Tom independently. "I picked these for use at home."

"Then what do you come here for, anyway, takin' up my time wid comin' to the door, when I'm busy gettin' supper?"

"I want to see Squire Hudson."

"I don't know if he's at home."

"Then you'd better find out and not keep me waiting."

"I never seen such impudence," cried the girl.

"I mean what I say," continued Tom stoutly. "I want to see the squire on important business."

"Much business you have wid him!" said the girl scornfully.

Tom, by this time, was out of patience.

"Go and tell your master that I wish to see him," he said firmly.

"I've a great mind to slam the door in your face," returned Bridget angrily.

"I wouldn't advise you to," said Tom calmly.

A stop was put to the contention by an irritable voice.

"What's all this, hey? Who's at the door, Bridget?"

"A boy wid berries, sir."

"Tell him I don't want any."

"I have told him, and he won't go."

—
11

"Won't go, hey?" and Squire Hudson came out into the hall. "What's all this, I say? Won't go?"

"I wish to see you, sir," said Tom, undaunted. "I have told the girl that I didn't come here to sell berries, but she objects to my seeing you."

Squire Hudson was far from an amiable man, and this explanation made him angry with the servant. He turned upon her fiercely.

"What do you mean, you trollop," he demanded, "by refusing to let the boy see me? What do you mean by your insolence, I say?"

Bridget was overwhelmed, for the squire's temper was like a tornado.

"I thought he wanted to sell berries," she faltered.

"That isn't true," said Tom. "I told you expressly that I picked the berries for use at home and had none to sell."

"Go back to the kitchen, you trollop!" thundered the squire. "You deserve to go to jail for your outrageous conduct."
Bridget did not venture to answer a word, for it would only have raised a more violent storm, but instead she retreated crestfallen to her own realm and left our hero in possession of the field. She contented herself with muttering under her breath what she did not dare to speak aloud.

"You are Tom Nelson, are you not?" asked the squire, adjusting his spectacles and looking more carefully at the boy.

"Yes, sir."

"Have you any message from your father?"

"No, sir."

"Then why did you come here to take up my time?" demanded the squire, frowning.

"I came to do you a service, Squire Hudson."

"You came—to—do—me—a—service?" repeated the squire slowly.

"Yes, sir."

"You may as well come in," said the rich man, leading into the sitting room.

Tom followed him into a handsomely furnished room, and the two sat down opposite each other.

CHAPTER III

TOM ASKS FOR A LOAN

"I don't know what service you can do me," said Squire Hudson incredulously. His manner implied, "I am a rich man and you are a poor boy. How can you possibly serve me?"

"Have you lost anything lately?" inquired Tom, coming at once to business.

I suppose most men, when asked such a question, would first think of their wallets. It was so with Squire Hudson. He hastily thrust his hand into his pocket and found a large hole, through which, doubtless, the wallet had slipped.

"I have lost my wallet," he said anxiously. "Have you found it?"

In reply Tom produced the missing article. The squire took it hurriedly, and, at once opening it, counted the money. It was all there, and he heaved a sigh of relief, for he was a man who cared for money more than most people.

"Where did you find it?" he asked.

Tom answered the question.

"It is very fortunate you came along before anyone else saw it. I rode that way on horseback this morning. I told Mrs. Hudson that my pocket needed repairing, but she put it off, according to her usual custom. If it had not been found, I would have kept her on short allowance for a year to come."

Tom felt rather embarrassed, for, of course, it would not do to join in with the squire in his complaints about his wife. Suddenly Squire Hudson asked, eying him keenly, "Do you know how much money there is in this wallet?"

"Yes, sir."

"Then you counted it?"

"Yes, sir."

"Why did you do it?"

"I wanted to know how much there was, so that no one might blame me if any were missing."

"Didn't you want to take any?" asked the squire bluntly.

"Yes," answered Tom promptly.

"Why didn't you? For fear you would be found out?"

"That may have had something to do with it, but it was principally because it would have been stealing and stealing is wrong."

"What would you have done with the money if you had taken it?"

"Started for California next week," answered Tom directly.

"Eh?" cried the squire, rather astonished. "Why do you want to go to California -- a boy like you?"

"To dig gold. I suppose a boy can dig gold as well as a man. There doesn't seem to be much chance for me here. There's nothing to do but to work on the farm, and father and Walter can do all there is to be done there."

"How is your father getting along?" asked the rich man, with an interest which rather surprised Tom.

"Poorly," said Tom. "He makes both ends meet, but we all have to do without a great many things that we need."

The squire looked thoughtful. He took half a dollar from his wallet and tendered it to Tom.

"You've done me a service," he said. "Take that."

Tom drew back.

"I would rather not take money for being honest," he said.

"That's all nonsense," said Squire Hudson sharply.

"That's the way I feel about it," said Tom stoutly.

"Then you're a fool."

"I hope not, sir."

"This would have been quite a large loss to me. I am perfectly willing to give you this money."

Then Tom gathered courage and said boldly, "You can do me a great favor, Squire Hudson, if you choose."

"What is it?"

"Lend me enough money to go to California," said Tom nervously.

"Good gracious! Is the boy crazy?" cried the astonished squire.

"No, sir, I am not crazy. I'll tell you what my plans are. I shall go to work directly when I get there and shall devote the first money I make to paying you. Of course, I shall expect to pay high interest. I am willing to pay you three hundred dollars for two; unless I am sick, I think I can do it inside of twelve months."

"How much money do you suppose you will need for this wild goose expedition?"

"About two hundred dollars, sir, and, as I just said, I will give you my note for three."

"A boy's note is worth nothing."

"Perhaps it isn't in law, but I wouldn't rest till it was paid back."

"What security have you to offer?"

"None, sir, except my word."

"Do you know what I would be if I lent you this money?"

"You would be very kind."

"Pish! I should be a fool."

"I don't think you'd lose anything by it, sir, but, of course, I can't blame you for refusing," and Tom rose to go.

"Sit down again," said the squire. "I want to talk to you about this matter. How long have you been thinking of California?"

"Only two or three days, sir."

"What made you think of it?"

"I wanted to help father."

"Who has told you about California?"

"I have read about it in the papers."

"Have you spoken to your father about going there?"

"I have spoken to him about leaving home and seeking my fortune, but I have not mentioned going to California because I thought it impossible to raise the necessary money."

"Of course. That's sensible, at least."

**An 1849 California Gold Rush flier advertising
steamship transportation**

Squire Hudson rose and walked thoughtfully about the room, occasionally casting a keen glance at Tom, who remained sitting, with his pail of huckleberries in his cap.

After a while the squire spoke again.

"Your father might let you have the money," he suggested.

"My father has no money to spare," said Tom quickly.

"Couldn't he raise some?"

"I don't know how."

"Then I'll tell you. I hold a mortgage for two thousand dollars on his farm. I suppose you know that?"

"Yes, sir."

"I might be willing to increase the mortgage to twenty-two hundred, and he could lend you the extra two hundred."

This was a new idea to Tom, and he took a little time to think it over.

"I don't like to ask father to do that," he said. "He finds it very hard now to pay the interest on the mortgage."

"I thought you intended to pay the money in a year," said the squire sharply.

"So I do," said Tom, and he began to think more favorably of the plan.

"In that case your father wouldn't suffer."

"You are right, sir. If father would only consent to do so, I would be happy. But I might die."

"Your father would have to take that risk. You can't expect me to."

This seemed fair enough, and, in fact, the danger didn't seem very great to Tom. He was about sixteen, and to a boy of sixteen death seems very far off, provided he is strong and vigorous, as Tom was. He rapidly decided that the squire's offer was not to be refused without careful consideration. It opened to him a career which looked bright and promising. Once in California, what could he not do? Tom was hopeful and sanguine and did not allow himself to think of failure.

"I understand that you are willing to advance the money, Squire Hudson?" he said, determined to know just what to depend upon.

"I will advance two hundred dollars, on the condition that your father will secure me with an increased mortgage. It is no particular object to me, for I can readily invest the money in some other way."

"I will speak to father about it, Squire Hudson, and meanwhile I am thankful to you for making the offer."

"Very well. Let me know as soon as possible," said the squire carelessly.

As Tom went out, the rich man soliloquized: "I have no faith in the boy's scheme, and I don't believe half the stories they tell about the California mines, but it will give me an extra hold on Nelson and hasten the day when the farm will come into my hands. When Mary Nelson refused my hand I resolved some day to have my revenge. I have waited long, but it will come at last. When she and her children are paupers, she may regret the slight she put upon me."

CHAPTER IV

TOM ASKS FOR A

LEAVE OF ABSENCE

Tom walked home slowly, but the distance seemed short, for he was absorbed in thought. In a way very unexpected he seemed to be likely to realize what he had regarded as a very pleasant, but impossible, dream. Would his father consent to the squire's proposal, and, if so, ought Tom to consent to expose him to the risk of losing so considerable a sum of money? If he had been older and more cautious he would probably have decided in the negative; but Tom was hopeful and sanguine, and the stories he had heard of California had dazzled him. There was, of course, an element of uncertainty in his calculations, but the fact that there seemed to be no prospect before him in his native village had an important influence in shaping his decision.

To ask his father the momentous question, however, was not easy, and he delayed doing it, hoping for a favorable opportunity of introducing the subject. His thoughtful manner excited attention and secured him the opportunity he sought.

"You seem deep in thought, Tom," said his mother.

"Yes, mother, I have a good deal to think about."

"Anybody would think Tom was overwhelmed with business," said Walter, next to Tom in age, with good-humored banter.

"I am," said Tom gravely.

"Won't you take me in partnership, then?" asked Walter.

Tom smiled.

"I don't think I could do that," he answered. "Not to keep you waiting, Squire Hudson has made me a business proposal this afternoon."

All were surprised and looked to Tom for an explanation.

"He offers to advance me two hundred dollars for a year, to help me out to California."

"Squire Hudson makes this offer to a boy of your age?" said his father slowly.

"Yes, or rather he makes the offer to you."

"To me?"

"Perhaps you will think me selfish for even mentioning it," said Tom rapidly, in a hurry to explain fully now that the ice was broken. "He will advance the money, on the condition that you increase the mortgage on the farm to twenty-two hundred dollars."

Mr. Nelson looked blank.

"Do you know, Tom," he said, "how hard I find it now to pay the interest on the mortgage, and how hopeless I am of ever paying it off?"

"I know all that, father, but I want to help you. If I keep my health and have a chance, I think I can help you. There's no chance for me here, and there is a chance in California. You remember what we have read in the Weekly Messenger about the gold fields and what large sums have been realized by miners."

"They are men, and you are a boy."

"That's true," said Tom, "but," he added, with natural pride, "I am pretty strong for a boy. I am willing to work, and I don't see why I can't dig gold as well as a man. I may not make as much, but if I only do half as well as some that we have read about, I can do a good deal for you."

"How far off is California?" asked Mrs. Nelson.

"Over three thousand miles, across the continent," answered her husband. "By sea it is a good deal more."

"Why, it is as far off as Europe," said Walter, who was fresh from his lesson in geography.

"It is farther than some parts of Europe -- England, for example," said his father.

"And a wild, unsettled region," said Mrs. Nelson soberly.

This 1852 map depicts the height of the Gold Rush in the United States.

"I don't think so much of that," said Mark Nelson. "Tom is no baby. He is a boy of good sense, not heedless, like some of his age, and I should feel considerable confidence in his getting along well."

"What, Mark, are you in favor of his going so far -- a boy who has never been away from home in his life?"

"I don't know what to say. I have not had time to consider the matter, as it has come upon me suddenly. I have a good deal of confidence in Tom, but there is one difficulty in my mind."

"What is that, father?" asked Tom anxiously.

"The expense of getting to California, and the method of raising the money; I don't like to increase the mortgage."

"I suppose you are right, father," said Tom slowly. "I know it is more than I have any right to ask. I wouldn't even have mentioned it if I hadn't hoped to help you to pay it back."

"That is understood, Tom," said his father kindly. "I know you mean what you say, and that you would redeem your promise if fortune, or rather Providence, permitted. It is a serious matter, however, and not to be decided in a hurry. We will speak of it again."

Nothing more was said about Tom's plan till after the children had gone to bed. Then, as Mark Nelson and his wife sat before the fire in the open fireplace, the subject was taken up anew.

"Mary," said Mark, "I am beginning to think favorably of Tom's proposal."

"How can you say so, Mark?" interrupted his wife. "It seems like madness to send a young boy so far away."

"Tom can't be called a young boy; he is now sixteen."

"But he has never been away from home."

"He must go some time."

"If it were only to Boston or New York ... but to go more than three thousand miles away!" and the mother shuddered.

"There are dangers as great in Boston or New York as in California, Mary, to a boy of Tom's age. He can't always be surrounded by home influences."

"I wish we could find employment for him in town," said Mrs. Nelson uneasily.

"That is a mother's thought, and it would be pleasant for all of us, but I doubt if it would be better for Tom."

"Why not?"

"A boy who is thrown upon his own guardianship and his own resources develops manliness and self-reliance sooner than at home. But we need not take that into consideration; there is nothing to do here, nor is there likely to be. He must go away from home to find employment. To obtain a job in Boston or New York requires influence and friends in those places, and we can hope for neither. In California he will become his own employer. The gold-mines are open to all, and he may earn in a year as much as he could in five years in the East."

"Do you favor his going, then, Mark?"

"Not against your will, Mary. Indeed, I should not feel justified in increasing the mortgage upon our little property against your wish. That concerns us all."

"I don't think so much of that. I am so afraid Tom would get sick in California. What would become of the poor boy in that case?"

"That is a mother's thought. I think Tom would find friends who would not let him suffer. He is a manly, attractive boy, though he is ours, and I think he is well calculated to make his way."

"That he is," said his mother proudly. "No one can help liking Tom."

"Then you see he is likely to find friends. Were he such a boy as Sinclair Hudson, I should feel afraid that he would fare badly, if he stood in need of help from others. Sinclair is certainly a very disagreeable boy."

"Yes, he is, and he isn't half as smart as Tom."

"A mother's vanity," said Mark Nelson, smiling. "However, you are right there. I should consider it a misfortune to have such a cross-grained, selfish son as Sinclair. Squire Hudson, with all his wealth, is not fortunate in his only child. There is considerable resemblance between father and son. I often wish that someone other than the squire held the mortgage on our farm."

"You don't think he would take advantage of you?"

"I don't think he would be very lenient on me if I failed to pay interest promptly. He has a grudge against me, you know."

"That is nonsense," said Mrs. Nelson, blushing, for she understood the allusion.

"I am glad he doesn't ask me to give him a mortgage on you, Mary."

"He has forgotten all that," said Mrs. Nelson. "I am no longer young and pretty."

"I think you more attractive than ever," said the husband.

"Because you are foolish," said his wife, but she was well pleased, nevertheless. Poor as her husband was, she had never dreamed of regretting her choice.

"Be it so, but about this affair of Tom -- what shall I say to him in the morning?"

Mrs. Nelson recovered her gravity instantly.

"Decide as you think right, Mark," she said. "If you judge that Tom had better go I will do my best to become reconciled to his absence and set about getting him ready."

"It is a great responsibility, Mary," said Mark slowly, "but I accept it. Let the boy go, if he wishes. He will leave our care, but we can trust him to the care of his heavenly Father, who will be as near to him in California as at home."

Thus Tom's future was decided. His father and mother retired to bed but not to sleep. They were parting already in imagination with their first-born, and the thought of that parting was sad indeed.

CHAPTER V

TOM RAISES THE MONEY

Tom got up early the next morning -- in fact, he was up first in the house -- and attended to his usual "chores." He was splitting wood when his father passed him on the way to the barn with the milk pail in his hand.

"You are up early, Tom," he said.

"Yes," answered our hero.

Tom could not help wondering whether his father had come to any decision about letting him go to California, but he did not like to ask. In due time he would learn, of course. He felt that he should like to have it decided one way or the other. While his plans were in doubt he felt unsettled and nervous.

At an early hour the family gathered about the breakfast table. Tom noticed that his father and mother looked grave and spoke in a subdued tone, as if they had something on their minds, but he did not know what to infer from this, except that they had his prospects still in consideration.

When breakfast was over, Mark Nelson pushed back his chair and said, "How soon can you get Tom ready to start, Mary?"

"Am I going, father?" asked Tom, his heart giving an eager bound.

"Is Tom really going?" asked the younger children, with scarcely less eagerness.

"If Squire Hudson doesn't go back on his promise. Tom, you can go with me to the squire's."

"How soon?"

"In about an hour. He doesn't eat breakfast as early as we do. I think he will be ready to receive us in about an hour."

"Thank you, father," said Tom. "You are doing a great deal for me."

"I can't do much for you, my boy. I can probably get you to California, and then you will be thrown upon your own exertions."

"I mean to work very hard. I think I shall succeed."

"I hope so at least, Tom. When the time comes for the other boys to start working, I shall be glad to have your help in doing it."

Tom was pleased to hear this, though it placed upon his shoulders a new and heavy responsibility. He was assuming the responsibility not only for his own future but for that of his brothers. But it made him feel more grown up, as if the period of his dependent boyhood were over, and he had become a young man all at once.

"I hope I sha'n't disappoint you, father," he said.

"If you do, I don't think it will be your fault, Tom," said his father kindly. "Fortune may be against you, but we must take that risk."

"I don't know what to think about it, Tom," said his mother, in a tone of doubt and mental disturbance. "I feel as if you were too young to go out in the wide world to seek your fortune."

"I am not so very young, mother. I am old enough to make my way."

"So your father says, and I have yielded to his judgment, but, Tom, I don't know how to let you go."

There were tears in Mrs. Nelson's eyes as she spoke. Tom was moved, and if he needed anything to strengthen him in the good resolutions he had formed, his mother's emotion supplied it.

"You sha'n't regret giving your consent, mother," he said manfully, and, rising from his seat, he went to his mother and kissed her.

"Mary," said Mr. Nelson, "you haven't answered my question. How long will it take to get Tom ready? If he is to go, he may as well start as soon as possible."

"Let me see," said Mrs. Nelson, "how many shirts have you got, Tom?"

"Five."

"Are they all in good order?"

"I believe one needs mending."

"I don't know whether that will be enough," said Mrs. Nelson doubtfully.

"Mary," said her husband, "don't provide too large a supply of clothing. Tom may find it a burden. Remember, in California, he will have to travel on foot and carry his own baggage."

"Then I think he is already pretty well provided. But some of his clothes may need mending. That won't take long, and I will attend to it at once."

"Perhaps Squire Hudson will go back on his word, after all," said Walter.

Tom's face was overcast. That would be a disappointment he could not easily bear.

"I shall soon know," he said.

An hour later Tom and his father set out for Squire Hudson's residence. Tom felt nervous; he could not well help it.

"Tom," said his father, "this is an important visit for you."

"Yes, sir," said Tom.

"You are feeling nervous, I see. Try to take it coolly and don't feel too low-spirited if things don't turn out as you hope."

"I will try to follow your advice, father, but I am not sure that I can."

"If you are disappointed, try to think it is for the best. A boy of your age had made all arrangements to visit Europe with a party of friends. The day before starting something happened which made it impossible for him to go. For weeks he had been looking forward with eager anticipation to his journey, and now it was indefinitely postponed."

"What a terrible disappointment!" said Tom.

"Yes, it seemed so, but mark the issue. The steamer was lost, and all on board were drowned. The disappointment saved his life."

"It might not always turn out so," objected Tom.

"No, that is true. Still, if we are willing to think that our disappointments are not always misfortunes, we shall go through life with more cheerfulness and content."

"Still, I hope I shall not be disappointed in this," said Tom.

"You are perhaps too young to be philosophical," said his father.

Mark Nelson had enjoyed only the usual advantages of education afforded by a common school, but he was a man of good natural capacity and more thoughtful than many in his vocation. From him Tom inherited good natural abilities and industrious habits. It would not be fair, however, to give all the credit to his father. Mrs. Nelson was a superior woman, and all her children were well endowed by nature.

As they turned into Squire Hudson's gravel path, the squire himself opened the front door.

"Were you coming to see me?" he asked.

"We would like to speak with you a few minutes, squire, if you can spare the time."

"Oh, yes, I have nothing pressing on hand," said the squire, with unusual affability. "Walk in, Mr. Nelson."

He led the way into the room where Tom had had his interview with him the day before.

"Your son did me a good turn yesterday," he said graciously. "He behaved in a very creditable manner."

"He told me that he found your wallet, Squire Hudson."

"Yes. It contained a large sum of money. Some boys would have kept it."

"None of my boys would," said Mark Nelson proudly.

"Of course not. They're too well brought up."

"Tom told me that you offered to advance money enough to get him to California," said Mr. Nelson, coming to business.

"On satisfactory security," added the squire cautiously.

"You proposed to increase the mortgage on my place?"

"Yes," said the squire. "I wouldn't have done it, though, Neighbor Nelson, but for the good turn the boy did me. I am not at all particular about increasing the amount of the mortgage, but, if by so doing I can promote Tom's views, I won't object."

"Thank you, sir," said Tom gratefully.

"It is a serious step for me to take," continued Mr. Nelson, "for I feel the encumbrance to be a heavy one already. In fact, it is with difficulty that I pay the interest. But the time has come when Tom should start in life, and in this village there seems to be no opening."

"None whatever," said the squire, in a tone of decision.

"What do you think of the prospects in California?" asked Mark Nelson. "You are a man of business and can judge better than I. Are the stories we hear of fortunes made in a short time to be relied upon?"

"As to that," said the squire deliberately, "I suppose we can't believe all we hear; we must make some allowances. But, after all, there's no doubt of the existence of gold in large quantities; I am sure of that."

"Then about the wisdom of sending out a boy like Tom, alone: do you think it best?"

"It depends altogether on the boy," responded the squire. "If he is honest, industrious, and energetic, he will make his way. You know your own boy better than I do."

"He is all you say, Squire Hudson. I have a great deal of confidence in Tom."

Tom looked at his father gratefully. Sometimes it does a boy good to learn that the older people have confidence in him.

"Then let him go," said the squire. "I stand ready to furnish the money. I think you said you needed two hundred dollars."

This question was put to Tom, and the boy answered in the affirmative.

"Very well," said the squire. "As soon as the necessary writings are made out, the money shall be ready."

"It's all settled!" thought Tom triumphantly.

At that moment Sinclair Hudson, the squire's only son, opened the door and looked into the room.

"Hello, Tom Nelson," said he rather rudely. "What brings you here?"

CHAPTER VI

TOM ARRIVES IN PITTSBURGH

"I came on business, Sinclair," answered Tom, smiling.

"Thomas is going to California, Sinclair," explained Squire Hudson.

Sinclair opened wide his eyes in amazement. "What for?" he asked.

"To dig gold and make my fortune," answered Tom complacently.

"Come out and tell me all about it."

"You can go, Thomas," said Squire Hudson graciously. "Your father and I will settle the business."

"Is it true that you are going to California?" asked Sinclair, when they were out in the front yard.

"Yes."

"How soon do you go?"

"I want to get away in a week."

"What has my father to do with it?" inquired Sinclair.

"He is going to lend me the money to get there."

"How much?"

"Two hundred dollars."

"Then he is a greater fool than I thought," said Sinclair, with characteristic politeness.

"Why do you say that?" demanded our hero, justly nettled.

"Because he'll never see the money again."

"Yes, he will. My father is responsible for it."

"Your father is a poor man."

"He is able to pay that, if I don't, but I hope he won't have to."

"Do you really expect to find gold?" asked Sinclair curiously.

"Certainly I do. Others have, and why shouldn't I? I am willing to work hard."

"Do you think you'll come home rich?"

"I hope so."

"I have a great mind to ask father to let me go with you," said Sinclair unexpectedly.

"You wouldn't like it. You haven't been brought up to work," said Tom, rather startled, and not much pleased with the proposal, for Sinclair Hudson was about the last boy he wished as a companion.

"Oh, I wouldn't go to work. I would go as a gentleman, to see the country. Wait a minute; I will run in and ask him."

So Sinclair ran into the house and made his request.

"That's a wild idea, Sinclair," said his father quickly.

"Why is it? I'm as old as Tom Nelson."

"He is going because it is necessary for him to earn his living."

"He will have a splendid time," grumbled the spoiled son.

"You shall travel all you want when you are older," said his father. "Now you must get an education."

"I want to travel now."

"I will take you to New York the next time I go."

"Give me five dollars besides."

The money was handed to him.

He went out and reported to Tom that he was going to travel all over the world when he was a little older and had decided not to go to California now.

"If you have money enough you can go with me," he added graciously.

"Thank you," said Tom politely, though the prospect of having Sinclair for a traveling companion did not exhilarate him much.

For a few days Mrs. Nelson was very busy getting Tom ready to go. It was well, perhaps, that so much needed to be done, for it kept her mind from the thought of the separation.

The question of which route to take, whether by steamer or across the plains, demanded consideration. It was finally decided that Tom should go overland. It was thought he might join some company at St. Joseph -- or St. Joe, as it was then, and is now, popularly called -- and pay his passage in services, thus saving a good share of the two hundred dollars. That was, of course, an important consideration.

"How shall I carry my money?" asked Tom.

"It will be best to take gold and carry it for safety in a belt around your waist," said his father. "You must be very prudent and careful, or you may be robbed. That would be a serious thing for you, as I could not forward you any more money."

29

"I will be very prudent, father," said Tom. "I know the value of money too well to risk losing it."

Well, the days of preparation were over at length, and Tom stood on the threshold, bidding goodbye to his parents and his brothers and sisters. He had not realized till now what it was to leave home on a long journey of indefinite duration. He wanted to be heroic, but in spite of himself his eyes moistened, and he came near breaking down.

"I don't know how to part with you, my dear child," said his mother.

Think that it is all for the best, mother," said Tom, choking. "Think of the time when I will come back with plenty of money."

"God bless you, Tom!" said his father. "Don't forget your good habits and principles when you are far away from us."

"I won't, father."

**Tom's family gathers at their humble farmhouse
to say goodbye to Tom.**

So Tom's long journey commenced.

Tom's plan was to go to St. Louis first. His father made some inquiries about the route and recommended going to Pittsburgh by train, then to take the boat on the Ohio River for Cincinnati. This seemed to Tom to afford a pleasant variety, and he gladly accepted the suggestion.

As they were approaching Pittsburgh, Tom occupied a whole seat on the left-hand side of the car. A brisk, plausible young man of twenty-five, passing through the aisle, observed the vacant seat and, pausing, inquired, "Is this seat engaged?"

"No, sir," answered Tom.

"Then, if you have no objection, I will occupy it."

"Certainly, sir."

The young man was nicely dressed. In his bosom sparkled a diamond pin, and he wore three or four rings on his fingers.

"He must be rich," thought Tom, who was of an observant turn.

"A pleasant day to travel," remarked the young man affably.

"Yes, it is," said Tom.

"Do you go farther than Pittsburgh?"

"Yes, I am going to California," answered Tom proudly.

"Is it possible? Are you alone?"

"Yes, sir."

"You are young to travel so far."

"I am sixteen -- that is, I shall be in two or three weeks."

"Still, you are young to take such a journey alone. Are you going to join friends there?"

"No, I am going to seek my fortune."

Once more the young man looked surprised and scanned Tom curiously.

"I presume you are from the city," he observed, with a smile which Tom would not have understood if he had noticed it. The truth is that Tom bore evident marks of being a country boy. I don't like to say that he looked "green," but he certainly lacked the air that distinguishes a town-bred boy. His companion evidently understood boy nature, for Tom was much flattered by the supposition that he was a city boy.

"No," he answered, almost as if apologizing for a discreditable fact. "I am from the country."

"You don't say so!" exclaimed the other, in apparent surprise. "I thought, from your appearance, that you were from the city. How do you go from Pittsburgh?"

"By river to Cincinnati."

"Do you really? I am glad to hear it; I am going there myself. We shall be fellow passengers. That will be pleasant."

Tom thought it would. His companion seemed very pleasant and social, and he had been feeling lonely, as was only natural.

"Yes, it will," he said.

"By the way, as we may be thrown together, more or less, we ought to know each other. My name is Milton Graham. My father is a rich merchant in New York. I am traveling partly on business for my father's firm and partly for pleasure."

"My name is Thomas Nelson; most people call me Tom," said our hero.

"Then I will call you Tom," said Graham. "I like the name. I have a favorite cousin named Tom. Poor boy!—he is an orphan. His father died two years ago, leaving him two hundred thousand dollars. My father is his guardian. He is about your age, only not quite so good-looking."

Tom blushed. He had not thought much of his own looks, but he was human, and no one is displeased at being considered good-looking. Mr. Graham spoke meditatively, as if he was not intending to pay a compliment, only mentioning a fact, and Tom did not feel called upon to thank him for this flattering remark.

"That is a great deal of money," he said.

"Yes, it is. All my relations are rich, that is, except one uncle, who probably is not worth over twenty thousand dollars."

Tom was impressed. A man who could talk of such a sum in such terms must certainly be very rich.

"Do you know, Mr. Graham," he inquired, "how soon the steamer will start after we reach Pittsburgh?"

"No, but I can find out after we reach there."

On arriving at Pittsburgh, inquiry was made, and it was ascertained that the steamer River Belle would leave at nine o'clock the following morning.

"We shall have to go to a hotel," said Graham.

"Is there any cheap hotel here?" asked Tom prudently.

"Yes, there is the Pittsburgh House. Suppose we both go there."

"All right."

Mr. Graham had only a small carpetbag, smaller than Tom's. They took them in their hands and walked for a short distance, till they reached a plain building, which, from the sign, Tom discovered to be the hotel which had been mentioned.

"Shall we room together? It will cost less," said Milton Graham carelessly.

"If you please," said Tom.

He was lonely and thought he would like company. Besides, it would be cheaper, and that was a weighty consideration.

—

CHAPTER VII

THE PITTSBURGH HOUSE

Tom and his companion entered the hotel. At the left was the clerk's desk. Milton Graham naturally took the lead. He took a pen from the clerk and entered his name with a flourish. Then he handed the pen to Tom, who followed his example, omitting the flourish, however.

"This young gentleman will room with me," said Graham.

"All right, sir," said the clerk. "Will you go up to your room now?"

"Yes."

The porter was summoned and handed the key of No. 16. He took the two carpetbags and led the way upstairs, for the Pittsburgh House had no elevator. Even in the best hotels at that time this modern convenience was not to be found.

The door of No. 16 was opened, revealing a plain room, about twelve feet square, provided, as Tom was glad to see, with two narrow beds.

"Have you got a quarter, Tom?" asked Graham.

Tom drew one from his pocket.

Graham took it and handed it to the porter, who expressed his thanks.

"It's always customary to tip the porter," he said carelessly, in answer to Tom's look of surprise.

"What for?"

"For bringing up the baggage."

"Twenty-five cents for bringing up two small carpetbags! That's pretty high. I'd have brought them up myself, if I had known," said Tom, dissatisfied, for he felt that this fee was hardly in accordance with his resolutions of economy.

"Oh, he expects it. It's his regular perquisite. When you've traveled more you'll understand."

"How much are we to pay for our accommodations?" asked Tom anxiously.

"About two dollars apiece, I reckon."

"That's more than I can afford," said Tom, alarmed.

"Perhaps it is less, as we room together."

"I hope so, for I can't afford to be extravagant."

"Do you call two dollars a day extravagant?" asked Graham, smiling.

"It is for me. My father is poor."

"Oh, it'll be all right. I'll fix it with the clerk. If you are ready, suppose we go down and have some supper."

To this Tom had no objection. He washed his hands and face and brushed his hair; then he declared himself ready.

Tom was hungry and did justice to the supper, which he found very good. As they left the table, and re-entered the office of the hotel, Milton Graham said, "I am going to make a call on some friends. Sorry to leave you, but we shall meet later in the evening."

"All right," said Tom.

On the whole he did not regret being alone. He began to doubt whether Graham would make a desirable traveling companion. Tom felt the need of economy, and he saw that his companion would make it difficult. If a fee must be paid, it was fair to divide it, but the porter's fee had come out of Tom's pocket.

"Didn't he have a quarter, I wonder?" thought our hero.

It was a small matter, but economy must begin in small matters, or it is not likely to be practiced at all.

He took the opportunity to go to the desk and ascertain the sum likely to be charged for his accommodations.

"How long do you stay?" asked the clerk pleasantly.

"Till tomorrow morning. I am going to sail in the River Belle."

"Then we shall charge you a dollar and a half."

This seemed large to Tom, but he made no objection.

"How much would it have been if I had roomed alone?" he asked.

"The same. We make no change in our terms on that account."

"Mr. Graham told me it would be cheaper to room together."

"He is your roommate, isn't he?"

"Yes, sir."

"He is mistaken, so far as our house is concerned. I suppose you have known him for some time."

"No, sir. I met him on the train yesterday afternoon for the first time."

"Then you don't know anything about him?"

"Oh, yes," answered Tom. "He is the son of a rich merchant in New York."

"Who told you that?"

34

"He did."

The clerk was a man of middle age. At home he had a son of Tom's age, and this led him to feel a friendly interest in our hero.

"I suppose you have never traveled much," he said.

"No, sir. This is my first journey."

"Are you going far?"

"To California."

"That is a long journey for a boy of your age," said the clerk, looking surprised.

"Yes, sir, but I can't find any work to do at home, and I am going to California to seek my fortune."

"I hope you will be successful," said the clerk, with hearty sympathy. "Will you let me give you a piece of advice?"

"I shall be very glad of it, sir," responded Tom. "I find I am quite inexperienced."

"Then don't trust strangers too readily. It is dangerous."

"Do you refer to Mr. Graham?" asked Tom, startled.

"Yes, I refer to him, or any other chance acquaintance."

"Don't you think he is all right?" asked our hero anxiously.

"I don't think he is the son of a rich merchant in New York."

"Then why should he tell me so?"

Tom was green, and I have no intention of concealing it.

"I can't tell what his designs may be. Did you tell him that you were going to California?"

"Yes, sir."

"Then he will, of course, conclude that you have money. Did you tell him where you keep it?"

"No, sir. I keep it in a belt around my waist."

"You are too ready to tell that, though with me the information is safe. You are to room together. What will be easier, then, for your companion to rob you during the night?"

"I'd better take a room alone," said Tom, now thoroughly alarmed.

"I should advise you to, in most cases, but at present it may be as well to let things remain as they are, as it will save an awkward explanation."

"But I don't want to be robbed."

"We have a safe in the office -- there it is -- in which we deposit articles of value entrusted to us by our guests. Then we become responsible for them. I advise you to leave your money with us overnight."

"I will," said Tom, relieved. "I shall have to go to my room to get it."

"Very well. If you have a watch, or any other valuable, it will be well to put those in our charge also."

"No, sir, I have nothing of consequence but the money."

The belt of money was deposited in the safe, and Tom felt relieved. He began to realize for the first time the need for prudence and caution. It had never occurred to him that a nice, gentlemanly-looking man like Milton Graham was likely to rob him of his scanty means. Even now he thought there must be some mistake. Still he felt that he had done the right thing in depositing the money with the clerk. The mere thought of losing it, and finding himself high and dry -- stranded, so to speak -- hundreds of miles from home, made him shudder. On the whole, Tom had learned a valuable, though unpleasant, lesson. The young are by nature trustful. They are disposed to put confidence in those whom they meet, even for the first time. Unhappily, in a world where there is so much evil as there is in ours, such confidence is not justified. There are too many who make it a business to prey on their fellows and select in preference the young and inexperienced.

It was only seven o'clock. Tom had a curiosity to see the city of Pittsburgh, with whose name he had been familiar. So, after parting with his treasure, he went out for a walk. He did not much care where he went, since all was new to him. He ascertained, on inquiry, that Smithfield Street was the principal business thoroughfare. He inquired his way thither and walked slowly through it, his attention fully occupied by what he saw.

CHAPTER VIII

GRAHAM IN HIS TRUE COLORS

Tom strayed into a street leading from the main thoroughfare. Presently he came to a brilliantly-lighted liquor saloon. As he paused in front of the door, a heavy hand was laid upon his shoulder, and, looking up, he met the glance of a well-dressed gentleman, rather portly, whose flushed face and uncertain gait indicated his condition. He leaned rather heavily upon Tom, apparently for support, for he seemed to have been drinking more than was good for him.

"My young friend," he said, "come in and take a drink."

"Thank you, sir, but I would rather not," said Tom, startled.

"It won't hurt you. It don't hurt me."

As he uttered these last words he came near falling. In his effort to save himself he clutched Tom by the arm and nearly pulled him over. Our hero was anxious to get away.

"Are you sure it don't hurt you?" he could not help saying.

"Do you think I'm drunk?" demanded the other.

"I think you've taken more than is good for you, sir," Tom answered bravely.

"I guess you're right," muttered the gentleman, trying to stand upright. "The drink's gone to my legs. That's strange. Does it ever go to your legs?"

"I never drink, sir."

"You're a most extraor'nary young man," hiccoughed Tom's new acquaintance.

"I must bid you good night, sir," said our hero, anxious to get away.

"Don't go. I can't get home alone."

"Where do you live, sir?"

"I live in the country."

"Are you staying at a hotel?"

"Yes -- Pittsburgh House. Know Pittsburgh House?"

"Yes, sir. I am staying there myself. Shall I lead you there? You'd better not drink any more."

"Jus' you say, my young frien'. You know best."

It was not a pleasant, or, indeed, an easy task to lead home the inebriate, for he leaned heavily on Tom, and, being a large man, it was as much as our hero could do to get him along. As they were walking along Tom caught sight of his roommate, Milton Graham, just turning into a saloon, in company with two other young men. They were laughing loudly and seemed in high spirits. Graham did not recognize Tom.

"I hope he won't come home drunk," thought our hero. "It seems to me it is fashionable to drink here."

Tom's experience of city life was very limited. It was not long before he learned that Pittsburgh was by no means exceptional in this respect.

He ushered his companion safely into the hotel, and then a servant took charge of him and led him to his room. Tom sat up a little while longer, reading a paper he found in the office, and then went to bed.

"I suppose Mr. Graham will come home late," he said to himself. "I must leave the door unlocked."

He soon went to sleep. How long he slept he did not know, but he suddenly awoke after an interval. Opening his eyes he became conscious that Graham had returned. He discovered something more. His roommate, partially undressed, and with his back turned to Tom, was engaged in searching our hero's pockets. This discovery set Tom broad awake at once. He was not frightened, but rather amused when he thought of Graham's disappointment. He did not think it best to speak but counterfeited sleep.

"I wonder where the boy keeps his money," he heard Graham mutter. "Perhaps it is in his coat pocket. No, there is nothing but a handkerchief. He's more careful than I gave him credit for. Perhaps it is under his pillow."

He laid down the clothes and approached the bed. Tom, with some effort, kept his eyes firmly closed.

Graham slid his hand lightly under the pillow but withdrew it with all exclamation of disappointment.

"He must have some money," he muttered. "Ah, I have it! It is in his valise."

He approached Tom's valise, but it was locked. He drew out a bunch of keys and tried one after the other, but it was in vain. Our hero feared he might resort to violent means of opening it, and he turned in bed. Graham wheeled round quickly.

—

38

Tom stretched and opened his eyes languidly.

"Is that you, Mr. Graham?" he asked.

"Yes," answered Graham nonchalantly, proceeding to undress himself. "Have you been abed long?"

"I don't know," answered Tom. "What time is it?"

"Haven't you got a watch?"

"No, I am not rich enough."

"It is one o'clock. I hadn't seen my friend for a long time and couldn't get away till late. By the way, have you got a key about you? I can't open my carpetbag."

Tom thought of suggesting the bunch of keys in Graham's pocket but decided not to.

"My key is in my pants' pocket."

"Suppose you get it," said Graham. "I don't like to feel in another person's pocket. There might be some money there."

This was very scrupulous for one who had already searched all Tom's pockets thoroughly.

Our hero got up, and got the key for his roommate.

"No, it won't fit," said the young man, after a brief trial. "It is too large."

Tom replaced the key in his pocket, confident that Graham would in the course of the night use it to open his valise. This, however, did not trouble him.

"He won't think it worth while to steal my shirts or stockings," he reflected, "and the handkerchiefs are not worth taking."

"It will be rather awkward if I can't find my keys," said Graham craftily. "I keep my money in my valise."

He thought his unsophisticated companion would reveal in turn where he kept his money, but Tom only said, "That is a good place," and, turning over, closed his eyes again.

During the night Tom's valise was opened, as he ascertained in a simple way. In the morning he found that the key was in the right hand-pocket instead of the left, in which he had placed it.

Upon Graham's last failure he began to suspect what Tom had done with his money.

"The boy isn't so green as I thought," he said to himself. "Curse his prudence! I must get the money somehow, for I am precious hard up."

He got up early, when Tom was yet asleep, and went down to the office.

"Good morning," he said to the clerk affably.

"Good morning, sir."

"My young friend and roommate left his money with you last night. Please deliver it to me."

"What is the number of your room?" asked the clerk quietly.

"No. 16. Tom Nelson is my roommate."

"Why doesn't he come for it himself?" inquired the hotel clerk, with a searching glance at Graham.

"He wishes me to buy his steamboat ticket," answered Graham coolly. "He is going down the river in my charge."

"Are you his guardian?"

"Yes," answered Graham, with cool effrontery. "He is the son of an acquaintance of mine, and I naturally feel an interest in the boy."

"He told me he never met you till yesterday."

Graham was rather taken aback, but he recovered himself quickly.

"That's pretty cool in Tom," he returned, shrugging his shoulders. "I understand it, though."

"I am glad you do," said the clerk sarcastically, "for it doesn't look to me at all consistent with what you represent."

"The fact is," said Graham plausibly, "Tom has a feeling of independence and doesn't like to have it supposed that he is under anybody's protection. That accounts for what he told you. It isn't right, though, to misrepresent. I must give him a scolding. I am in a little of a hurry, so if you will kindly give me the boy's money -- "

"It won't do, Mr. Graham," said the clerk very firmly. "The money was put in our charge by the boy, and it will be delivered only to him."

"You seem to be very suspicious," said Graham loftily. "Hand me my bill, if you please. I will breakfast elsewhere."

The bill was made out and paid. Five minutes later Milton Graham, with an air of outraged virtue, stalked out of the hotel, quite forgetting the young friend who was under his charge.

When Tom came downstairs he was told of the attempt to get possession of his money.

"I am much obliged to you for not letting him have it," he said. "He searched my clothes and valise during the night, but I said nothing, for I knew he would find nothing worth taking."

"He is a dangerous companion. If you ever meet him again, I advise you to give him a wide berth."

40

"I certainly shall follow your advice. If you had not warned me against him he would have stolen my money during the night."

CHAPTER IX

THE "RIVER BELLE"

As Tom took his place at the breakfast table, he mechanically lifted his eyes and glanced at his neighbors. Directly opposite him sat the gentleman whom he had brought home the evening before. Now he looked sober and respectable. Indeed, he looked as if he might be a person of some prominence. He met Tom's glance and recognized him.

"I think you are the boy who came home with me last evening," he said.

"Yes, sir," answered Tom, rather embarrassed.

"I am afraid I was not quite myself," continued the stout gentleman.

"Not quite, sir."

"I ought to be ashamed of myself, and I am. I don't often allow myself to be caught in that way. You did me a good service."

"You are quite welcome, sir."

"I had a good deal of money with me, and, if I had drank any more, I should probably have been robbed."

"Why did you run such a risk, sir?" Tom could not help asking.

"Because I was a fool," said the other bluntly. "I have taste for drink, but when I am at home I keep it under control."

"Then you don't live in Pittsburgh, sir?"

"No. My home is in one of the river towns in Ohio. I came to Pittsburgh to collect money due to me for produce, and but for you I should probably have carried none of it home."

"I am very glad to be of service to you," said our hero sincerely.

"What are your plans, my young friend? I suppose you are only a visitor in this city."

"I am on my way to California. I expect to sail in the River Belle at nine o'clock."

"Then we shall be fellow passengers, and I shall have a chance to become better acquainted with you. You are young to go to California alone. You are alone -- are you not?"

"Yes, sir."

They went down to the boat together, and on the way Tom told his story. He learned that his acquaintance was Mr. Nicholas Waterbury, that he had been a member of the Ohio Legislature, and, as he inferred, that he was a prominent citizen of the town in which he lived.

"I should be very much ashamed to have them hear at home how I had forgotten myself," said Mr. Waterbury.

"It need not be known," said Tom. "I shall not mention it to any one."

"Thank you," said Mr. Waterbury. "I would rather you did not, as the news might reach my home."

"Where do you live, sir?"

"In Marietta. I shall be glad to have you leave the boat there and stay a day or two with me."

"Thank you, sir, but I am in a hurry to reach California, on my father's account. I want to send back as soon as possible the money he raised to pay my expenses out."

"That is very commendable; I can enter into your feelings. I should like to show my obligation to you in some way."

"It is not worth thinking about, sir," said Tom modestly.

"Permit me to disagree with you. Why, my young friend, how much money do you think I had with me?"

"I don't know, sir."

"Upward of six hundred dollars."

As Mr. Waterbury uttered these words, a young man, very dark, with narrow black whiskers, passed them. He darted a quick glance at the speaker and walked rapidly on. Tom noticed him but not with attention.

"That is a good deal of money, sir," he remarked.

"It would have been a good deal to lose," said Mr. Waterbury, "and I have no doubt I should have lost it if it had not been for you."

"I haven't so much money as you, but I came near losing it last night."

"How was that?" asked Tom's new acquaintance, with curiosity.

Tom explained the attempt of his roommate to rob him.

"It would have been a serious loss to you, my young friend."

"It would have broken up all my plans, and I should have had to work my way home, greatly disappointed."

You will need to be careful about forming acquaintances. There are exceptions, however. I am a new acquaintance, but I don't think you need fear me."

"No, sir," said Tom, smiling.

"While I have received a great service from you, who are a new acquaintance. But here we are at the steamer."

The River Belle lay at her pier. Tom and his companion went on board. Both secured tickets, and Tom provided himself with a stateroom, for he expected to remain on board till they reached Cincinnati. Freight of various kinds was being busily stowed away below. It was a busy and animated scene, and Tom looked on with interest.

"Have you ever been on a steamboat before?" asked Mr. Waterbury.

"No, sir. I have never traveled anywhere to speak of before leaving home on this journey," replied Tom.

"It will be a pleasant variety for you, then, though the scenery is tame. However, some of the river towns are pretty."

"I am sure I shall like it, sir."

"I wish I were going all the way with you -- I mean as far as Cincinnati," said Mr. Waterbury.

"I wish you were, sir."

"I have a great mind to do it," said the gentleman musingly. "I should have to go very soon on business, at any rate, and I can attend to it now just as well as later."

"I shall be very glad if you can make it convenient, sir. We might occupy the same stateroom."

"Are you not afraid that I shall follow the example of your Pittsburgh roommate?" asked Mr. Waterbury.

"I have less to lose than you," answered Tom. "Besides, I shall have to have a roommate, as there are two berths."

"Precisely, and I might be safer than some. I have a great mind to keep on. I shall see someone on the pier in Marietta by whom I can send word to my family. By the way, I have a son about your age and a daughter two years younger."

"Have you, sir?" asked Tom, with interest.

"I should like you to meet them. Perhaps you may some day."

"I hope I may," said Tom politely.

"I am a manufacturer," continued Mr. Waterbury, "and sell my goods chiefly in Pittsburgh and Cincinnati. From these places they are forwarded farther east and west."

"I suppose that's a pretty good business, sir?"

"Sometimes, but there are intervals of depression. However, I have no right to complain. I began a poor boy, and now I am moderately rich."

"Were you as poor as I am?" inquired Tom, beginning to feel a personal interest in his companion's career.

"Quite so, I fancy. At the age of sixteen I couldn't call myself the owner of five dollars."

"And you have become rich?" said Tom, feeling very much encouraged.

"Moderately so. I am probably worth fifty thousand dollars and am just fifty years of age."

"That seems to me very rich," said Tom.

"I should have said the same thing at your age. Our views change as we get older. Still, I regard myself as very well off, and, with prudent management, I need not fear reverses."

"I should think not," said Tom.

"You don't know how easy it is to lose money, my boy. I am not referring to robbery, but to mismanagement."

"Your success encourages me, Mr. Waterbury," said Tom. "I am willing to work hard."

"I think you will succeed. You look like a boy of good habits. Energy, industry, and good habits can accomplish wonders. But I think we are on the point of starting."

Just before the gangplank was drawn in, two persons hastily crossed it.

One was the dark young man who had passed them on the way down to the boat; the other was Milton Graham.

"Mr. Waterbury," said Tom hurriedly, "do you see that man?"

"Yes."

"He is the man that tried to rob me."

"We must be on our guard, then. He may be up to more mischief."

CHAPTER X

ON THE STEAMER

In half an hour the River Belle was on her way. Tom watched the city as it receded from view. He enjoyed this new mode of travel better than riding on the cars. He had never before been on any boat except a ferryboat and congratulated himself on his decision to journey by boat part of the way.

Tom continues his journey on the River Belle ferryboat.

Milton Graham had passed him two or three times, but Tom, though seeing him, had not volunteered recognition. Finding that he must make the first advances, Graham finally stopped short, looked full at our hero, and his face wore a very natural expression of surprise and pleasure.

"Why, Tom, is that you?" he said, offering his hand, which Tom did not appear to see.

"Yes," said our hero coldly.

"I didn't expect to see you here."

"I told you I intended to sail on the River Belle."

"So you did, but I thought you had changed your mind."

It made very little difference to Tom what Mr. Graham thought, and he turned from him to watch the scenery past which the boat was gliding.

"I suppose," continued the young man, "you were surprised to find me gone when you came downstairs to breakfast."

"Yes, I was."

"He resents it because I left him," thought Graham. "I guess I can bring him around."

"The fact was," explained Graham, in a plausible manner, "I went out to call on a friend, meaning to come back to breakfast, but he made me breakfast with him, and when I did return you were gone. I owe you an apology, Tom. I hope you will excuse my unintentional neglect."

"Oh, certainly," said Tom indifferently, "it's of no consequence."

Mr. Graham looked at him sharply. He could not tell whether our hero was aware of his dishonest intentions or not, but as Tom must still have money, which he wanted to secure, he thought it best to ignore his coldness.

"No," said he, "it's of no consequence as long as we have come together again. By the way, have you secured a stateroom?"

"Yes."

"If the other berth is not taken, I should like very much to go in with you," said Graham insinuatingly.

"I have a roommate," said Tom coolly.

"You have? Who is it?" demanded Graham, disappointed.

"That gentleman," answered Tom, pointing out Mr. Nicholas Waterbury.

"Humph! Do you know him?"

"I met him at the Pittsburgh House."

"My young friend," said Graham, with the air of a friendly mentor, "I want to give you a piece of advice."

"Very well."

"Don't be too ready to trust strangers. This Mr. Waterbury may be a very good man, but, on the other hand, he may be a confidence man. Do you understand me?"

"I think so."

"Now, I suppose you have money?"

"A little."

"Take care that he doesn't get possession of it. There are men who go about expressly to fleece inexperienced strangers."

"I suppose you know all about that," Tom could not help saying.

"What do you mean?" demanded Graham suspiciously.

—

47

"You are an old traveler and must know all about the sharpers."

"Oh, to be sure," said Graham, immediately dismissing his suspicions. "You couldn't leave your companion, could you, and come into my stateroom?"

"I don't think I could."

"Oh, very well. It's of no consequence. Keep a good lookout for your roommate."

Graham turned away and resumed his walk. Soon Tom saw him in company with the dark young man, to whom reference has already been made.

"Well," said the latter, "how did you make out with the boy?"

"He's offish. I don't know if he suspects me. I wanted to get him into my stateroom, but he has already taken up with another man -- that stout party over there."

"So I suspected. I can tell you something about that man."

"What?"

"He carries six hundred dollars about him."

"You don't say so! How did you find out?"

"I overheard him telling the boy so."

"That's important news. The boy must have a couple of hundred, or thereabouts, as he is on his way to California."

"Eight hundred dollars together! That would make a good haul."

"So it would, but it won't be easy to get it."

While this conversation was going on Tom informed Mr. Waterbury of what had passed between Graham and himself.

"So he warned you against me, did he?" said Mr. Waterbury laughingly.

"Yes, he thought I would be safer in his company."

"If you want to exchange, I will retire," said Mr. Waterbury, smiling.

"Thank you; I would rather not. I am glad I met you, or he might have managed to get in with me."

It was not long before they came to a landing. It was a small river village, whose neat white houses, with here and there one of greater pretensions, presented an attractive appearance. A lady and her daughter came on board here. The lady was dressed in black and appeared to be a widow. The girl was perhaps fourteen years of age, with a bright, attractive face. Two trunks were put on the boat with them, and as they were the only passengers from this landing, Tom inferred that they were their property.

"That's quite a pretty girl," said Mr. Waterbury.

"Yes," answered Tom.

"You ought to get acquainted with her," said Mr. Waterbury jocosely.

"Perhaps," said Tom shyly, "you will get acquainted with them, and then you can introduce me."

"You are quite sharp," said Mr. Waterbury, laughing. "However, your hint is a good one. I may act upon it."

It happened, however, that Tom required no introduction. As the lady and her daughter walked across the deck, to occupy some desirable seats on the other side, the former dropped a kid glove, which Tom, espying, hastened forward and, picking up, politely tendered to the owner.

"You are very kind," said the lady, in a pleasant voice. "I am much obliged."

"Mama is quite in the habit of dropping her gloves," said the young girl, with a smiling glance at Tom. "I really think she does it on purpose."

"Then, perhaps, I had better keep nearby to pick them up," said Tom.

"Really, Jennie," said her mother, "you are giving the young gentleman a strange impression of me."

"Well, mama, you know you dropped your gloves in the street the last time you were in Pittsburgh, but there was no gentleman to pick them up, so I had to. Are you going to Cincinnati?" she asked, turning to Tom.

"Yes, and farther; I am going to California," replied Tom.

"Dear me, you will be quite a traveler. I wish I were going to California."

"You wouldn't like to go there on the same business that I am."

"What is that?"

"I am going to dig gold."

"I don't know. I suppose it isn't girl's work, but if I saw any gold about, I should like to dig for it. Is that your father that was standing by you?"

"No," answered Tom. "I hadn't met him till yesterday. We were staying at the same hotel in Pittsburgh."

"He seems like quite a nice old gentleman."

Mr. Waterbury was not over fifty, but to the young girl he seemed an old gentleman.

"I find him very pleasant."

There was a seat next to Jennie, and Tom ventured to occupy it.

"What is your name?" asked the young lady sociably.

"Thomas Nelson, but most people call me Tom."

"My name is Jane Watson, but everybody calls me Jennie."

"That is much prettier than Jane."

"So I think. Jane seems old-maidish, don't you think so?"

"Are you afraid of becoming an old maid?" asked Tom, smiling.

"Awfully. I wouldn't be an old maid for anything. My school teacher is an old maid. She's horribly prim. She won't let us laugh, or talk, or anything."

"I don't think you'll grow up like that."

"I hope not."

The sociable Jennie Watson

"How you run on, Jennie!" said her mother. "What will this young gentleman think of you?"

"Nothing very bad, I hope," said Jennie, smiling archly on Tom. "I suppose," she continued, addressing him, "I ought to be very quiet and reserved, as you are a stranger."

"I hope you won't be," said Tom heartily.

"Then I won't. Somehow you don't seem like a stranger. You look a good deal like a cousin of mine. I suppose that is the reason."

So they chatted on for an hour or more. Jennie was very vivacious and occasionally droll, and Tom enjoyed her company. The mother saw that our hero was well-behaved and gentlemanly, and she made no objection to the sudden intimacy.

CHAPTER XI

THE FIRST DAY ON THE RIVER

About half-past twelve lunch was announced.

"I hope you'll sit next to us, Tom," said Jennie Watson.

"I will, if I can."

It happened that Milton Graham entered the saloon at the same time with the new friends. He took the seat next to Jennie, much to that young lady's annoyance.

"Will you be kind enough to take the next seat?" she asked. "That young gentleman is to sit next to me."

"I am sorry to resign the pleasure, but anything to oblige," said Graham. "Tom, I congratulate you," he continued, with a disagreeable smile.

"Thank you," said our hero briefly.

"He calls you Tom. Does he know you?" inquired Jennie, in a low voice.

"I made his acquaintance yesterday for the first time."

"I don't like his looks; do you?"

"Wait till after dinner, and I will tell you," said Tom, fearing that Graham would hear.

Milton Graham saw that Jennie was pretty and desired to make her acquaintance.

"Tom," said he -- for he sat on the other side of our hero -- "won't you introduce me to your young lady friend?"

Tom was not well versed in etiquette, but his good sense told him that he ought to ask Jennie's permission first.

"If Miss Watson is willing," he said, and asked her the question.

Jennie was not aware of Graham's real character, and she gave permission. She was perhaps a little too ready to make new acquaintances.

"Do you enjoy this mode of travel, Miss Watson?" said Graham, after the introduction.

"Oh, yes. I think it very pleasant."

"I suppose you wouldn't like the ocean as well. I went to Havana last winter -- on business for my father -- and had a very rough passage. The steamer pitched and tossed, making us all miserably seasick."

"I shouldn't like that."

"I don't think you would, but we businessmen must not regard such things."

Tom listened to him with incredulity. Only the day before he would have put full confidence in his statement, but he had learned a lesson, thanks to Graham himself.

"How far are you going, Miss Watson?" continued Graham.

"To Cincinnati. My mother and I are going to live there."

"It is a very pleasant city. I have often been there -- on business."

"What is your business, Mr. Graham?" Tom could not help asking.

"I see you are a Yankee," said Graham, smiling. "Yankees are very inquisitive -- always asking questions."

"Are you a Yankee, Mr. Graham?" asked Jennie. "You asked me where I was going."

"A fair hit," said Graham. "No, I am not a Yankee. I am a native of New York."

"And I of New Jersey," said Tom.

"Oh, you are a foreigner then," said Graham. "We always call Jerseymen foreigners."

"It is a stupid joke, I think," said Tom, who was loyal to his native state.

"You didn't answer Tom's question," said Jennie, who was a very straightforward young lady.

"Oh, my father is a commission merchant," answered Graham.

"What does he deal in?"

"Articles too numerous to mention. Tom, will you pass me the potatoes?"

Lunch was soon over, and the passengers went upon deck. Graham lit a cigar.

"Have a cigar, Tom?" he said.

"No, thank you. I don't smoke."

"You'll soon learn. I'll see you again soon."

"Tom," said Jennie, "tell me about this Mr. Graham. What do you know about him?"

"I don't like to tell what I know," said Tom hesitating.

"But I want you to. You introduced me, you know."

"What I know is not to his advantage. I don't like to talk against a man."

"You needn't mind telling me."

On reflection Tom decided that he ought to tell what he knew, for he felt that Jennie ought to be put on her guard against a man whom he did not consider a suitable acquaintance for her.

"Very well," said he, "if you promise not to let him know that I have told you."

"I promise."

"He was my roommate last night at the Pittsburgh House," said Tom, in a low voice. "During the night he tried to rob me."

"You don't say so!" cried Jennie, in round-eyed wonder.

"I will tell you the particulars."

This Tom did. Jennie listened with indignation.

"But I don't understand," she said. "Why should the son of a merchant need to rob a boy like you? He looks as if he had plenty of money."

"So I thought, but the hotel clerk told me that sharpers often appeared like this Mr. Graham, if that is his name."

"How strange it seems!" said Jennie. "I wish you hadn't introduced me."

"I didn't want to, but he asked, and at the table I couldn't give my reasons for refusing."

"My dear child," said her mother, "you are too ready to form new acquaintances. Let this be a lesson for you."

"But some new acquaintances are nice," pleaded Jennie. "Isn't Tom a new acquaintance?"

"I will make an exception in his favor," said Mrs. Watson, smiling pleasantly.

"Thank you," said Tom. "How do you know that I am not a pickpocket?" he continued, addressing Jennie.

"As I have only ten cents in my pocket I will trust you," said the young lady merrily. "I'd trust you with any amount, Tom," she added impulsively.

"Thank you for your good opinion, Miss Jennie."

"Don't call me Miss Jennie. If you do, I'll call you Mr. Tom."

"I shouldn't know myself by that title. Then I'll call you Jennie."

"I wish you were going to live in Cincinnati," said the young lady. "It would be nice to have you come and see us."

"I should like it, but I mustn't think so much of pleasure as business."

"Like Mr. Graham."

"I must work hard at the mines. I suppose I shall look pretty rough when I am there."

"When you've made your pile, Tom -- that's what they call it, isn't it? -- you'll come back, won't you?"

"Yes."

"You must stop in Cincinnati on your way home."

"I wouldn't know where to find you."

"I will give you our address before we part. But that will be some time yet."

About this time Graham, who had finished smoking his cigar, strolled back.

"Miss Watson," said he, "don't you feel like having a promenade?"

"Yes," said Jennie suddenly. "Tom, come walk with me."

Our hero readily accepted the invitation, and the two walked up and down the deck.

"That's what I call a snub," said Graham's friend, the dark-complexioned young man, who was within hearing.

Graham's face was dark with anger.

"Curse her impudence -- and his too!" he muttered. "I should like to wring the boy's neck."

"He can't help it, if the girl prefers his company," said the other, rather enjoying Graham's mortification.

"I'll punish him all the same."

By this time Tom and Jennie were near him again, on their return.

"You don't treat me with much ceremony, Miss Watson," said Graham, with an evil smile.

"My mother doesn't like me to make too many acquaintances," said Jennie demurely.

"She is very prudent," sneered Graham. "You have known your present companion quite a long time."

"I hope to know him a long time," said the young lady promptly. "Let's continue our walk, Tom."

In discomfiture which he was unable to hide, Graham walked away.

"Evidently, Graham, you are no match for those two youngsters," said his friend in amusement, which Graham did not share.

Graham did not reply but seemed moody and preoccupied.

—

Tom and his companion noticed Graham's displeasure, but they felt indifferent to it. They had no desire to continue his acquaintance. Our hero introduced Mr. Waterbury to his new friends, and this gentleman, who was a thorough gentleman, except on the rare occasion when he yielded to the temptation of strong drink, made a favorable impression upon both.

So the day passed. Tom enjoyed it thoroughly. The river banks afforded a continuous panorama, while the frequent stops gave him an opportunity of observing the different towns in detail. Two or three times he went ashore, accompanied by Jennie, and remained till the steamer was ready to start.

Finally night came, and one by one the weary passengers retired to rest.

"Good night, Tom," said Jennie Watson. "Be up early in the morning."

"So as to get an appetite for breakfast?" asked Tom, with a smile.

"I think we shall both have appetites enough, but it will be pleasant to breathe the fresh morning air."

Tom promised to get up, if he wakened in time.

"If you don't mind, I will occupy the lower berth," said Mr. Waterbury. "I can't climb as well as you."

"All right, sir. It makes no difference to me."

CHAPTER XII
NO. 61 AND NO. 62

The stateroom was small, as most staterooms on river boats are. There appeared to be no means of ventilation. Mr. Waterbury was a stout man and inclined to be short-breathed. After an hour he rose and opened the door, so as to leave it slightly ajar. With the relief thus afforded he was able to go to sleep, and sleep soundly. Tom was already asleep and knew nothing of what had happened.

The number of the stateroom was 61. Directly opposite was 62, occupied by Milton Graham and his companion.

If Graham did not go to sleep it was because his brain was busily scheming how to obtain possession of the money belonging to his neighbors.

"Won't your key fit?" asked Vincent, for this was the name of the dark-complexioned young man.

"No use, even if it does. Of course they will lock it inside and probably leave the key in the lock."

About midnight, Graham, who had not fully undressed, having merely taken off his coat, got up, and, opening the door, peered out. To his surprise and joy he saw that the door of No. 61 was ajar. He at first thought of rousing Vincent, who was asleep, but a selfish thought suggested itself. If he did this, he must share with Vincent anything he might succeed in stealing; if not, he could keep it all himself.

He left his stateroom silently, and looked cautiously around him. No one seemed to be stirring in the cabin. Next he stepped across and, opening wider the door of 61, looked in. The two inmates were, to all appearances, sleeping soundly.

"So far, so good," he said to himself.

He stepped in, moderating even his breathing, and took up a pair of pants which lay on a chair. They belonged to Mr. Waterbury, for Tom had merely taken off his coat and lain down as he was. His belt of gold he therefore found it unnecessary to take off.

Graham saw at once, from the size of the pants, that they must belong to the elder passenger. This suited him, however, as he knew from Vincent's information that Mr. Waterbury had six hundred dollars, and Tom could not be supposed to have anything like this sum. He felt eagerly in the pockets, and to his great joy his hand came in contact with a pocketbook. He drew it out without ceremony. It was a comfortable-looking wallet, fairly bulging with bills.

"He's got all his money inside," thought Graham, delighted. "What a fool he must be to leave it so exposed -- with his door open, too!"

At this moment Graham heard a stir in the lower berth. There was no time to wait. He glided out of the room and reentered his own stateroom. Immediately after his departure Mr. Waterbury, who had awakened in time to catch sight of his receding figure, rose in his berth and drew toward him the garment which Graham had rifled. He felt in the pocket and discovered that the wallet had been taken.

Instead of making a fuss, he smiled quietly and said, "Just as I expected. I wonder if they have robbed Tom, too," he said to himself.

He rose, closed the door, and then shook Tom with sufficient energy to awaken him.

"Who's there?" asked Tom, in some bewilderment, as he opened his eyes.

"It's I -- Mr. Waterbury."

"Is it morning? Have we arrived?"

"No, it is about midnight."

"Is there anything the matter?"

"I want you to see if you have been robbed.'"

Tom was broad awake in an instant.

"Robbed!" he exclaimed, in alarm. He felt for his belt and was relieved.

"No," he answered. "What makes you ask?"

"Because I have had a wallet taken. It makes me laugh when I think of it."

"Makes you laugh!" repeated Tom, under the transient impression that his companion was insane. "Why should you laugh at the loss of your money?"

"I saw the thief sneak out of the stateroom," continued Mr. Waterbury, "but I didn't interfere with him."

"You didn't!" said Tom, completely mystified. "I would. Did you see who it was?"

"Yes, it was your friend and late roommate."

"Mr. Graham?"

"As he calls himself. I don't suppose he has any rightful claim to the name."

"Surely, Mr. Waterbury, you are not going to let him keep the money," said Tom energetically. "I'll go with you, and make him give it up. Where is his stateroom?"

"Just opposite -- No. 62."

"We had better go at once," said Tom, sitting up in his berth.

"Oh, no. He's welcome to all there is in the pocketbook."

"Wasn't there anything in it?"

"It was stuffed full."

Tom was more than ever convinced that his roommate was crazy. He had heard that misfortune sometimes affected a man's mind, and he was inclined to think that here was a case in point.

"You'll get it back," said he soothingly. "Graham can't get off the boat. We will report the matter to the captain."

"I don't care whether I get it back or not," said Mr. Waterbury.

Tom looked so confused and bewildered that his companion felt called upon to end the mystification.

"I know what is in your mind," he said, smiling. "You think I am crazy."

"I don't understand how you can take your loss so coolly, sir."

"Then I will explain. That wallet was a dummy."

"A what, sir?"

"A sham -- a pretense. My pocketbook and money are safe under my pillow. The wallet taken by your friend was filled with imitation greenbacks -- in reality, business circulars of a firm in Marietta."

Tom saw it all now.

"It's a capital joke," he said, laughing. "I'd like to see how Graham looks when he discovers the value of his prize."

"He will look green and feel greener, I suspect," chuckled Mr. Waterbury. "You are certain you have lost nothing, Tom?"

"Perfectly certain, sir."

"Then we won't trouble ourselves about what has happened. I fancy, however, it will be best to keep our own door locked for the remainder of the night, even at the risk of suffocation."

"That's a capital trick of yours, Mr. Waterbury," said Tom admiringly.

"It has more than once saved me from robbery. I have occasion to travel considerably and so am more or less exposed."

"I wonder if Graham will discover the cheat before morning."

"I doubt it. The staterooms are dark, and the imitation is so good that on casual inspection the strips of paper will appear to be genuine greenbacks."

Mr. Waterbury retired to his berth and was soon asleep again. Tom, as he lay awake, from time to time laughed to himself, as he thought of Graham's coming disappointment, and he congratulated himself that he and that young man were no longer roommates.

When Graham returned to his stateroom Vincent, who was a light sleeper, was aroused by the slight noise he made.

"Are you up, Graham?" he asked.

"Yes. I got up a minute."

"Have you been out of the stateroom?"

"Yes."

"What for?"

"To get a glass of water."

There was a vessel of water in the cabin, and this seemed plausible enough.

"Any chance of doing anything tonight?"

"No, I think not."

Vincent sank back on his pillow, and Graham got back into his berth. Quietly he drew the wallet from his pocket, in which he had placed it, and eagerly opened it. The huge roll of bills was a pleasant and welcome sight.

"There's all of six hundred dollars here!" he said to himself. "I mustn't let Vincent know that I have them."

It occurred to Graham that, of course, Mr. Waterbury would proclaim his loss in the morning, and it also occurred to him that he might be able to fasten suspicion upon Tom, who, as his roommate, would naturally have the best chance to commit the robbery. One thing might criminate him -- the discovery of the wallet upon his person. He therefore waited till Vincent was once more asleep and, getting up softly, made his way to the deck. He drew the bills from the wallet, put them in an inside pocket, and threw the wallet into the river.

"Now I'm safe," he muttered, with a sigh of relief. "The money may be found on me, but no one can prove it is not my own."

He gained his berth without again awakening his companion.

"A pretty good night's work!" he said to himself, in quiet exultation. "Alone I have succeeded, while Vincent lies in stupid sleep. He is no match for me, much as he thinks of himself. I have stolen a march upon him this time."

It is not in accordance with our ideas of the fitness of things that a man who has committed a midnight robbery should be able to sleep tranquilly for the balance of the night, but it is at any rate certain that Graham slept soundly till his roommate awakened him in the morning.

"Rouse up, Graham," he said. "Breakfast is nearly ready."

"Is it?" asked Graham.

"Instead of sleeping there, you ought to be thinking how we can make a forced loan from our acquaintances in 61."

"To be sure," said Graham, smiling. "I am rather stupid about such things. Have you any plan to suggest?"

"You seem very indifferent all at once," said Vincent.

"Not at all. If you think of anything practical I am your man."

He longed to get rid of Vincent, in order to have an opportunity of counting his roll of bills.

CHAPTER XIII

GRAHAM'S DISAPPOINTMENT

Milton Graham, on reaching a place where he could do so unobserved, drew from his pocket the roll of bills, with a smile of exultation. But the smile faded, and it was succeeded by a look of dismay, when he recognized the worthlessness of his booty. An oath rose to his lips, and he thrust the roll back into his pocket, as he noticed the approach of a passenger.

"It's a cursed imposition!" he muttered to himself, and he really felt that he had been wronged by Mr. Waterbury.

"What are you doing out here, Graham?" asked Vincent, for it was his confederate who approached.

"Nothing in particular. Why?" responded Graham.

"What makes you look so glum?"

"Do I look glum?"

"You look as if you had but one friend in the world, and you were about to lose him."

"That may be true enough," muttered Graham.

"Come, man, don't look so downcast."

"I'm out of luck, and out of cash, Vincent."

"We're both in the same boat, as far as that goes, but that isn't going to last. How about our stout friend? Can't we make him contribute to our necessities?"

"I don't believe he's got any money."

"No? Why, I heard him tell the boy he had six hundred dollars."

"Where does he keep it?"

"In his pocketbook probably."

"Will you oblige me by stating how we are going to get hold of it?"

"I look to you for that."

"He's too careful. I leave you to try your hand."

"Let me go in to breakfast. There's nothing like a full stomach to suggest ideas."

So the two went to the breakfast table, and Graham, in spite of his disappointment, managed to eat a hearty meal.

An hour later Mr. Waterbury and Tom were standing on deck, conversing with Jennie Watson and her mother, when Graham and Vincent approached arm in arm. As soon as they were within hearing distance Mr. Waterbury purposely remarked, "By the way, Mrs. Watson, I met with a loss last night."

"Indeed!" returned the lady.

Graham was about to push on, not wishing Vincent to hear the disclosure, as it might awaken his suspicions, but the latter's curiosity was aroused.

"Wait, Graham," he said, and Graham, against his will, was compelled to slacken his pace.

"A man entered my stateroom during the night, and stole a wallet from my coat pocket."

Graham changed color a little, and Vincent seemed amazed.

"Did you hear that, Graham?" he asked.

"Yes."

"What does it mean?"

"How can I tell?"

"I hope you did not lose much," said Mrs. Watson, in a tone of sympathy.

"I lost the wallet," said Mr. Waterbury, laughing.

"Was there nothing in it?"

"It was full of bills."

Vincent looked at Graham with new-born suspicion, but Graham looked indifferent.

"It appears to me that you take the loss cheerfully," said Mrs. Watson, puzzled.

"I have reason to. The fact is, I was prepared for the visit and had filled the wallet with bogus bills. I fancy they won't do my visitor much good."

The lady smiled.

"You were fortunate, Mr. Waterbury," said she. "Do you suspect any one of the theft?"

"I know pretty well who robbed me," returned Mr. Waterbury, and he suffered his glance to rest on Graham, who seemed in a hurry to get away.

"Come along, Vincent," he said sharply.

Vincent obeyed. Light dawned upon him, and he determined to verify his suspicions.

"Graham," said he, in a low voice, "you did this."

—

"Did what?"

"You got that wallet."

Graham concluded that he might as well make a clean breast of it, since it had become a matter of necessity.

"Well," said he, "suppose I did?"

"You were not going to let me know of it," said Vincent suspiciously.

"That is true. I was ashamed of having been imposed upon."

"When did you find out that the money was bogus?"

"Immediately."

"If it had been good, would you have shared with me honorably?"

"Of course. What do you take me for?"

Vincent was silent. He did not believe his companion. He suspected that the latter had intended to steal a march on him.

"You might have told me of it," he continued, in a tone of dissatisfaction.

"There was no need to say anything, as there was nothing to divide."

"Have you got the wallet with you now?"

"No, I threw it overboard."

"And the bills?"

"You may have them all, if you like."

"Come into the stateroom, where we can be unobserved, and show them to me."

Graham complied with his suggestion.

"It would have been a good haul if they had been genuine," said Vincent, as he unfolded the roll.

"Yes, but they are not; worse luck!"

"I didn't give the old fellow credit for being so sharp."

"Nor I. There's more in him than I supposed there was."

"Well, what is to be done?"

"Nothing. The old man is on his guard, and, besides, he suspects me. He was probably awake when I entered the stateroom. He and the boy have probably laughed over it together. I hate that boy."

"Why?"

"Because he is a green country boy, and yet he has succeeded in thwarting me. I am ashamed whenever I think of it."

"Would you like to play a trick on him in turn?"

"Yes."

"Then give me this roll of bills."

"What do you want to do with them?"

"Put them in his pocket."

"Can you do it unobserved?"

"Yes. The fact is, Graham, I served an apprenticeship as a pickpocket, and flatter myself I still have some dexterity in that line."

"Very well, it will be some satisfaction, and if the old man didn't see me enter the stateroom, he may be brought to believe that the boy robbed him. If that could be, I should feel partly compensated for my disappointment. I should like to get that boy into trouble."

"Consider it done, so far as I am concerned. Now let us separate, so as to avoid suspicion."

Vincent began to pace the deck in a leisurely manner, in each case passing near Tom, who was still engaged in conversation with Jennie Watson and her mother. For a time he was unable to effect his purpose, as our hero was sitting down. But after a while Tom rose and stood with his back to Vincent. He wore a sack coat, with side pockets. This was favorable to Vincent, who, as he passed, adroitly slipped the bills into one of them, without attracting the attention of our hero.

Presently Tom thrust his hand into his pocket mechanically. They encountered the bills. In surprise he drew them out and looked at them in amazement.

"What's that, Tom?" asked Jennie, with great curiosity.

"It looks like money," answered Tom, not yet understanding what had happened.

"You seem to be rich."

"By gracious! -- it's Mr. Waterbury's money," exclaimed Tom. Then he colored, as it flashed upon him that its presence in his pocket might arouse suspicion. "I don't see how it got there," he continued, in a bewildered way.

Just then Mr. Waterbury came up and was made acquainted with the discovery.

"I don't know what you'll think, Mr. Waterbury," said Tom, coloring. "I haven't the slightest idea how the money came in my pocket."

"I have," said Mr. Waterbury quietly.

Tom looked at him to discover whether he was under suspicion.

"The companion of your friend Graham slipped it into your pocket. He was very quick and adroit, but I detected him. He wanted to throw suspicion upon you."

"It is lucky you saw him, sir."

"Why?"

"You might have suspected me."

"My dear boy, don't trouble yourself about that. No circumstantial evidence will shake my confidence in your integrity."

"Thank you, sir," said Tom gratefully.

"What a wicked man to play a trick on you, Tom!" exclaimed Jennie indignantly.

"I see there is somebody else who has confidence in you, Tom," said Mr. Waterbury, smiling.

"I'd like to give him a piece of my mind."

"I am ready to forgive him," said Mr. Waterbury, "as he has restored the money. It will do as a bait for the next thief."

CHAPTER XIV

COMING TO AN UNDERSTANDING

"I believe, Tom," said Mr. Waterbury, "that I will come to an understanding with these officious acquaintances of yours. I will intimate to them that their persecution must cease."

"Will they mind what you say, sir?"

"I think they will," answered his friend quietly.

Graham and Vincent were standing together, and apart from the rest of the passengers, when Mr. Waterbury approached them.

"A word with you, gentlemen," said he gravely.

"I don't know you, sir," blustered Vincent.

"Perhaps not. Permit me to remark that I have no special desire for your acquaintance."

"Then why do you take the liberty of addressing me?"

"I rather admire the fellow's impudence," said Mr. Waterbury to himself.

" Are you associated with this gentleman?" he asked, indicating Graham.

"We are friends."

"Then I will address an inquiry to him. I am not in the habit of receiving calls in my stateroom during the hours of sleep."

"I don't understand you, sir," said Milton Graham, with hauteur.

"Oh, yes, you do, unless your memory is singularly defective. Our staterooms are close together. You entered mine last night."

"You must have been dreaming."

"If so, I was dreaming with my eyes open. Perhaps it was in my dreams that I saw you extract a wallet from my coat pocket."

"Do you mean to insult me, sir?" demanded Graham.

"Really, sir, your remarks are rather extraordinary," chimed in Vincent.

"Do you mean to say that I robbed you?" demanded Graham, confident in the knowledge that the booty was not on his person.

"I find a wallet missing. That speaks for itself."

"Let me suggest that your roommate probably took it," said Vincent.

"Extremely probable," said Graham. "He roomed with me in Pittsburgh, and I caught him at my pockets during the night."

"Did you ever hear the fable of the wolf and the lamb, Mr. Graham?" asked Mr. Waterbury.

"Can't say I have."

"It's of no consequence. I am reminded of it, however."

"Come to think of it," said Vincent, "I saw the boy with a roll of bills. You had better search him. If he is innocent, he can't object."

"I see your drift," returned Mr. Waterbury, after a pause. "I saw you thrust the bills into his pocket, as he stood with his back turned, conversing with one of the passengers. It was very skillfully done, but I saw it."

Vincent started, for he had supposed himself unobserved.

"I see you are determined to insult us," he said. "I will charitably conclude that you are drunk."

"I can't be so charitable with you, sir. I believe you are a pair of precious scoundrels, who, if you had your deserts, would be in the penitentiary instead of at large."

"I have a mind to knock you down," said Vincent angrily.

As Vincent was several inches shorter and much slighter than the person whom he threatened, this menace sounded rather ridiculous.

"You are at liberty to try it," said the latter, smiling. "First, however, let me warn you that, if you continue to annoy us, it will be at your peril. If you remain quiet I shall leave you alone. Otherwise I will make known your true character to the captain and passengers, and you will undoubtedly be set ashore when we reach the next landing. I have the honor to wish you good morning."

"It strikes me, Graham," said Vincent, as Mr. Waterbury left them, "that we have tackled the wrong passenger."

"I believe you are right," said Graham. "Just my luck."

"There isn't much use in staying on the boat. He will keep a good lookout for us."

"True, but I don't want to give up the boy."

"He is under the guardianship of this determined old party."

"They will separate at Cincinnati."

"Well?"

"He has money enough to take him to California. He is worth following up."

"Then you are in favor of going on to Cincinnati?"

"By all means."

"Very well. There are always chances of making an honest penny in a large city."

"Money or no money, I want to get even with the boy."

So the worthy pair decided to go on to Cincinnati.

CHAPTER XV

THE ALLEGHANY HOUSE

It was a bright, sunny morning when the River Belle touched her pier at Cincinnati. The passengers gathered on deck and discussed their plans. In one group were Tom, Mr. Waterbury, Jennie Watson and her mother.

"I am sorry you are going to leave us, Tom," said Jennie. "I shall feel awfully lonely."

"So shall I," said Tom.

"What's the use of going to that hateful California? Why can't you stay here with us?"

"Business before pleasure, Jennie," said her mother. "You mustn't forget that Tom has his fortune to make."

"I wish he could make it in Cincinnati, mother."

"So do I, but I must admit that California presents a better prospect just at present. You are both young, and I hope we may meet Tom in a few years."

"When I have made my pile," suggested Tom.

"Precisely."

"You won't go right on, Tom, will you?" asked Jennie. "You'll stay here a day or two."

"Yes. I should like to see something of Cincinnati."

"And you'll call on us?"

"I shall be very happy to do so. Where are you going to stay?"

"At the Burnet House. Won't you come there, too?"

"Is it a high-priced hotel?"

"I believe it is."

"Then I can't afford to stay there, but I can call on you all the same."

"Stay there as my guest, Tom," said Mr. Waterbury cordially. "It shall not cost you anything."

"Thank you, sir. You are very kind, but I don't like to accept unnecessary favors. I will put up at some cheap hotel and call upon you both."

"You would be heartily welcome, my boy," said Mr. Waterbury.

"I don't doubt it, sir, and the time may come when I will gladly accept your kindness," replied Tom.

"But now you mean to have your own way, is that it, Tom?"

"You won't be offended, sir?"

"On the contrary, I respect you for your manly independence. You won't forget that I am your friend?"

"I don't want to forget that, sir."

So it happened that while Mrs. Watson, Jennie and Mr. Waterbury registered at the Burnet House, Tom, carpetbag in hand, walked through the streets till he came to a plain inn, bearing the name Alleghany House. It is not now in existence, having given way to an imposing business block.

"That looks as if it might suit my purse," thought Tom.

He walked in and, approaching the desk, inquired, "How much do you charge at this hotel?"

"A dollar a day," answered the clerk. "Will you have a room?"

"Yes, sir."

"Please register your name." Tom did so.

"Cato," called the clerk -- summoning a colored boy, about Tom's size -- "take this young man to No. 18."

"All right, sar," said Cato, showing his ivories.

"When do you have lunch?" asked Tom.

"One o'clock."

Preceded by Cato, Tom walked upstairs and was ushered into a small, dingy room on the second floor. There was a single window, looking through dingy panes upon a back yard. There was a general air of cheerlessness and discomfort, but at any rate it was larger than the stateroom on the River Belle.

"Is this the best room you have?" asked Tom, not very favorably impressed.

"Oh, no, sar," answered Cato. "If your wife was with you, sar, we'd give you a scrumptious room, 'bout twice as big."

"I didn't bring my wife along, Cato," said Tom, amused. "Are you married?"

"Not yet, sar," answered his colored guide, with a grin.

"I think we can wait till we are a little older."

"Reckon so, sar."

"Just bring up a little water, Cato. I feel in need of washing."

"Dirt don't show on me," said Cato, with a guffaw.

"I suppose you do wash, now and then, don't you?"

"Yes, sar, sometimes," answered Cato equivocally.

When Tom had completed his washing he found that it was but ten o'clock. He accordingly went downstairs, intending to see a little of the city before lunch.

CHAPTER XVI

THE EVENTS OF A MORNING

Graham and Vincent had kept quiet during the latter part of the voyage. They had a wholesome fear of Mr. Waterbury and kept aloof from him and Tom. They even exchanged their stateroom for one at a different part of the boat. All was satisfactory to Tom and his companion.

When the worthy pair reached Cincinnati they were hard up. Their united funds amounted to but seven dollars, and it seemed quite necessary that they should find the means of replenishing their purses somewhere. They managed to ascertain that Tom and his friend were going to separate, and this afforded them satisfaction, since it made their intentions upon our hero more feasible. At a distance they followed Tom to the Alleghany House and themselves took lodgings at a small, cheap tavern nearby. Like Tom, they set out soon after their arrival in quest of adventure.

"We must strike a vein soon, Graham," said Vincent, "or we shall be in a tight place."

"That's so," answered Graham.

"Thus far our trip hasn't paid very well. It's been all outgo and no income."

"You're right, partner, but don't give up the ship," responded Graham, whose spirits returned, now that he was on dry land. "I've been in the same straits about once a month for the last five years."

"I've known you for three years, Graham, and, so far as my knowledge extends, I can attest the truth of what you say. By the way, you never say anything of your life before that date."

A shadow passed over Graham's face.

"Because I don't care to think of it; I never talk of it," he said.

"Pshaw, man, we all of us have some ugly secrets. Suppose we confide in each other. Tell me your story, and I will tell you mine. It won't change my opinion of you."

"Probably not," said Graham. "Well, there is no use in holding back. For this once I will go back to the past. Five years ago I was a favorite in society. One day an acquaintance introduced me into a gambling house, and I tried my hand successfully. I went out with fifty dollars more than I brought in. It was an unlucky success, for it

---

73

made me a frequent visitor. All my surplus cash found a market there, and when that was exhausted I borrowed from my employer."

"Without his knowledge?"

"Of course. For six months I evaded discovery. Then I was detected. My friends interceded and saved me from the penitentiary, but I lost my job and was required to leave the city. I went to New York, tried to obtain a position there, failed, and then adopted my present profession. I need not tell you the rest."

"My dear friend, I think I know the rest pretty well. But don't look sober. A fig for the past. What's the odds, as long as you're happy?"

"Are you happy?" inquired Graham.

"As long as I'm flush," answered Vincent, shrugging his shoulders. "I'm nearly dead-broke now, and of course I am miserable. However, my story comes next in order. I was a bank teller, appropriated part of the funds of the bank, fled with it, spent it, and then became an ornament to our common profession."

"Where was the bank?"

"In Canada. I haven't been there since. The climate don't suit me. It's bleak, but I fear it might prove too hot for me. Now we know each other."

"You don't allow it to worry you, Vincent," said Graham.

"No, I don't. Why should I? I let the dead past bury its dead, as Longfellow says, and act in the living present. That reminds me, we ought to be at work. I have a proposal to make. We won't hunt in couples, but separate, and each will try to bring home something to help the common fund. Is it agreed?"

"Yes."

"Au revoir, then!"

"That fellow has no conscience," thought Graham. "Mine is callous, but he goes beyond me. Perhaps he is the better off."

Graham shook off his transient dull spirits and walked on, keeping a sharp lookout for a chance to fleece somebody. In front of a railroad ticket office he espied a stolid-looking German, who was trying to read the placard in the window.

Graham approached him and said politely, "My friend, perhaps I can help you. Are you thinking of buying a railroad ticket?"

The German turned, and his confidence was inspired by the friendly interest of Graham's manner.

"I go to Minnesota," he said, "where my brother live."

—

"Exactly, and you want a ticket to go there?"

"Yes, I want a ticket. Do they sell him here?"

"No," said Graham. "That is, they do sell tickets here, but they ask too much."

"I will not pay too much," said the German, shaking his head decisively.

"Of course not; I will take you to a cheaper place."

"That is good," said the German, well pleased. "It is luck I meet a friend like you."

"Yes," said Graham, linking his arm in that of his new acquaintance. "I don't like to see a worthy man cheated. Come with me. How much money have you?"

This inquiry ought to have excited the suspicions of the German, but he was trustful and answered promptly, "Two hundred dollar."

Graham's eyes sparkled.

"If I could only get the whole of it," he thought. But that didn't seem easy.

They walked through street after street till Graham stopped in front of an office.

"Now," said he, "give me your money, and I will buy the ticket."

"How much money?" asked his new acquaintance.

"I don't know exactly," said Graham carelessly. "Just hand me your pocketbook, and I will pay what is needed."

But here the German's characteristic caution came in.

"I will go with you," he said.

"If you do, I can't get the tickets so cheap. The agent is a friend of mine, and if he thinks it is for me he will give it to me for less. Don't give me all your money. Fifty dollars will do. I will buy the ticket, and bring you the rest of the money."

This seemed plausible enough, and Graham would have got what he asked for, but for the interference of Tom, who had come up just in time to hear Graham's proposal. He had no difficulty in comprehending his purpose.

"Don't give him the money," he said. "He will cheat you."

Both Graham and his intended victim wheeled round and looked at our hero.

"Clear out of here, you young vagabond!" said Graham angrily.

"This man wants to cheat you," persisted Tom. "Don't give him your money."

The bewildered foreigner looked from one to the other.

"This is no ticket office," said Tom. "I will lead you to one, and you shall buy a ticket for yourself."

"He wants to swindle you," said Graham quickly.

"You shall keep your money in your own hands," said Tom. "I don't want it."

"I go with you, my young friend," said the German, convinced by Tom's honest face. "The other man may be all right, but I go with you."

Graham protested in vain. His victim went off with Tom, who saw that he was provided with the ticket he wanted. His new friend tried to force a dollar upon him, but this Tom steadily refused.

"I'll get even with you yet!" said Graham furiously, but our hero was not disturbed by this menace.

Vincent, meantime, was making a tour of observation, ready for any adventure that might put an honest or dishonest penny into his pocket. About half an hour later he found himself on the leading retail street in Cincinnati. In front of him walked a lady, fashionably attired, holding a mother-of-pearl portemonnaie carelessly in her hand. He brushed by her, and at the same moment the pocketbook was snatched from her hand.

The lady screamed and instinctively clutched Vincent by the arm.

"This man has robbed me, I think," she said. The crowd began to gather about Vincent, and he saw that he was cornered. Among the crowd, unluckily for himself, was Tom. By a skilful movement Vincent thrust the portemonnaie into our hero's pocket.

"You are mistaken, madam," he said coolly. "I saw that boy take your money."

Instantly two men seized Tom.

"Search him," said Vincent, "and see if I am not right."

The portemonnaie was taken from Tom's pocket, amid the hootings of the crowd.

"So young, and yet so wicked!" said the lady regretfully.

"I didn't take the money, madam," protested Tom, his face scarlet with surprise and mortification.

"Don't believe him, ma'am. I saw him take it," said Vincent virtuously.

Poor Tom looked from one to another, but all faces were unfriendly. It was a critical time for him.

CHAPTER XVII

TOM'S ARREST

To one who is scrupulously honest a sudden charge of dishonesty is almost overwhelming. Now, Tom was honest, not so much because he had been taught that honesty was a virtue, as by temperament and instinct. Yet here he saw himself surrounded by hostile faces, for a crowd soon collected. Not one believed in his innocence, not even the lady, who thought it was such a pity that he was "so young and yet so wicked."

"Will somebody call a policeman?" asked Vincent.

A policeman soon made his appearance. He was a stout, burly man, and pushed his way through the crowd without ceremony.

"What's the row?" he inquired.

"This boy has picked a lady's pocket," exclaimed Vincent.

The officer placed his hand roughly on Tom's shoulder.

"You were a little too smart, young feller!" said he. "You must come along with me."

"I didn't take the money," protested Tom, pale, but in a firm voice.

"That's too thin," said Vincent, with a sneer.

"Yes, it's too thin," repeated two or three in the crowd.

"It's true," said Tom.

"Perhaps you'll tell us how the money came in your pocket," suggested a bystander.

"That man put it in," answered Tom, indicating Vincent.

The latter shrugged his shoulders.

"He says so, because I exposed him," he remarked, turning to the crowd.

"Of course; that's a common game," interposed the policeman.

"Have you any reason for what you say, my boy?" asked a quiet-looking man, with a pleasant face.

"Of course he hasn't," replied Vincent hastily.

"I spoke to the boy, sir."

"I have a reason," answered Tom. "A friend of this man roomed with me at Pittsburgh and during the night tried to rob me. We were both passengers on the River Belle on the last trip. During the trip he entered our stateroom and stole a wallet from my roommate. This man slyly put it into my pocket, in order to escape suspicion."

"It's a lie!" exclaimed Vincent uneasily. "Gentlemen, the boy is very artful, and the greatest liar out."

"Of course he is!" assented the policeman. "Come along, young feller!"

"Wait a minute," said the quiet man. "Have you any proof of your statements, my boy, except your own word?"

"Yes, sir. My roommate will tell you the same thing."

"Who is he? Where can he be found?"

"He is Mr. Nicholas Waterbury, of Marietta. He is now at the Burnet House."

"That's all gammon!" said the officer roughly. "Come along. I can't wait here all day."

"Don't be in a hurry, officer," said the quiet man. "I know Mr. Waterbury, and I believe the boy's story is correct."

"It ain't any of your business!" said the officer insolently. "The boy's a thief, and I'm goin' to lock him up."

"Look out, sir!" said the quiet man sternly. "You are overstepping the limits of your duty and asserting what you have no possible means of knowing. There is reason to believe that this man" -- pointing out Vincent -- "is the real thief. I call upon you to arrest him."

"I don't receive no orders from you, sir," said the policeman. "I'm more likely to take you along."

"That's right, officer," said Vincent approvingly. "The man is interfering with you in the exercise of your duty. You have a perfect right to arrest him."

"I have a great mind to," said the officer, who was one of the many who are puffed up by a little brief authority and lose no opportunity of exercising it.

The quiet man did not seem in the least alarmed. He smiled and said, "Perhaps, officer, it might be well for you to inquire my name, before proceeding to arrest me."

"Who are you?" demanded the officer insolently.

"I am Alderman Morris."

A great change came over the policeman. He knew now that the quiet man before him was President of the Board of Aldermen, and he began to be alarmed, remembering with what rudeness he had treated him.

"I beg your pardon, sir," he said humbly. "I didn't know you."

"What is your name, sir?" demanded the alderman, in a tone of authority.

"Jones, sir."

"How long have you been on the force?"

"Six months, your honor."

"Then you ought to be better fitted for your position by this time."

I hope you won't take no offense at what I said, not knowing you, alderman."

"That's no personal offense, but I object to your pronouncing upon the guilt of parties arrested when you know nothing of the matter."

"Shall I take the boy along, sir?"

"Yes, and this man also. I don't wish to interfere with the exercise of justice, but it is my opinion that the boy is innocent."

"I protest against this outrage," said Vincent nervously. "Am I to be punished because I expose a thief?"

"Come along, sir," said the policeman. "The alderman says so."

"I appeal to the gentlemen present," said Vincent, hoping for a forcible deliverance.

"Madam," said the alderman to the lady who had been robbed, "did you see the boy take your pocketbook?"

"No, sir! I thought it was the man, till he told me it was the boy, and the money was found on the boy."

"I should think that told the story," said Vincent. "Any man here might be arrested as soon as I. Fellow citizens, is this a free country, where a man of reputation can be summarily arrested at the bidding of another? If so, I would rather live under a monarchy."

There was a murmur of approval, and some sympathy was excited.

"There will be no injustice done, sir," said the alderman. "I propose to follow up this matter myself. I will see my friend, Mr. Waterbury, and I can soon learn whether the boy's story is correct."

"He may lie, too!" said Vincent, who had very good reasons for fearing Mr. Waterbury's testimony.

"Mr. Waterbury is a gentleman of veracity," said Alderman Morris sharply. "I see you recognize the name."

"Never heard of him," said Vincent. "I suppose it is one of the boy's confederates."

"I will answer for him," said the alderman. "My boy," he said, "I hope we shall be able to prove your innocence. Be under no anxiety. Go with the officer, and I will seek out Mr. Waterbury. Officer, take care to treat him gently."

"All right, sir."

There was no fear now that Tom would be roughly treated. He had too much regard for his own interest, and his tenure of office, to disoblige a man so influential and powerful as Alderman Morris.

Notwithstanding there had been such a turn in his favor, Tom felt humiliated to feel that he was under restraint, and his cheeks burned with shame as he walked beside the officer. Vincent, upon the other side, gnashed his teeth with rage, as he thought of his unexpected detention. Just as revenge was in his grasp, he had been caught in the same trap which he had so willingly set for Tom.

"That Alderman Morris is a fool!" he said. "He isn't fit to be in office."

"Don't you say nothin' against him!" said the policeman. "It won't be best for you. He's one of our leadin' citizens, Alderman Morris is."

"He snubbed you!" sneered Vincent. "He talked to you as if you were a dog."

"No, he didn't. You'd better shut up, prisoner."

"Oh, well, if you're willing to be trampled upon, it isn't any of my business. I wouldn't stand it, alderman or no alderman. Such things wouldn't be allowed in New York, where I live."

"Oh, New York's a model city, so I've heard," retorted the policeman, in a tone of sarcasm. "We don't pretend to come up to New York."

Finding that nothing was to be gained by continuing his attacks upon the alderman, Vincent became silent, but his brain was active. He felt that Mr. Waterbury's testimony would be fatal to him. He must escape, if possible. Soon a chance came. He seized his opportunity, shook off the grasp of the officer, and darted away. Not knowing what to do with Tom, who was also under arrest, the officer paused an instant, then, leaving our hero, hastened in pursuit.

"Now's your chance to escape, boy!" said a sympathetic bystander to him.

"I don't want to escape," answered Tom. "I want my innocence proved. I shall stay where I am till the officer returns."

—

And he kept his word. Ten minutes later the officer came back, puffing and panting, after an unsuccessful pursuit, prepared to find Tom gone also.

"What, are you there?" he asked, staring in wonder.

"Yes," said Tom. "I don't want to escape. I shall come out right."

"I believe you will," said the officer, with a revulsion of sentiment in Tom's favor. "Just walk along beside me, and I won't take hold of you. I'm not afraid of your running away now."

CHAPTER XVIII

TOM GETS OUT OF HIS DIFFICULTY

Tom had not been long in the stationhouse when Alderman Morris, accompanied by Mr. Waterbury, entered. The latter looked at Tom with a humorous smile.

"You don't appear to get along very well without my guardianship, Tom," he said.

"No, sir," answered Tom. "The trouble is, some of my other friends can't let me alone."

"Was it in a fit of emotional insanity that you relieved the lady of her pocketbook?" asked Mr. Waterbury, bent on keeping up the joke.

"If I ever do such a thing, you may be sure it is because I am insane," answered Tom positively.

"I shall," said Mr. Waterbury seriously. "Now, where is this precious acquaintance of ours who got you into this scrape?"

"He has escaped."

"Escaped!" exclaimed the alderman hastily. "How is that?"

Here the policeman took up the story and explained that Vincent had taken advantage of his double charge to effect his escape.

"I suppose, officer," said Mr. Waterbury, "that you were unwilling to leave Tom in order to pursue him."

"I did leave him, sir, and didn't expect to find him when I got back. But there he was, waiting for me as quietly as -- anything."

"Didn't you feel tempted to escape, too, my boy?"

"Why should I, sir? I had done nothing; I had nothing to fear."

"Innocence is not always a protection, for justice is sometimes far from clear-sighted. In the present case, however, I think you will not suffer for your confidence."

Tom was not brought to trial. Mr. Waterbury's statement of what had passed on the voyage of the River Belle was held to be sufficient to establish Tom's innocence, and he was allowed to walk out with Mr. Waterbury.

"Have you anything to do this morning, Tom?" asked his friend.

"No, sir."

"Then come around and dine with me at the Burnet House. Afterward we will call upon your friends, the Watsons."

Mrs. Watson and Jennie had altered their plans and gone to a boarding house, preferring that to a hotel.

"That will be agreeable to me, sir."

The lunch was excellent, and Tom did full justice to it.

"At one time this morning, Tom, it looked as if you would dine at quite a different place," said Mr. Waterbury, when they were eating the dessert.

"Yes, sir."

"You won't think much of Cincinnati's hospitality, eh, Tom?"

"Any place would be the same, where Vincent was," returned Tom.

"Very true; he and Graham will bring discredit on any city which they adopt as a home. How long shall you remain here?"

"I should like to stay long enough to see something of the city, but I cannot afford it. I must reach California as soon as possible."

"No doubt you are right, in your circumstances. I have been inquiring for you and find that St. Joseph, in Missouri, is the usual starting-point for travelers across the plains. I find an acquaintance here in the hotel, who will start tomorrow for that place. I have mentioned you to him, and he says he shall be glad to have your company so far. Whether you keep together afterward will depend upon yourselves."

"I shall be glad to have company, sir," said Tom. Though manly and self-reliant, he realized that it was quite a serious undertaking for a boy of his age to make the trip alone. He was not sure of meeting with another friend like Mr. Waterbury, and there might be danger of falling in with another brace of worthies like Graham and Vincent.

"My friend's name is Ferguson -- a Scotchman, rather sedate, but entirely trustworthy. I will introduce you this evening."

"Thank you, sir."

After lunch they walked to Mrs. Watson's boarding house. Somewhere on Vine Street, Mr. Waterbury paused in front of a jewelry store.

"I want to step in here a minute, Tom," he said.

"Certainly, sir."

Tom remained near the door, while Mr. Waterbury went into the back part of the store where he was occupied for a few minutes with one of the proprietors. When he came back he held a small box in his hand.

"Please carry this for me, Tom," he said.

"With pleasure, sir."

They went out into the street together.

"Do you know what is in the box, Tom?" asked Mr. Waterbury.

"No, sir," answered our hero, a little surprised at the question.

"You didn't see what I was buying, then?" continued Mr. Waterbury.

"No, sir. I was watching the crowds on the sidewalk."

"If you have any curiosity, you may open the box."

Previously Tom had felt no curiosity. Now he did feel a little.

Opening the box, his eye rested on a neat silver watch, with a chain attached. The case was a pretty one, and Tom glanced at it with approval.

"It is very pretty, sir," he said, "but I thought you had a watch already."

"I didn't buy it for myself."

"For your son?" asked Tom innocently.

Mr. Waterbury smiled.

"I thought of asking your acceptance of it," he said.

"You don't mean that you are going to give it to me, sir?" said Tom eagerly.

"If you will accept it."

"How kind you are, Mr. Waterbury!" exclaimed Tom gratefully. "There is nothing in the world that I should like so much. How can I thank you?"

"By considering it a proof of my interest in you. I was sure you would like it. Before I had reached your age the great object of my ambition was a watch. I received one from my uncle, as a gift, on my seventeenth birthday. I believe I looked at it once every five minutes on an average during the first day."

"I dare say it will be so with me, sir," said Tom, who, at the moment, had the watch in his hand, examining it.

"As you are to rough it, I thought it best to get you a hunting case watch, because it will be less liable to injury. When you become a man I hope you will be prosperous enough to buy a gold watch and chain, if you prefer them. While you are a boy silver will be good enough."

"Gold wouldn't correspond very well with my circumstances," said Tom. "I didn't dream of even having a silver watch and chain for years to come. I shall write home this evening, and tell mother of my good luck."

—

"Will you mention that you have already been under arrest?" asked Mr. Waterbury, smiling.

Tom shook his head.

"I am not proud of that," he answered, "and it would only trouble them at home to have an account of it. When I get home, I may mention it sometime."

"Better put on your watch and chain, Tom, before we reach Mrs. Watson's."

Tom needed no second invitation.

"It's lucky mother put a watch pocket in my vest," he said. "We didn't either of us suppose there would be any occasion for it, but I asked her to do it."

In a nice-looking brick boarding house -- for brown-stone houses were not then often to be found -- Tom and his friend found Mrs. Watson and Jennie.

"I'm so glad to see you, Tom," said Jennie. "I've missed you awfully."

"Thank you," said Tom. "I've come to bid you goodbye."

"Goodbye! You don't mean that?"

"I expect to start for St. Joseph tomorrow. I am in a hurry to get to California."

"That's real mean. I don't see why you can't stay in Cincinnati a week."

"I should like to."

"Then why don't you?" persisted the young girl.

"Jennie," said her mother, "we must remember that Thomas is not traveling for pleasure. He is going to California to seek his fortune. It won't do for him to linger on his way."

"A week won't make much difference; will it, Tom?"

"I am afraid it will, Jennie. Besides, a friend of Mr. Waterbury will start tomorrow, and he has agreed to take me with him."

"I suppose you've got to go, then," said Jennie regretfully. "Oh, where did you get that watch, Tom?"

"A kind friend gave it to me."

"Who do you mean -- Mr. Graham?" she asked archly.

"He would be more likely to relieve me of it. No, it is Mr. Waterbury."

"I am going to kiss you for that, Mr. Waterbury," said Jennie impulsively, and she suited the action to the word.

"What will Mr. Waterbury think, Jennie?" said her mother.

—

86

"He thinks himself well repaid for his gift," answered that gentleman, smiling, "and half inclined to give Tom another watch."

"Isn't it my turn, now?" asked Tom, with a courage at which he afterward rather wondered, but he was fast getting rid of his country bashfulness.

"I never kiss boys," said Jennie demurely.

"Then I will grow into a man as fast as I can," said Tom, "and give somebody a watch, and then -- But that will be a good while to wait."

"I may kiss you goodbye," said Jennie, "if I feel like it."

She did feel like it, and Tom received the kiss.

"It strikes me, Tom," said Mr. Waterbury, as they were walking home, "that you and Jennie are getting along fast."

"She kissed you first," said Tom, blushing.

"But the kiss she gave me was wholly on your account."

"She seems just like a sister," said Tom. "She's a tip-top girl."

CHAPTER XIX

A MISSOURI TAVERN

The next day Tom started on his way. His new companion, Donald Ferguson, was a sedate Scotchman and a thoroughly reliable man. He was possessed to the full of the frugality characteristic of the race to which he belonged, and, being more accustomed to traveling than Tom, saved our hero something in the matter of expense. He was always ready to talk of Scotland, which he evidently thought the finest country in the world. He admitted that Glasgow was not as large a city as London, but that it was more attractive. As for New York, that city bore no comparison to the chief city of Scotland.

"You must go to Scotland some time, Tom," he said. "If you can't visit but one country in the Old World, go to Scotland."

Privately Tom was of opinion that he should prefer to visit England, but he did not venture to hurt the feelings of his fellow-traveler by saying so.

"I wonder, Mr. Ferguson," he could not help saying one day, "that you should have been willing to leave Scotland, since you so much prefer it to America."

"I'll tell you, my lad," answered the Scotchman. "I would rather live in Scotland than anywhere else on God's footstool, but I won't be denying that it is a poor place for a man to make money, if compared with a new country like this."

Mr. Donald Ferguson

"There are no gold mines, I suppose, sir?"

"No, and the land is not as rich as the land here. It is rich in historical associations, but a man, you know, can't live on those," he added shrewdly.

"No, I should think not," said Tom. "It would be a pretty dry diet. How long have you been in the country, Mr. Ferguson?"

"A matter of three months only, my lad. It's the gold mines that brought me over. I read of them in the papers at home, and I took the first ship across the Atlantic."

"Have you a family, Mr. Ferguson?"

"I've got an old mother at home, my lad, who looks to me for support. I left fifty pounds with her when I came away. It'll last her, I'm thinkin', till I can send her some from California."

"Then Mr. Ferguson, you are like me," said Tom. "I am going to California to work for my father and mother. Father is poor, and I have brothers and sisters at home to provide for. I hope I shall succeed, for their sake."

"You will, my lad," said the Scotchman, in a tone of calm confidence. "It is a noble purpose, and if you keep to it God will bless you in your undertaking, and give you a good fortune."

"I hope we shall both be fortunate."

—

"I have no fear. I put my trust in the Lord, who is always ready to help those who are working for him."

Tom found that Mr. Ferguson, though his manner was dry and unattractive, was a religious man, and he respected and esteemed him for his excellent traits. He was not a man to inspire warm affection, but no one could fail to respect him. He felt that he was fortunate in having such a man for his companion, and he was glad that Mr. Ferguson appeared to like him in turn.

He also found that the Scotchman, though a man of peace and very much averse to quarreling, was by no means deficient in the trait of personal courage.

One evening they arrived at a small tavern in a Missouri town. Neither Tom nor his companion particularly liked the appearance of the place nor its frequenters, but it appeared to be the only place of entertainment in the settlement.

The barroom, which was the only public room set apart for the use of the guests, was the resort of a party of drunken roisterers, who were playing poker in the corner and betting on the game. At the elbow of each player was set a glass of whisky, and the end of each game was marked by a fresh glass all around.

Tom and Mr. Ferguson took a walk after supper and then sat down quietly at a little distance from the card-players, attracting at first but little attention from them.

Presently, at the close of a game, glasses were ordered for the party, at the expense of those who had suffered defeat.

"What'll you have, strangers?" inquired a tipsy fellow, with an Indian complexion and long black hair, staggering toward Ferguson.

"Thank you, sir," said the Scotchman, "but I don't drink."

"Don't drink!" exclaimed the former, in evident surprise. "What sort of a man, pray, may you be?"

"I am a temperance man," said Ferguson, adding indiscreetly, "and it would be well for you all if you would shun the vile liquor which is destroying soul and body."

"—your impudence!" cried the other, in a rage. "Do you dare to insult gentlemen like us?"

"I never insult anybody," said the Scotchman calmly. "What I have said is for your good, and you would admit it if you were sober."

"Do you dare to say I'm drunk?" demanded the man, in a fury.

"Mr. Ferguson," said Tom, in a low voice, "I wouldn't provoke him if I were you."

But the Scotchman was no coward, and, though generally prudent, he was too fond of argument to yield the point.

"Of course, you're drunk," he said calmly. "If you will reflect, you show all the signs of a man that has taken too much liquor. Your face is flushed, your hand is unsteady, and -- "

He was interrupted by a volley of execrations from the man whom he was coolly describing, and the latter, in a fit of fury, struck the Scotchman in the face. Had the blow been well directed it would, for the time, have marred the small share of personal beauty with which nature had endowed Mr. Ferguson, but it glanced aside and just struck him on his prominent cheekbone.

"A ring! A ring!" shouted the men in the corner, jumping to their feet in excitement. "Let Jim and the Scotchman fight it out."

"Gentlemen," said Mr. Ferguson, "I don't wish to fight with your friend. He is drunk, as you can see plainly enough. I don't wish to fight with a drunken man."

"Who says I am drunk?" demanded the champion of whisky. "Let me get at him."

But his friends were now holding him back. They wanted to see a square fight, according to rule. It would prove, in their opinion, a pleasant little excitement.

"I meant no offense," said Ferguson. "I only told the truth."

"You are a -- liar!" exclaimed the man, known as Jim.

"I do not heed the words of a man in your condition," said the Scotchman calmly.

"Pull his nose, Jim! Make him fight!" exclaimed the friends of the bully. "We'll back you!"

The hint was taken. Jim staggered forward, and, seizing the Scotchman's prominent nose, gave it a violent tweak.

Now there are few men, with or without self-respect, who can calmly submit to an insult like this. Certainly Mr. Donald Ferguson was not one of them. The color mantled his high cheekbones, and anger gained dominion over him. He sprang to his feet, grasped the bully in his strong arms, dashed him backward upon the floor of the barroom, and, turning to the companions of the fallen man, he said, "Now come on, if you want to fight. I'll take you one by one, and fight the whole of you, if you like."

Instead of being angry, they applauded his pluck. They cared little for the fate of their champion but were impressed by the evident strength of the stranger.

"Stranger," said one of them, "you've proved that you're a man of honor. We thought you were a coward. It's a pity you don't drink. What may your name be?"

"Donald Ferguson."

"Then, boys, here's to the health of Mr. Ferguson. He's a bully boy, and no coward."

"Gentlemen," said the Scotchman, "it's a compliment you mean, no doubt, and I'm suitably thankful. If you'll allow me, I'll drink your health in a liquor which will not injure any one. I'll wish you health and prosperity in a glass of cold water, if the barkeeper happens to have any of that beverage handy. Tom, join with me in the toast."

Tom did so, and the speech was well received.

"As for this gentleman," said Mr. Ferguson, addressing Jim, who had struggled to his feet and was surveying the scene in rather a bewildered way, "I hope he won't harbor malice; I've only got even with him. We may as well forgive and forget."

"That's the talk! Jim, drink the stranger's health!"

Jim looked a little doubtful, but when a glass of whisky was put into his hand he could not resist the seductive draft and tossed it down.

"Now shake hands!" said one of the players.

"With all my heart," said Ferguson, and the two shook hands, to the great delight of the company.

"You got off pretty well, Mr. Ferguson," said Tom, when they retired for the night.

"Yes, my lad, better than I expected. I thought once I would have to fight the whole pack. Poor fellows! I pity them. They are but slaves to their appetites. I hope, my lad, you'll never yield to a like temptation."

"No fear for me, Mr. Ferguson. I feel as you do on the subject."

The journey continued till one day, about noon, they reached the town of St. Joseph, popularly called St. Joe.

CHAPTER XX

ST. JOE

St. Joe was at that time the fitting-out point for overland parties bound for California. As a matter of course it presented a busy, bustling appearance, and it seemed full of life and movement. There was a large transient population, of a very miscellaneous character. It included the thrifty, industrious emigrant, prepared to work hard and live poorly, till the hoped-for competence was attained. But there was also the shiftless adventurer, whose chief object was to live without work, and the unscrupulous swindler, who was ready, if opportunity offered, to appropriate the hard earnings of others.

"It's a lively place, Mr. Ferguson," said Tom.

"It is, indeed, my young friend," said the cautious Scot, "but it is a place, to my thinking, where it behooves a man to look well to his purse."

"No doubt you are right, Mr. Ferguson. I have learned to be cautious since my adventure with Graham and Vincent."

"There's many like them in the world, Tom. They are like lions, going about seeking whom they may devour."

St. Joseph could not at that time boast any first-class hotels. Inns and lodging houses it had in plenty. At one of these -- a two-story building, dignified by the title of "The Pacific Hotel" -- our hero and his Scotch friend found accommodations. They were charged two dollars and a half per day -- the same price they charged at first-class hotels in New York and Boston, while their rooms and fare were very far from luxurious. The landlord was a stout, jolly host, with a round, good-natured face.

"You and your son will room together, I suppose," he said.

"He isn't my son, but a young friend of mine," said Mr. Ferguson.

"I thought he didn't look much like you," said the landlord.

"I am hard and weather-beaten, while he is young and fresh."

"Well, gentlemen, I wish you both good luck. What will you take? I have a superior article of whisky that I can recommend."

"Thank you, but I beg you will excuse me, sir," said Ferguson. "I never drink."

"Nor I," said Tom, "but I am much obliged to you all the same."

"Well, that beats me," said the landlord. "Why, you don't know what's good. You ain't a minister, are you?" turning to Ferguson.

"I have not that high distinction, my friend. I am an unworthy member of the church of Scotland."

"I don't think your countrymen generally refuse whisky."

"So much the worse for them. They are only too fond of it. My own brother died a miserable death, brought on by his love of liquor."

"Then I won't press you, but I say, strangers, you won't find many of your way of thinking in the country you're going to."

"I don't doubt he's right, Tom," said Ferguson to Tom, as they entered the chamber assigned to them. "We may not be together always. I hope you won't be led away by them who offer you strong drink. It would be the ruin of you, boy."

"Don't fear for me, Mr. Ferguson. I have no taste for it."

"Sometimes it's hard to refuse."

"It won't be hard for me."

"I am glad to hear you say that, my lad. You are young, strong, and industrious. You'll succeed, I'll warrant, if you steer clear of that quicksand."

Later in the day the two friends began to make inquiries about overland travel. They had no wish to remain long at St. Joe. Both were impatient to reach the land of gold, and neither cared to incur the expense of living at the hotel any longer than was absolutely necessary. Luckily this probably would not be long, for nearly every day a caravan set out on the long journey, and doubtless they would be able to join on agreeing to pay their share of the expenses. It was a great undertaking, for the distance to be traversed was over two thousand miles, through an unsettled country, some of it a desert, with the chances of an attack by hostile Indians, and the certainty of weeks, and perhaps months, of privation and fatigue. Mr. Donald Ferguson looked forward to it with some apprehension, for, with characteristic Scotch caution, he counted the cost of whatever he undertook and did not fail to set before his mind all the contingencies and dangers attending it.

"It's a long journey we're going on, my lad," he said, "and we may not reach the end of it in safety."

"It isn't best to worry about that, Mr. Ferguson," said Tom cheerfully.

—

"You are right, my lad. It's not for the best to worry, but it is well to make provision for what may happen. Now, if anything happens to me, I am minded to make you my executor."

"But don't you think I am too young, Mr. Ferguson?"

"You are o'er young, I grant, but you are a lad of good parts, temperate, steady and honest. I have no other friend I feel like trusting."

"I hope, Mr. Ferguson, there will be no occasion to render you any such service, but whatever I can I will do."

"It will be very simple. You will take my money, and see that it is sent to my mother, in Glasgow. I will give you her address now, and then, if any sudden fate overtakes me, there will be no trouble. You will know just what to do."

Tom was flattered by this mark of confidence. It was evident that the cautious Scotchman had formed a very favorable opinion of him, or he would not have selected so young a boy for so important a trust.

"Will you do the same for me, Mr. Ferguson?" he asked, with the sudden reflection that, young as he was, there was no absolute certainty of his living to reach California.

"Surely I will, my lad."

"If I should die I should want any money I might have left sent to my father."

"Give me his address, my lad, and it shall be done. It is a good precaution, and we shan't either of us die the sooner for doing our duty, to the best of our ability, by those who would mourn our loss."

Tom and his friend instituted inquiries, and ascertained that two days later a caravan was to start on its way across the continent. They ascertained, also, that the leader of the expedition was a pioneer named Fletcher, who was making his home at the California Hotel. They made their way thither and were fortunate enough to find Mr. Fletcher at home. He was a stout, broad-shouldered man and a practical farmer, who was emigrating from Illinois. Unlike the majority of emigrants, he had his family with him, namely, a wife, and four children, the oldest a boy of twelve.

"My friend," said Ferguson, "I hear that you are soon leaving here with a party for California."

"I leave day after tomorrow," answered Fletcher.

"Is your party wholly made up?"

"We are about full, but we might receive one or two more."

95

"My young friend and I wish to join some good party, as we cannot afford to remain here, and we are anxious to get to work as soon as possible."

Some care needed to be exercised in the choice of a party, as there were some who would only give trouble and annoyance, or perhaps fail to pay their proper share of the expenses. But Ferguson's appearance was sufficient guarantee of his reliability, and no one was likely to object to Tom.

"Of course," added Ferguson, "we are ready to bear our share of the expense."

"Then you can come," said Fletcher. "You will both need revolvers, for we may be attacked by Indians and must be able to defend ourselves."

"Certainly, we will do our part, if need be."

This was an expense which Tom had not foreseen, but he at once saw the importance of being armed when crossing such a country as lay before them, and he went with Ferguson to make the needful purchase. His Scotch friend instructed him in the method of using his new weapon, and Tom felt a boy's natural pride in his new acquisition. He felt years older then he did on the morning when he left his country home. He had gained some knowledge of the world and felt a greater confidence in himself on that account. He looked forward to the remainder of his journey with pleasurable excitement and lost no time in making the necessary preparations.

CHAPTER XXI

HOW THINGS WENT ON AT HOME

While Tom was slowly making his way westward, there was one place where tidings from him were anxiously awaited and where nightly prayers were offered for his health and safe progress. Of course this was the dear, though humble, farmhouse, which had been his home.

Twice a week Tom wrote, and his letters were cheerful and reassuring.

"Don't trouble yourself about me, dear mother," he wrote from Cincinnati. "I am making friends and learning how to travel. I feel years older and rely much more on myself than when, an inexperienced boy, I bade you goodbye. I am a thousand miles from you, and the longest and most difficult part of the journey lies before me, but with health and strength, and prudence, I hope to arrive in good condition at my destination. As to health I never felt better in my life, and I have taken lessons in prudence and caution which will be of essential service to me. I have found that a boy who goes out into the world to seek his fortune cannot trust everybody he falls in with. He will find foes as well as friends, and he will need to be on his guard.

"I start tomorrow for St. Joseph, in Missouri, going by way of St. Louis. Mr. Donald Ferguson, a middle-aged Scotchman, is my companion. A younger and livelier companion might prove more agreeable, but perhaps not so safe. Mr. Ferguson is old enough to be my father, and I shall be guided by his judgment where my own is at fault. He is very frugal, as I believe his countrymen generally are, and that, of course, just suits me. I don't know how long I shall be in reaching St. Joseph, but I shall write you once or twice on the way. Give my love to father, Sarah, Walter, and Harry, and keep a great deal for yourself.

"Your loving son,

"Tom."

"Tom is growing manly, Mary," said Mark Nelson to his wife. "It's doing him good to see a little of the world."

"I suppose it is, Mark," said his wife, "but the more I think of it the more I feel that he is very young to undertake such a long journey alone."

97

"He is young, but it will make a man of him."

"He must be having a tip-top time," said Walter. "I wish I were with him."

"You would be more of a hindrance than a help to him, Walter," said Mark Nelson.

"You are only a child, you know," said Sarah, in an elder-sister tone.

"What do you call yourself?" retorted Walter. "You are only two years older than I am."

"Girls always know more than boys of the same age," said Sarah condescendingly. "Besides, I haven't said anything about going out to California."

"No, I should think not. A girl that's afraid of a mouse had better stay at home."

Walter referred to an incident of the day previous, when the sudden appearance of a mouse threw Sarah into a panic.

"Are there any mouses in California?" asked little Harry, with interest.

"If there are I could carry a cat with me," returned Sarah good-humoredly.

Mark Nelson, though he felt Tom was a boy to be trusted, did ask himself occasionally whether he had been wise in permitting him to leave home under the circumstances. Suppose he continued in health, there were doubts of his success. His golden dreams might not be realized. The two hundred dollars which he had raised for Tom might be lost and bring in no return, and this would prove a serious loss to Mark, hampered as he was already by a heavy mortgage on his farm. Would Squire Hudson be forbearing, if ill-luck came? This was a question he could not answer. He only knew that such was not the squire's reputation.

"Well, Mr. Nelson, what do you hear from Tom," asked the squire, one day about this time. "How far is he on his way?"

"We received a letter from Cincinnati yesterday. He then was about starting for St. Joseph."

"Does he seem to enjoy the journey?"

"He writes in excellent spirits. He says he has met with good friends."

"Indeed! How does his money hold out?"

"He does not speak of that."

"Oh, well, I dare say he is getting along well," and the squire walked on.

"Does he feel interested in Tom, or not?" queried Mark Nelson, as he looked thoughtfully after the squire, as he walked on with stately steps, leaning slightly on his gold-headed cane. He might have been enlightened on this point, if he could have heard a conversation, later in the day, between Squire Hudson and his son Sinclair.

"I saw Mark Nelson this morning," he observed at the supper table.

"Has he heard from Tom?"

"Yes. His son wrote him from Cincinnati."

"I wish I could go to Cincinnati," grumbled Sinclair. "I think I have a better right to see the world than Tom Nelson."

"All in good time, my son. Tom is not traveling for pleasure."

"Still, he is getting the pleasure."

"He will have to work hard when he reaches California. Probably he won't have a cent left when he gets there."

"What will he do then?"

"He must earn money."

"Do you think he will do well, father?"

"He may, and then again he may not," answered the squire judicially.

"If he don't, how is he going to pay you back the money you lent him?"

"I always thought your father was foolish to lend his money to a boy like that," said Mrs. Hudson querulously.

"Women know nothing about business," said the squire, with an air of superior wisdom.

"Sometimes men don't know much," retorted his wife.

"If you refer to me, Mrs. Hudson," said her husband, "you need have no anxiety. I did not lend the money to the boy, but to his father."

"That isn't much better. Everybody knows that Mark Nelson has all that he can do to get along. His wife hasn't had a new dress for years."

The squire's face grew hard and stern. He had never loved his wife, and never forgiven Mrs. Nelson, whom he had loved as much as he was capable of doing, for refusing his hand.

"She has made her bed, and she must lie upon it," he said curtly. "She might have known that Mark Nelson would never be able to provide for her."

"Perhaps she never had any other offer," said Mrs. Hudson, who was ignorant of a certain passage of her husband's life.

"Probably she did, for she was a very pretty girl."

"Then she's faded," said Mrs. Hudson, tossing her head.

Squire Hudson did not reply, but as his eyes rested on the sharp, querulous face of his helpmate, and he compared it mentally with the pleasant face of Mrs. Nelson, he said to himself that, faded or not, the latter was still better looking than his wife had been in the days of her youth. Of course it would not do to say so, for Mrs. Hudson was not amiable.

"Mark Nelson has given me security," said the squire, returning to the point under discussion. "I hold a mortgage on his farm for the whole amount he owes me."

"Do you think you shall have to foreclose, father?" asked Sinclair.

"If Tom does not succeed in California, I probably shall," said the squire.

"Do you think he will succeed?"

"He may be able to make a living, but I don't think he will be able to help his father any."

"Then why did you lend him the money?"

"He wanted to go and was willing to take the risk. I lent the money as a business operation."

"Suppose Mr. Nelson loses his farm, what will he do?" inquired Sinclair.

"I really don't know," answered the squire, shrugging his shoulders. "That is no concern of mine."

"Tom wouldn't put on so many airs if his father had to go to the poorhouse," said Sinclair.

"Does he put on airs?"

"He seems to think he is as good as I am," said Squire Hudson's heir.

"That is perfectly ridiculous," said Mrs. Hudson. "The boy must be a fool."

"He is no fool," said the squire, who did not allow prejudice to carry him so far as his wife and son. "He is a boy of very fair abilities, but I apprehend he will find it harder to make his fortune than he anticipated. However, time will show."

"Most likely he'll come home in rags and grow up a day-laborer," said Sinclair complacently. "When I'm a rich man I'll give him work. He won't feel like putting on airs, then."

"What a good heart Sinclair has!" said Mrs. Hudson admiringly.

Squire Hudson said nothing. Possibly the goodness of his son's heart was not so manifest to him.

CHAPTER XXII

THE YOUNG MAN FROM BOSTON

Soon after leaving St. Joe, the emigrant train which Tom had joined entered the territory of Kansas. At that early day the settlement of this now prosperous State had scarcely begun. Its rich soil was as yet unvexed by the plow and the spade, and the tall prairie grass and virgin forest stretched for many and many a mile westward in undisturbed loneliness.

One afternoon, toward the setting of the sun, the caravan halted on the site of the present capital of the state, Topeka. The patient oxen, wearied with the twenty miles they had traveled, were permitted to graze. The ten baggage wagons or "ships of the plain," as they were sometimes called, came to anchor in a sea of verdure. They were ranged in a circle, the interior space being occupied as a camping ground. Then began preparations for supper. Some of the party were sent for water. A fire was built, and the travelers, with a luxurious enjoyment of rest, sank upon the grass.

The caravan stops to rest. ("Nooning on the Platte" by Albert Bierstadt)

Donald Ferguson looked thoughtfully over the vast expanse of unsettled prairie, and said to Tom, "It's a great country, Tom. There seems no end to it."

"That's the way I felt when I was plodding along today through the mud," said Tom, laughing.

"It's because the soil is so rich," said the Scotchman. "It'll be a great farming country some day, I'm thinking."

"I suppose the soil isn't so rich in Scotland, Mr. Ferguson?"

"No, my lad. It's rocky and barren and covered with dry heather, but it produces rare men, for all that."

Mr. Ferguson was patriotic to the backbone. He would not claim for Scotland what she could not fairly claim, but he was all ready with some compensating claim.

"How do you stand the walking, Mr. Ferguson?"

"I'm getting used to it."

"Then it's more than I am. I think it's beastly."

These words were not uttered by Tom, but by rather a dandified-looking young man, who came up limping. He was from Boston and gave his name as Lawrence Peabody. He had always lived in Boston, where he had been employed in various genteel avocations, but in an evil hour he had been lured from his comfortable home by the seductive cry of gold and, laying down his yardstick, had set out for California across the plains. He was a slender young man, with limbs better fitted for dancing than for tramping across the prairie, and he felt bitterly the fatigue of the journey.

"Are you tired, Mr. Peabody?" asked Tom.

"I am just about dead. I didn't bargain for walking all the way across the prairies. Why couldn't old Fletcher let me ride?"

"The oxen have had all they could do today to draw the wagons through the mud."

"Look at those boots," said the Bostonian ruefully, pointing to a pair of light calfskin boots, which were so overlaid with mud that it was hard to tell what was their original color. "I bought those boots in Boston only two weeks ago. Everybody called them stylish. Now they are absolutely disreputable."

"It seems to me, my friend," said the Scotchman, "that you did not show much sagacity in selecting such boots for your journey. My young friend, Tom, is much better provided."

"His boots are cowhide," said Mr. Lawrence Peabody disdainfully. "Do you think I would wear cowhide boots?"

"You would find them more serviceable, Mr. Peabody," said Tom. "Besides, I don't believe anybody could tell the difference now."

"How much did you pay for them?" asked the Bostonian.

"A dollar and a half."

"Humph! I thought so," returned Peabody contemptuously. "We don't wear cowhide boots in Boston."

103

"You are not in Boston now."

"I wish I was," said Peabody energetically. "I wouldn't have started if I had known what was before me. I expected to travel like a gentleman, instead of wading through this cursed mud till I'm ready to drop. Look at my pantaloons, all splashed with mire. What would my friends say if I should appear in this rig on Washington Street?"

"They might take you for a bogtrotter," said Tom, smiling.

"I have always been particular about my appearance," said Peabody plaintively. "'He looks just as if he'd come out of a bandbox,' some of my lady friends used to say. How do I look now?"

"Like a dirty-handed son of toil," said Tom humorously.

"So do you," retorted Peabody, who felt that this was uncomplimentary.

"I admit it," said Tom, "and that's just what I expect to be. You don't expect to dig gold with kid gloves on, do you, Mr. Peabody?"

"I wish I had brought some with me," said the Bostonian seriously. "It would have saved my hands looking so dingy."

Mining for gold was not easy work. Here, a miner sifts for gold on the American River in California, 1850.

"How came you to start for California, my friend?" inquired Ferguson.

"The fact is," said Peabody, "I am not rich. There are members of our family who are wealthy, but I am not one of the lucky number."

"You were making a living at home, were you not?"

"Yes, but my income was only enough for myself."

"I suppose you were in love, then," said Tom.

"I don't mind saying that I was, confidentially, of course," said Mr. Peabody complacently.

"Was your love returned?"

"I may say it was. The young lady was the daughter of a merchant prince. I saw that she loved me, but her father would not consent to our union, on account of my limited means. I read in the Transcript of the gold discoveries in California. I determined to go out there and try my fortune. If I am successful I will go home and, with a bag of gold in each hand, demand the hand of Matilda from her haughty sire. When he asks me for my credentials, I will point to the gold and say, 'Behold them here!'"

"If both your hands are full I don't see how you can point to the bags of gold," said Tom, who liked to tease the young Bostonian.

"There are a great many things you don't understand," said Mr. Peabody, irritably.

"He is right, Tom," said Ferguson, with a quiet smile.

"If you are both against me, I will give it up," said Tom. "All I can say is, I hope you'll get the two bags of gold, Mr. Peabody, and that you'll get the young lady, too."

Here Fletcher came up, and called upon Tom to assist in preparations for supper. Our hero readily complied with the request. Indeed, he always showed himself so obliging that he won the favorable regards of all.

Mr. Peabody continued the conversation with Mr. Ferguson.

"Do you think there's as much gold in California as people say?" he asked.

"No," answered the Scotchman.

"You don't?" exclaimed the Bostonian, in dismay.

"No. People always magnify when they talk of a new country. Now, my friend, how much do you expect to get in the first year?"

"Well, about fifty thousand dollars," answered Peabody.

"And how much were you earning in Boston -- a thousand dollars?"

"About that," answered Peabody vaguely. In fact, he had been working on a salary of twelve dollars a week in a retail dry-goods store on Washington Street.

"Then you expect to make fifty times as much as at home?"

"Don't you think I will?"

"I have never had such large expectations. If I make three or four thousand dollars in twelve months it will satisfy me."

"But a man would never get rich, at that rate," said Lawrence Peabody uneasily.

"I don't know about that. It depends as much on what a man does with his money, as on the amount he makes," said the prudent Scot.

"I am afraid I did wrong in leaving Boston," said Peabody gloomily. "If I am to travel many weeks through the mud and get no more than that, I shall feel that I am poorly paid."

"You don't feel like my young friend Tom. He is full of hope and enjoys everything."

"He hasn't been brought up as I have," said Peabody. "A country boy in cowhide boots is tough and don't mind roughing it."

Ferguson did not have a chance to answer, for there was a summons to supper -- a welcome call that made even Mr. Lawrence Peabody look cheerful for the time being.

CHAPTER XXIII

MR. PEABODY'S TROUBLES

When the party camped for the night the custom was to arrange the baggage wagons in a semicircle, and provide a resting place for the women and children inside. As they were passing through a country occupied by Indians it was necessary to post one or more sentinels to keep watch through the night and give notice of any who might be seen lurking near the camp. Fortunately, however, an Indian attack was seldom made at night. The time generally selected was in the morning, when the party were preparing to start on their day's march. Tom, as a boy, would have been excused taking his turn, but this did not suit him. He requested as a favor that he might stand watch with the rest.

"Can he be relied upon? Is he not too young?" asked Fletcher, the leader, of Mr. Ferguson.

"You can depend upon him," said the Scotchman confidently. "There's more manliness in Tom than in many men of twice his years."

"Then I will put his name on the list," said Fletcher.

"That's right. I'll answer for him."

But there was one of the travelers who was by no means eager to stand on watch. This was Lawrence Peabody, the young man from Boston. He sought an interview with Fletcher and asked to be excused.

"On what grounds, Mr. Peabody?" asked Fletcher, surprised.

"It doesn't agree with me to lose my night's sleep," said Peabody. "I am naturally delicate, and --"

"Your excuse is not satisfactory, Mr. Peabody. We are banded together in a little community, having mutual rights and mutual obligations. In the arrangements made for the common safety it is your duty to bear your part."

"I am willing to provide a substitute," said Peabody eagerly.

"Where will you find a substitute?"

"I have been talking with Tom Nelson. He says he is willing to serve in my turn."

"He will serve when his own turn comes; that will be all we can expect of him."

"But he is only a boy. Why should he be expected to take his turn?"

"If he is old enough to be a substitute, he is old enough to stand watch for himself."

"But, Mr. Fletcher, I am very delicate," protested Lawrence Peabody. "I must have my regular sleep, or I shall be sick."

"We must take our chances of that, Mr. Peabody."

"I shall be very likely to go to sleep on my post."

"I wouldn't advise you to," said Fletcher seriously. "It might be dangerous."

"Dangerous!" cried Peabody nervously.

"Precisely. If a lurking Indian should surprise you, you might wake up to find yourself scalped."

"Good gracious!" exclaimed the Bostonian, his teeth chattering, for he was not of the stuff of which heroes are made. "Do you … think there is any danger of that?"

"Considerable, if you neglect your duty."

"But perhaps I can't help falling asleep."

"Mr. Peabody," said Fletcher sternly, "you must keep awake. Not only your own safety, but that of the whole camp, may depend upon your vigilance. If you choose to risk your own life, I don't complain of that, but you shall not imperil ours. I therefore give you notice, that if you fall asleep on guard you will be drummed out of camp and left to shift for yourself."

"But I couldn't find my way on the prairie," said Peabody, very much alarmed.

"You had better think of that when you are tempted to close your eyes, Mr. Peabody," replied Fletcher.

Lawrence Peabody walked off, feeling very much disconcerted. Fervently he wished himself back in Boston, where there are no Indians and a man might sleep from one week's end to another without any danger of losing his scalp.

"What's the matter, Mr. Peabody?" asked Tom, observing his melancholy appearance.

"I don't think I shall ever live to see California," answered Mr. Peabody plaintively.

"Why, what's the matter now?" asked Tom, checking an inclination to laugh. "Are you sick?"

"I don't feel very well, Tom. I'm very delicate, and this journey is almost too much for my strength."

"Oh, cheer up, Mr. Peabody! Think of the gold that awaits you at the end of the journey."

"It's all that keeps me up, I do assure you. But I am afraid I shall never live to get there," said Peabody, with a groan.

"Don't think of such things, Mr. Peabody. Of course none of us is sure of living, but the chances are that we shall reach California in health, make our fortunes, and go home rich. At any rate, that's what I am looking forward to."

"I wouldn't mind so much but for one thing, Tom."

"What is that?"

"Fletcher insists that I shall take my turn in standing guard. If I were not so delicate I wouldn't mind, but I know I can't stand it. I'll give you two dollars to take my place, every time my turn comes."

"I am willing, if Mr. Fletcher is," said Tom, who was by no means averse to making a little extra money.

"But he isn't. I proposed it to him, for I was sure I could arrange with you, but he refused."

"I suppose," said Tom slyly, "he thought I couldn't fill your place. You are a brave, resolute man, and I am only a boy."

"Tom -- I -- I don't mind telling you, but I am afraid I am not brave."

"Oh, nonsense, Mr. Peabody! That is only your modesty."

"But I assure you," said the young Bostonian earnestly, "I am speaking the truth. If I should see an Indian crawling near the camp I'm really afraid I should faint."

"You won't know how brave you are till you are put to the test."

"But do you think there is any chance of my being put to the test? Do you think there are any Indians near?" asked Lawrence Peabody, wiping the damp perspiration from his brow.

"Of course there must be," said Tom. "We are passing through their hunting grounds, you know."

"Why did I ever leave Boston?" said Mr. Peabody sadly.

"You came, as I did, to make your fortune, Mr. Peabody."

"I'm afraid I can't keep awake, Tom. Mr. Fletcher tells me, if I don't, that he will turn me adrift on the prairie. Isn't that hard?"

"I am afraid it is a necessary regulation. But you won't fall asleep. Your turn will only come about once in two weeks, and that isn't much."

"The nights will seem very long."

"I don't think so. I think it'll be fun, for my part."

109

"But suppose -- when you are watching -- you should all at once see an Indian, Tom?" said Peabody, with a shiver.

"I think it would be rather unlucky for the Indian," said Tom coolly.

"You are a strange boy, Tom," said Mr. Peabody.

"What makes you think so?"

"You don't seem to care anything about the danger of being scalped."

"I don't believe I should like being scalped any more than you do."

"You might have got off from standing watch, but you asked to be allowed to."

"That is quite true, Mr. Peabody. I want to meet my fair share of danger and fatigue."

"You can stand it, for you are strong and tough. You have not my delicacy of constitution."

"Perhaps that's it," said Tom laughing.

"Would you mind speaking to Fletcher and telling him you are willing to take my place?"

"I will do it, if you wish me to, Mr. Peabody."

"Thank you, Tom. You are a true friend," and Mr. Peabody wrung the hand of his young companion.

Tom was as good as his word. He spoke to Fletcher on the subject, but the leader of the expedition was obdurate.

"Can't consent, my boy," he said. "It is enough for you to take your turn. That young dandy from Boston needs some discipline to make a man of him. He will never do anything in a country like California unless he has more grit than he shows at present. I shall do him a favor by not excusing him."

Tom reported the answer to Peabody, who groaned in spirit, and nervously waited for the night when he was to stand watch.

CHAPTER XXIV

A SAD SIGHT

A day later, while the wagon train was slowly winding through a mountain defile, they encountered a sight which made even the stout-hearted leader look grave. Stretched out stiff and stark were two figures, cold in death. They were men of middle age, apparently. From each the scalp had been removed, thus betraying that the murderers were Indians.

"I should like to come across the red devils who did this," said Fletcher.

"What would you do with them?" asked Ferguson.

"Shoot them down like dogs, or if I could take them captive they should dangle upon the boughs of yonder tree."

"I hope I shall be ready to die when my time comes," said Ferguson, "but I want it to be in a Christian bed and not at the hands of a dirty savage."

Just then Lawrence Peabody came up. He had been lagging in the rear, as usual.

"What have you found?" he inquired, not seeing the bodies at first, on account of the party surrounding them.

"Come here, and see for yourself, Peabody," said one of the company.

Lawrence Peabody peered at the dead men -- he was rather nearsighted -- and turned very pale.

"Is it the Indians?" he faltered.

"Yes, it's those devils. You can tell their work when you see it. Don't you see that they are scalped?"

"I believe I shall faint," said Peabody, his face becoming of a greenish hue. "Tom, let me lean on your shoulder. Do -- do you think it has been done lately?"

"Yesterday, probably," said Ferguson. "The bodies look fresh."

"Then the Indians that did it must be near here?"

"Probably."

"These men were either traveling by themselves or had strayed away from their party," said Fletcher. "It shows how necessary it is for us to keep together. In union there is strength."

The bodies were examined. In the pocket of one was found a letter addressed to James Collins, dated at some town in Maine. The writer appeared to be his wife. She spoke of longing for the time when he should return with money enough to redeem their farm from a heavy mortgage.

"Poor woman!" said Ferguson. "She will wait for her husband in vain. The mortgage will never be paid through his exertions."

Tom looked sober, as he glanced compassionately at the poor emigrant.

"He came on the same errand that I did," he said. "I hope my journey will have a happier ending."

"Always hope for the best, Tom," said his Scotch friend. "You will live happier while you do live, and, if the worst comes, it will be time enough to submit to it when you must."

"That is good philosophy, Mr. Ferguson."

"Indeed it is, my lad. Don't borrow trouble."

"We must bury these poor men," said Fletcher. "We can't leave them out here, possibly to be devoured by wild beasts. Who will volunteer for the service?"

"Come, Peabody," said John Miles, a broad-shouldered giant, who had a good-natured contempt for the young man from Boston. "Suppose you and I volunteer."

Lawrence Peabody shrank back in dismay at the unwelcome proposition.

"I couldn't do it," he said shivering. "I never touched a dead body in my life. I am so delicate that I couldn't do it, I assure you."

"It's lucky we are not all delicate," said Miles, "or the poor fellows would be left unburied. I suppose if anything happens to you, Peabody, you will expect us to bury you?"

"Oh, don't mention such a thing, Mr. Miles," entreated Peabody, showing symptoms of becoming hysterical. "I really can't bear it."

"It's my belief that nature has made a mistake, and Peabody was meant for a woman," said Miles, shrugging his shoulders.

"I will assist you, my friend," said the Scotchman. "It's all that remains for us to do for the poor fellows."

"Not quite all," said Tom. "Somebody ought to write to the poor wife. We have her address in the letter you took from the pocket."

"Well thought of, my lad," said Fletcher. "Will you undertake it?"

"If you think I can do it properly," said Tom modestly.

"It'll be grievous news, whoever writes it. You can do it as well as another."

In due time Mrs. Collins received a letter revealing the sad fate of her husband, accompanied with a few simple words of sympathy.

Over the grave a rude cross was planted, fashioned of two boards, with the name of James Collins, cut out with a jack-knife, upon them. This inscription was the work of Miles.

"Somebody may see it who knows Collins," he said.

It happened that, on the second night after the discovery of Collins and his unfortunate companion, Lawrence Peabody's turn came to stand watch. He was very uneasy and nervous through the day. In the hope of escaping the ordeal he so much dreaded he bound a handkerchief round his head.

"What's the matter, Mr. Peabody?" asked Fletcher.

"I've got a fearful headache," groaned Peabody. "It seems to me as if it would split open."

"Let me feel of it," said Fletcher. "It doesn't feel hot. It doesn't throb," he said.

"It aches terribly," said Peabody. "I'm very subject to headaches. It is the effect of a delicate constitution."

"The fellow is shamming," said Fletcher to himself, and he felt disgust rather than sympathy.

"It's a little curious, Mr. Peabody, that this headache should not come upon you till the day you are to stand on watch," remarked the leader, with a sarcasm which even the young man from Boston detected.

"Yes, it's strange," he admitted, "and very unlucky, for of course you won't expect a sick man to watch."

"You don't look at it in the right light, Mr. Peabody. I regard it as rather lucky than otherwise."

Lawrence Peabody stared.

"I don't understand you, Mr. Fletcher," he said.

"If you have the headache, it will prevent you from going to sleep, and you remember you expressed yourself as afraid that you might. If you were quite well, I might feel rather afraid of leaving the camp in your charge. Now, I am sure you won't fall asleep."

Mr. Peabody listened in dismay. The very plan to which he had resorted in the hope of evading duty was likely to fasten that duty upon him.

"He'll be well before night," thought Fletcher shrewdly, and he privately imparted the joke to the rest of the party. The result was that Mr. Peabody became an object of general attention.

In half an hour the young man from Boston removed his handkerchief from his head.

"Are you feeling better, Mr. Peabody?" asked Tom.

"Very much better," said Peabody.

"Your headache seems to pass off suddenly."

"Yes, it always does," said the young Bostonian. "I am like mother in that. She had a delicate constitution, just like mine. One minute she would have a headache as if her head would split open, and half an hour afterward she would feel as well as usual."

"You are very fortunate. I was afraid your headache would make it uncomfortable for you to watch tonight."

"Yes, it would, but, as the captain said, it would have kept me awake. Now I don't believe I can keep from sleeping on my post."

"Why don't you tell Fletcher so?"

"Won't you tell him, Tom? He might pay more attention to it if you told him."

"No, Mr. Peabody. You are certainly the most suitable person to speak to him. What makes you think he would pay more attention to me, who am only a boy?"

"He seems to like you, Tom."

"I hope he does, but really, Mr. Peabody, you must attend to your own business."

Fletcher was at the head of the train, walking beside the first wagon. Hearing hurried steps, he turned, and saw Mr. Lawrence Peabody, panting for breath.

"Have you got over your headache, Mr. Peabody?" he asked, with a quiet smile.

"Yes, Mr. Fletcher, it's all gone."

"I am glad to hear it."

"It would have kept me awake tonight, as you remarked," said Peabody. "Now, I am really afraid that I shall fall asleep."

"That would be bad for you."

"Why so?"

"You remember those two poor fellows whom we found scalped the other day?"

"I shall never forget them," said Lawrence Peabody, with a shudder.

"Better think of them tonight. If you go to sleep on watch, those very Indians may serve you in the same way."

"Oh, good gracious!" cried Peabody, turning pale.

"They or some of their tribe are, no doubt, near at hand."

"Don't you think you could excuse me, Mr. Fletcher?" stammered Peabody, panic-stricken.

"No!" thundered Fletcher, so sternly that the unhappy Bostonian shrank back in dismay.

For the credit of Boston, it may be said that John Miles -- a broad-shouldered young giant, who did not know what fear was -- more honorably represented the same city.

CHAPTER XXV

A NIGHT PANIC

Lawrence Peabody's feelings when night approached were not unlike those of a prisoner under sentence of death. He was timid, nervous and gifted with a lively imagination. His fears were heightened by the sad spectacle that he had recently witnessed. His depression was apparent to all, but I regret to say that it inspired more amusement than sympathy. Men winked at each other as they saw him pass, and, with the exception of Tom and his Scotch friend, probably nobody pitied the poor fellow.

"He's a poor creature, Tom," said Donald Ferguson, "but I pity him. We wouldn't mind watching tonight, but I doubt it's a terrible thing to him."

"I would volunteer in his place, but Mr. Fletcher won't agree to it," said Tom.

"He is right. The young man must take his turn. He won't dread it so much a second time."

"What would the poor fellow do if he should see an Indian?"

"Faint, likely, but that is not probable."

"Mr. Fletcher thinks there are some not far off."

"They don't attack in the night, so I hear."

"That seems strange to me. I should think the night would be most favorable for them."

"It's their way. Perhaps they have some superstition that hinders."

"I am glad of it, at any rate. I can sleep with greater comfort."

The rest were not as considerate as Tom and Ferguson. They tried, indeed, to excite still further the fears of the young Bostonian.

"Peabody," said Miles, "have you made your will?"

"No," answered Peabody nervously. "Why should I?"

"Oh, I was thinking that if anything happened to you tonight you might like to say how your things are to be disposed of. You've got a gold watch, haven't you?"

"Yes," said Peabody nervously.

"And a little money, I suppose."

"Not very much, Mr. Miles."

"No matter about that. Of course if you are killed you won't have occasion for it," said Miles, in a matter-of-fact tone.

"I wish you wouldn't talk that way," said Peabody irritably. "It makes me nervous."

"What's the use of being nervous? It won't do any good."

"Do you really think, Mr. Miles, there is much danger?" faltered Peabody.

"Of course there is danger. But the post of danger is the post of honor. Now, Peabody, I want to give you a piece of advice. If you spy one of those red devils crouching in the grass, don't stop to parley, but up with your revolver, and let him have it in the head. If you can't hit him in the head, hit him where you can."

"Wouldn't it be better," suggested Peabody, in a tremulous voice, "to wake you up, or Mr. Fletcher?"

"While you were doing it the savage would make mincemeat of you. No, Peabody, fire at once. This would wake us all up, and if you didn't kill the reptile we would do it for you."

"Perhaps he would see me first," suggested Peabody, in a troubled tone.

"You mustn't let him. You must have your eyes all about you. You are not near-sighted, are you?"

"I believe I am -- a little," said Peabody eagerly, thinking that this might be esteemed a disqualification for the position he dreaded.

"Oh, well, I guess it won't make any difference, only you will need to be more vigilant."

"I wish I was blind, just for tonight," thought Peabody to himself, with an inward sigh. "Then they would have to excuse me."

John Miles overtook Fletcher, who was with the head wagon.

"Captain Fletcher," he said, "I am afraid Peabody will make a mighty poor watch."

"Just my opinion."

"He is more timid than the average woman. I've got a sister at home who has ten times his courage. If she hadn't I wouldn't own the relationship."

"I am not willing to excuse him."

"Of course not, but I'll tell you what I'll do. I'll keep an eye open myself, so that we sha'n't wholly depend on him."

"If you are willing to do it, Miles, we shall all be indebted to you. Don't let him know it, though."

"I don't mean to. He shall suppose he is the only man awake in camp."

At a comparatively early hour the party stretched themselves out upon the ground, inviting sleep. Generally they did not have to wait long. The day's march brought with it considerable physical fatigue. Even those who were light sleepers at home slept well on the trip across the plains. Few or none remained awake half an hour after lying down. So Peabody knew that he would soon be practically alone.

With a heavy heart he began to pace slowly forward and back. He came to where Tom lay.

"Tom -- Tom Nelson," he called, in a low voice.

"What's the matter?" asked Tom, in a sleepy tone.

"Are you asleep?"

"No, but I soon shall be."

"Won't you try to keep awake a little while? It won't seem so lonesome."

"Sorry I can't accommodate you, Mr. Peabody, but I'm awfully tired and sleepy."

"Who's that talking there?" drowsily demanded the nearest emigrant. "Can't you keep quiet, and let a fellow sleep?"

"Good night, Mr. Peabody," said Tom, by way of putting an end to the conversation.

"Good night," returned the sentinel disconsolately.

The hours passed on, and Lawrence Peabody maintained his watch. He was in no danger of going to sleep, feeling too timid and nervous. He began to feel a little more comfortable. He could see nothing suspicious and hear nothing except the deep breathing of his sleeping comrades.

"It is not so bad as I expected," he muttered to himself.

He began to feel a little self-complacent and to reflect that he had underrated his own courage. He privately reflected that he was doing as well as any of his predecessors in duty. He began to think that after he had got back to Boston with a fortune, gained in California, he could impress his friends with a narrative of his night-watch on the distant prairies. But his courage had not yet been tested.

He took out his watch to see how time was passing.

It pointed to twelve o'clock.

Why there should be anything more alarming in twelve o'clock than in any other hour I can't pretend to say, but the fact none will question. Mr. Peabody felt a nervous thrill when his eyes rested on the dial. He looked about him, and the darkness seemed blacker and more awe-inspiring than ever, now that he knew it to be midnight.

"Will it ever be morning?" he groaned. "Four long hours at least before there will be light. I don't know how I am going to stand it."

Now, there was attached to the wagon-train one of those universally despised but useful animals, a donkey, the private property of a man from Iowa, who expected to make it of service in California. The animal was tethered near the camp and was generally quiet. But tonight he was wakeful, and managed about midnight to slip his tether, and wandered off. Peabody did not observe his escape. His vigilance was somewhat relaxed, and with his head down he gave way to mournful reflection. Suddenly the donkey, who was now but a few rods distant, uplifted his voice in a roar which the night stillness made louder than usual. It was too much for the overwrought nerves of the sentinel. He gave a shriek of terror, fired wildly in the air, and sank fainting to the ground. Of course the camp was roused. Men jumped to their feet, and, rubbing their eyes, gazed around them in bewilderment.

It was not long before the truth dawned upon them. There lay the sentinel, insensible from fright, his discharged weapon at his feet. The almost equally terrified donkey was in active flight, making the air vocal with his peculiar cries.

There was a great shout of laughter, in the midst of which Peabody recovered consciousness.

"Where am I?" he asked, looking about him wildly, and he instinctively felt for his scalp, which he was relieved to find still in its place.

"What's the matter?" asked the leader. "What made you fire?"

"I -- I thought it was the Indians," faltered Peabody. "I thought I heard their horrid war-whoop."

"Not very complimentary to the Indians to compare them with donkeys," said Miles.

Lawrence Peabody was excused from duty for the remainder of the night, his place being taken by Miles and Tom in turn.

It was a long time before he heard the last of his ridiculous panic, but he was not sensitive as to his reputation for courage, and he bore it, on the whole, pretty well.

CHAPTER XXVI

MR. PEABODY IS WORSTED

The traveler of today who is whirled across the continent in six days and a half has little conception of what the overland journey was in the year 1850. Week after week and month after month slipped away between the start and the arrival on the western slope of the Sierra Nevadas. Delicate women and children of tender years developed extraordinary endurance and showed remarkable fortitude on the wearisome trip. But the hope of bettering their fortunes was the magnet that drew them steadily on, day after day, in their march across the plains.

The travelers are looking forward to searching for gold. Pictured here are miners in the Sierra Nevada Mountains in 1852.

Tom was at an age when adventure has a charm. His feet were often weary, but he never tired of the journey. Every morning found him active, alert, and ready for the toilsome walk. He was, indeed, impatient for the time to come when he could be earning something to pay up his debt to Squire Hudson, and so relieve his father from the additional burden assumed for his sake. Otherwise he was quite content to plod on, seeing something new every day.

"You're always cheerful, Tom, my lad," said Ferguson one day.

"Yes," said Tom. "I am having a good time."

"Youth is aye the time for enjoyment. When I was a lad like you I might have been the same."

"Don't you enjoy the journey, Mr. Ferguson?" asked Tom.

"I'm getting tired of it, Tom. I look upon it as a means to an end. I'm in a hurry to reach the mines."

"So am I, Mr. Ferguson, for that matter."

"And I can't help thinking, what if they don't turn out as well as we expect? Then there'll be months lost, besides a good bit of money," replied Ferguson.

"Oh, I'm sure there is plenty of gold, and we shall get our share," said Tom confidently. "That is, if we have our health."

"I hope it'll be as you say, my lad. Indeed, I think you are right. You have taught me a lesson."

"Have I, Mr. Ferguson? What is it?"

"Always to look on the bright side. It is a lesson worth learning. It makes a man feel happier and often gives courage to press on to the accomplishment of his purpose."

"I suppose it is natural to me," said Tom.

"It is a happy gift. It is a pity that poor creature from Boston hadn't it."

Lawrence Peabody was approaching, and this no doubt led to the allusion. He was limping along, looking decidedly down in the mouth, which, indeed, was not unusual.

"What is the matter with you, Mr. Peabody?" asked Tom.

"I'm almost gone," groaned Peabody. "My strength is exhausted, and, besides, I've got a terrible corn on my left foot."

"How long has that been?"

"For two or three days. It's torture for me to walk. I don't know but you'll have to leave me here on the prairie to perish."

"Not so bad as that, Mr. Peabody, I hope. Perhaps Mr. Chapman will lend you his donkey to ride upon."

The owner of the donkey was within hearing distance, and at once expressed a willingness to lend his animal to Mr. Peabody.

"That will be better than perishing on the prairies," said Tom cheerfully.

"I am not much used to riding," said Peabody cautiously.

"He won't run away with you, Peabody," said the owner. "He's too lazy."

Lawrence Peabody was already aware of this fact, and it gave him courage to accept the offered help. He mounted Solomon -- as the donkey was called, for some unknown reason -- and for a time enjoyed the relief from the toil of walking. He became quite cheerful and was disposed to congratulate himself upon his success, when an unfortunate fit of obstinacy came over Solomon. It dawned upon the sagacious animal that it would be much easier to travel without a load, and, turning his head, he looked thoughtfully at his rider.

"Get up, Solomon!" exclaimed Peabody, striking the animal on the haunch.

Solomon felt that this was taking a personal liberty and he stood stock-still, his face expressive of obstinacy.

"Why don't he go on?" asked Peabody, perplexed.

"He's stopping to rest," said Tom. "I am afraid he is lazy."

"Go along!" exclaimed Peabody, again using his whip. But the animal did not budge.

"This is really very provoking," murmured the rider. "What shall I do?"

"Don't give up to him," advised one of the company. "Here, let me whip him."

"Thank you. I wish you would."

It was an unlucky speech. The other complied with the request and delivered his blow with such emphasis that Solomon's equanimity was seriously disturbed. He dashed forward with what speed he could command, Mr. Peabody holding on, in a sort of panic, till he was a hundred yards away. Then he stopped suddenly, lowering his head, and his hapless rider was thrown over it, landing some distance in advance. Solomon looked at him with grim humor, if a donkey is capable of such a feeling and, apparently satisfied, turned and walked complacently back to the wagon-train.

Several of the company, witnessing the accident, hurried forward to Mr. Peabody's assistance. They picked him up, groaning and bewildered, but not much hurt.

"None of your limbs broken," said Miles. "I guess you'll do."

"I'm badly shaken up," moaned Peabody.

"It will do you good," said Miles bluntly.

"You had better try it yourself, then," retorted Peabody, with unwonted spirit.

"Good for you!" laughed Miles. "I suspect you are not dead yet."

"What made you put me on such a vicious beast?" asked Peabody of the owner.

"Solomon isn't vicious; he's only lazy," said Chapman. "We can't blame him much."

"I think he ought to be shot," said Peabody, painfully rising and stretching out one limb after another to make sure that none was broken.

"You seem to be unlucky, Mr. Peabody," said Tom.

"I'm always unlucky," moaned Peabody.

"Will you ride again, Mr. Peabody?" asked Chapman. "I'll catch Solomon for you, if you like."

"Not for fifty dollars!" exclaimed Peabody energetically. "It is as much as anybody's life is worth."

"If you will make me the same offer, I won't refuse, Mr. Chapman," said Tom.

"You can mount him, if you like."

Tom waited for no second invitation. He approached Solomon cautiously, vaulted upon his back, and the animal, disagreeably surprised, had recourse to the same tactics which had proved so successful in the case of the young man from Boston. But he had a different kind of a rider to deal with. Tom had been accustomed to ride from the time he was six years of age, and he stuck to his seat in spite of all attempts to dislodge him. So far from feeling alarmed, he enjoyed the struggle.

"It's no go, Solomon!" he said gaily. "You've tackled the wrong customer this time. Better make up your mind to go as I want you to."

Solomon came to the same conclusion after a time. He had tried his ordinary tactics, and they had proved unavailing. The struggle had been witnessed with some interest by the other members of the company.

"You can ride, youngster; that's a fact," said the owner of the donkey. "I didn't say anything, but I rather expected to see you follow Peabody."

"I'm used to riding," said Tom modestly. "Mr. Peabody is not."

"Every lad ought to know how to ride," said Ferguson. "It's a deal manlier than smoking a cigar, to my thinking."

"I can smoke a cigar," said Peabody, desirous probably of appearing to possess one manly accomplishment.

"You will hardly find it as useful as riding in the new country you are going to, Mr. Peabody," said Ferguson dryly.

"I'd give something for a good cigar myself," said John Miles.

"I prefer riding," said Tom. "I never smoked a cigar in my life."

"You are just as well off without it, my lad," said the Scotchman. "It don't do men any good, and always harms boys."

Peabody never again mounted Solomon. One trial was sufficient, and, footsore and lame as he was, he decidedly preferred to walk.

CHAPTER XXVII

THE LOST HORSE

Day followed day, and every sunset found the party from eighteen to twenty miles nearer the land of gold. They had not yet been molested by Indians, though on more than one occasion they had encountered the remains of those whom the savages had ruthlessly slaughtered. When they witnessed such a spectacle they were moved less by fear than indignation.

"I didn't think I should ever thirst for a fellow creature's blood," said John Miles, "but if I could meet the savages that did this bloody work, I would shoot them down like dogs and sleep all the more soundly for it. How is it with you, friend Ferguson?"

"I am inclined to agree with you," said the Scotchman. "When an Indian makes himself a beast of prey he should be treated accordingly."

"Are there any Indians in California?" asked Peabody nervously.

"I don't think we shall have any trouble with them there, Mr. Peabody," said Ferguson.

"Then I wish I was there now. It must be terrible to be scalped," and the young man from Boston shuddered.

"I don't think it would be an agreeable surgical operation," said Fletcher, who had just come up. "Let us hope that we shall not be called upon to undergo it."

The next morning, when breakfast was over and the party was preparing to start, an unpleasant discovery was made. One of the most valuable horses was missing. He must have slipped his tether during the night and strayed away. As they were situated, the loss of such an animal would be felt.

"He can't be far away," said Fletcher. "Some of us must go after him."

"Let Peabody mount the mustang and undertake to find him," suggested John Miles, winking at the captain.

"Mr. Peabody," said Captain Fletcher gravely, "will you undertake to recover the horse? We shall all feel under great obligations to you."

"I -- I hope you will excuse me, Captain Fletcher," stammered Peabody in great alarm. "I know I couldn't find the horse. I shouldn't know where to look."

"This is where he got away. You can see his trail in the grass," said Scott, a young man from Indiana. "All you will have to do will be to follow the trail, Mr. Peabody."

"I'm very nearsighted," pleaded Peabody. "I should lose my way, and never come back."

"Carrying the mustang with you? That would be a loss indeed," said John Miles pointedly. "On the whole, Captain Fletcher, we had better excuse Mr. Peabody."

"Mr. Peabody is excused," said the leader.

"Thank you," said Peabody, looking relieved. "I would go, I am sure, if I could do any good, but I know I couldn't."

"Who will volunteer?" asked Fletcher.

"Let me go," said Tom eagerly.

"You are not afraid of losing your way, Tom?" said Miles.

"No, or if I do, I will find it again."

"That boy is more of a man now than Peabody will ever be," said Miles, in a low voice to Ferguson.

"That he is," said the Scotchman, who was a firm friend of our young hero. "There is the making of a noble man in him."

"I believe you."

"I have no objection to your going, Tom," said Fletcher, "but it is better that you should have company. Who will go with the boy?"

"I," said several, among them John Miles and Henry Scott.

"You may go, Scott," said the leader. "I have work for Miles at camp. The sooner you get started the better."

"All right, captain. Come along, Tom."

The two were in the saddle before two minutes had passed and, guided by the trail, struck out upon the prairie.

Scott was a tall, broad-shouldered young farmer, not over twenty-five, strong and athletic, and reported, the best runner, wrestler, and vaulter in the party. Tom was very well pleased to have his company.

CHAPTER XXVIII

INDIAN CASUISTRY

"I should like to know when the horse got away," said Scott, as he and Tom rode on side by side, "then we could calculate how far we should have to go before overtaking him."

"He wouldn't be likely to travel all the time, would he?" asked Tom.

"Probably not. He may have gone only a mile or two. Are your eyes good?"

"Pretty good."

"Look about, then, and see if you can anywhere see anything of the rover."

Scott and Tom, drawing rein, looked searchingly in all directions, but nowhere was the lost animal visible.

"Somebody may have found him," suggested Tom.

"That may be. If so, we have a harder job before us."

The prairie was not quite level but was what is called a rolling prairie, and this limited the view. Otherwise it would have been easy for a person, whose sight was keen, to have distinguished an object as large as a horse at a distance of many miles.

"Are you sure we are on the right track, Mr. Scott?" asked Tom.

"Yes, I can see by the trail."

"I can see no hoof-marks."

"Not just here, but look closely, and you will see slight marks of disturbance in the grass. As long as these signs last we need have no doubts as to our being on the right track."

"The same trail will lead us back to our party," said Tom.

"Yes, I shouldn't like to part from them in this country. It would be rather a bad place to be lost without provisions."

They had ridden about five miles when the trail became clearer and better defined. In fact, the marks in the prairie grass appeared more numerous than a single horse would be likely to make.

Scott looked grave.

"We will halt here a moment, Tom," he said. "I want to examine the trail."

"Shall I get off my horse?"

"No, it is not necessary."

Scott dismounted and walked about, closely examining the marks in the grass.

Finally he looked up.

"I begin to think it doubtful whether we shall recover Dan," he said.

"Why?"

"He has been found and carried off," was the reply. "Do you see the double trail?"

"Yes," said Tom, after a brief examination.

"It means that a horseman has found Dan and led him away. This rather complicates matters."

"What do you think we had better do?" inquired Tom.

"That requires consideration. I could tell better if I knew by whom the horse had been found. The finder may be honest and would, in that case, surrender it on our appearing and claiming him. But, again, he may be dishonest, and resist our claims."

"We are two to one," said Tom stoutly.

"We don't know that. The man may belong to a party."

"The members of his party would know that the horse was not his."

"Quite true, if the party was composed of decent persons, like our own, but that is not certain."

"Then will you go back without Dan?" asked Tom.

"I don't want to do that. In fact I should be ashamed to. Captain Fletcher would conclude that he might as well have sent Peabody, and I am not anxious to be classed with him."

"Nor I," said Tom, smiling.

"So the only thing is to push on, and make what discoveries we may."

"All right," said Tom cheerfully.

They rode on for a couple of miles, having no difficulty in following the trail, until they reached the brow of a small eminence. Here they were greeted with a sight that startled them. A group of a dozen Indians were reclining on the grass, with their horses fastened near them. Startled as they were, they detected the animal of which they were in search among the Indian horses.

"We've walked into a trap with our eyes open, Tom," said Scott, halting his horse mechanically. His bronzed face was a little pale, for he knew well the character of the savages before him, the hopelessness of escape, and the terrible fate that probably awaited them.

"Shall we turn and fly, Mr. Scott?" asked Tom hurriedly.

"It would be of no use, Tom. We must stay and face the music."

Upon the appearance of the two friends the Indians had sprung to their feet, and the colloquy was scarcely over before there was an Indian at each bridle-rein. They made signs, easily understood, for Tom and Scott to dismount.

"Stop a minute," said Scott, with creditable coolness, considering the great peril in which he knew himself to be. "Is there any one here who speaks English?"

An elderly Indian stepped forward quickly and said, "Speak, white man. I speak English a little."

"Good," said Scott. "Then I want you to tell your friends here that I came after a horse that left our camp last night. Do you understand?"

The Indian inclined his head.

"There he is," continued Scott, pointing with his finger to Dan. "Give him to me, and I will go away."

The interpreter turned to his companions and repeated what Scott had said. Evidently it was not favorably received, as Scott could see by the menacing looks that were turned upon him. He waited, with some anxiety, for the answer to his claim. He had to wait for some minutes, during which the Indians appeared to be consulting. It came at last.

"The white man has lied," said the Indian sententiously. "The horse is ours."

"That's pretty cool, eh, Tom?" said Scott, provoked not only by the denial of his claim, but by the charge of falsehood.

Tom did not answer, thinking silence more prudent.

The Indian interpreter looked suspiciously from one to the other. He understood what "cool" meant, but was not familiar with the special sense in which Scott used it.

"I will prove that the horse is ours," said Scott. "Here, Dan!"

The horse whinnied and tried to reach Scott, upon hearing his name pronounced.

"There," said Scott triumphantly, "you see the horse knows me. I have not lied."

The speech was an imprudent one. Indians are not lawyers, but they understand the familiar saying that "possession is nine points of the law." That the horse was a valuable one they understood, and they had no intention of parting with him. Still more, they looked with covetous eyes at the horses ridden by Scott and the boy, and they had already made up their minds to seize them also.

"The white man is a magician," said the interpreter. "He has bewitched the horse. The horse is ours. He has always belonged to us."

"It's no use, Tom," said Scott. "They are bound to keep Dan, and I don't see how we can help it. We had better give him up and get away if we can. All the same, the fellow is an outrageous liar."

He spoke in a low voice, and the interpreter, though listening attentively, did not quite catch what was said.

"I guess you are right," said Tom.

Scott turned to the interpreter.

"Well, if you think it is yours, squire, I reckon you will keep it. So we'll say good morning and go."

He pulled the rein, but the Indian at his bridle did not let go.

"Good morning, gentlemen," said Scott. "We are going."

"White man must stay," said the Indian interpreter decisively.

"Why?" demanded Scott impatiently.

"He has tried to steal Indian's horse," said the wily savage.

"Well, by gosh, that's turning the tables with a vengeance," cried Scott. "They're rather ahead of white rogues, Tom. Will you let the boy go?" he asked.

"White boy stay, too," answered the interpreter, after a brief reference to the leader of the Indian party.

"Tom," said Scott rapidly and not appearing to be excited, lest his excitement should lead to suspicion, "none of them are mounted. Lash your horse, and tear from the grasp of the man that holds him. Then follow me. It is our only chance."

Tom's heart beat rapidly. He knew that all his nerve was called for, but he did not falter.

"Give the signal," he said.

"One, two, three!" said Scott rapidly. Simultaneously both lashed their horses. The startled animals sprang forward. The grips of the Indians, who were not suspecting any attempts at escape, were already relaxed, and before they were fully aware of what was intended our two friends were galloping away.

CHAPTER XXIX

A RACE FOR LIFE

The Indians were taken by surprise. They so outnumbered their intended captives that they had not anticipated an attempt at escape. But they had no intention of losing their prey. There was a howl of surprise and disappointment. Then they sprang for their horses and, with little delay, were on the track of our two friends.

The delay was small, but it was improved by Scott and Tom. Pressing their animals to their highest speed they gained a lead of several hundred feet before their savage pursuers had fairly started. It was well that Tom was a good rider, or he might not have been able to keep his seat. In fact, he had never ridden so rapidly before, but he felt that he was riding for his life and was only anxious to ride faster. Scott had felt a little anxious on this point, but his anxiety vanished when he saw how easily and fearlessly his boy companion kept at his side.

"Well done, Tom!" he said as they flew over the prairie. "Keep up this pace, and we will escape yet."

"I can do it, if my horse holds out," returned Tom briefly.

Scott looked over his shoulder, and, brave man as he was, it almost made him shudder. The whole party of Indians was on his track. He could see their dusky faces, distorted by wrath, and the longing for a vicious revenge. He knew that Tom and he had little to hope for if they were caught. Fortunately their horses were strong and fleet, and not likely to break down.

"Ride for your life, Tom!" he shouted. "They will show us no mercy if they catch us."

"All right, Mr. Scott!" said Tom, his face flushed and panting with excitement. If he had not felt that so much depended upon it; if he could have thrust out from his mind the sense of the awful peril in which he stood, he would have enjoyed the furious pace at which his horse was carrying him.

The horses ridden by the Indians were not equal in speed or endurance to those which the two friends bestrode. They were fresher indeed, but they did not make up for the difference between

---

them. There was one exception, however: Dan, the stolen horse, was not only equal to either of their horses but had the advantage of being fresher. This, after a while, began to tell. It was ridden by a young Indian brave, a brother of the leader. Soon he drew away from his companions and, yard by yard, lessened the distance between himself and the pursued. At the end of three miles he was close upon them, and at least fifty rods in advance of his comrades. Scott saw this in one of his backward glances.

"Tom," said he, "the redskin on Dan is overhauling us."

"Will he catch us?"

"I mean to catch him," said Scott coolly.

Tom did not need to ask for an explanation. Scott wheeled round, took hasty but accurate aim at the Indian, and fired. The hapless warrior reeled in his saddle, loosed his hold of the reins, and fell to the ground, while his horse, continuing in his course, his pace accelerated by fright, soon galloped alongside of Scott. There was a howl of rage from the main body of Indians, who saw the fate of their comrade without being able to help him.

"Now, Tom, ride as you never rode before!" shouted Scott. "We will circumvent those Indian devils yet and bring Dan safe into camp. Come along, Dan, old fellow. You're doing nobly."

Dan recognized the familiar voice. He entered into the spirit of the race and, relieved from the weight of his rider, dashed forward with increased speed till he led, and Scott and Tom were forced to follow.

The Indians were mad with rage. Their comrade had received a fatal wound. They saw the round hole in his breast, from which the life-blood was gushing, and they thirsted for vengeance.

Should two palefaces, one of them a boy, escape from them? That would be a disgrace, indeed. The blood of their brother called for blood in return.

Could they have inspired their horses with the same spirit which animated themselves, they might, perhaps, have overtaken their intended captives, but, happily for our two friends, the horses were less interested than their riders.

The danger was well-nigh over. It was scarcely two miles to the camp. There they would be so reinforced that the Indians would not venture an attack. That was the goal they had in view. Already they could see in the distance the wagon-train, ready for a start. They were surely safe now. But at this unlucky moment Tom's horse stumbled. The motion was so rapid that he could not retain his seat. He was thrown over the horse's head, and lay stunned and insensible upon the ground. His horse kept on his way to the camp.

CHAPTER XXX

TOM BECOMES AN INDIAN

Scott did not immediately notice Tom's mishap. The boy had shown himself so good a rider that such an accident had not occurred to him as likely to happen. When he did look back there was already a considerable distance between them. In fact, Tom lay midway between the Indians and himself.

What was he to do?

If he returned there was no hope of rescuing Tom, and he would infallibly fall into the hands of the Indian pursuers. In that case his fate was sealed. He had killed an Indian warrior, and his life would pay the forfeit. By going on he could head a rescuing party from the camp. His heart ached for Tom. It was hard to leave him in the hands of the savage foe; but Tom was a boy, and there was hope that he would be spared. So, he felt that it was better to continue his flight.

There was a shout of fierce joy when the Indians saw Tom's fall. They would have preferred to capture Scott, for he it was who had killed their comrade, but they were glad to have one prisoner. They reined up their horses and halted beside the still insensible boy. They held a brief consultation and decided not to continue the pursuit. They could see the encampment, which Scott was sure to reach before he could be overtaken. They could not tell the number of the party to which he belonged, but, being few in numbers themselves, the risk would be a hazardous one. They decided to retire with their prisoner. Tom was lifted to a seat in front of one of the party, and they rode leisurely back.

This was the position in which our hero found himself when he roused from his stupor. One glance revealed to him the whole. His heart sank within him. They might kill him. Remembering the ghastly sights he had seen on his trip across the plains, he thought it likely that they would. Life was sweet to Tom. To what boy of sixteen is it not? It seemed hard to be cut off in the threshold of an active career, and to but cut off by savage hands. But there was an additional pang in the thought that now he would be unable to help his father. The result of his plan would only be to impose an additional burden upon the modest home which his father found it so hard to keep up. Tom sighed, and, for the first time in his life, he felt discouraged.

He looked about him, scanning the dark, grave faces, and read no hope or encouragement in any. Finally the Indians came to a halt at their old camping-ground, and Tom was lifted from the horse. He was placed upon the ground, in the center of the group. Then followed a consultation. From the glances directed toward him Tom understood that he was the subject of deliberation. In fact, his fate was being decided.

It was certainly a trying ordeal for our young hero. He was not sure of half an hour's life. An unfavorable decision might be followed by immediate execution. Tom felt that his best course was to remain perfectly passive. He could not understand what was said, but we are able to acquaint the reader with the general purport of the conference.

Several of the Indians favored immediate death.

"Our brother's blood calls for vengeance," they said. "The white boy must die."

"The boy did not kill him," said others. "It was the white warrior who spilled our brother's blood. He must be pursued and slain."

"What, then, shall be done with the boy? Shall he go?"

"No, we will keep him. He has strong limbs. We will adopt him into our tribe. He will make a brave warrior."

"He shall be my brother," said the chief. "I will take him in place of my brother who is dead."

There was a low murmur of approval. Even those who had first recommended the infliction of death seemed to have changed their minds. They looked at the boy as he lay stretched out upon the ground. He was stout, comely and strongly made. He had proved that he was an admirable rider. If he should join them he would grow up into a warrior who would do credit to their tribe.

So the matter was settled. The only thing that remained was to acquaint the prisoner with the decision.

The interpreter approached Tom, and said, "White boy, you are our captive. Why should we not kill you?"

"You can if you wish," answered Tom, "but why should you kill me? I have done you no harm."

"Our brother is killed. He lies dead upon the plain."

"I did not kill him," said Tom.

"The white boy speaks truth. He did not kill our brother, but his white friend took his life."

"You ought not to kill me for that," said Tom, gathering courage, for he inferred he was to live.

"The white boy speaks truth, and therefore he shall live, but he must join us. He must live with us, hunt with us, and fight for us."

"You want me to become an Indian!" cried Tom.

"We will take you in place of the warrior that is gone," said the interpreter.

Tom looked thoughtful. He did not enjoy the prospect before him, but it was, at all events, better than death. While there was life there was hope of escape. He concluded to make one appeal for freedom and, if that was denied, to accept the proposal.

"I have a father and mother far away," he said. "I have brothers and a sister, who will mourn for me. My father is poor; he needs my help. Let me go back to them."

The interpreter communicated Tom's words to his companions, but it was easy to see that they were not favorably received. The original advocates of the death penalty looked at our hero with hostile eyes, and he saw that he had made a mistake.

"The white boy must become one of us; he must take our brother's place, or he must die," said the interpreter.

Tom very sensibly concluded that it would be better to live with the Indians than to be killed and signified his acceptance of the offer. Upon this the Indians formed a circle about him and broke into a monotonous chant, accompanied with sundry movements of the limbs, which appeared to be their way of welcoming him into their tribe.

It seemed like a dream to Tom. He found it very hard to realize his position, so unexpectedly had he been placed in it. He could not help wondering what the family at home would say when they should learn that he had joined an Indian tribe far beyond the Mississippi.

CHAPTER XXXI

TOM GIVES A MAGICAL SOIREE

Tom had no intention of passing his life with the Indians. In joining them he submitted to necessity. It gave him a respite and a chance to devise plans of escape. He understood very well that, if he made the attempt and failed, his life would be the forfeit. But Tom determined to take the risk, though his life was sweet to him. Of course, he had to wait for a favorable opportunity.

There was a chance of his being rescued by his party, but this chance was diminished by the decision of his Indian captors to break camp and proceed in a northerly direction, while the course of the emigrant train was, of course, westward. Little time was wasted. The Indians mounted their horses, Tom being put on the horse of the fallen brave. The leader put himself at the head, and Tom was placed in the center, surrounded by Indians. It was evident that they were not willing to trust him yet. They meant to afford him no chance of escape.

As the only one of the band with whom Tom could converse was the interpreter, who rode at the head with the chief, he rode in silence. The Indians on either side of him never turned their heads toward him but, grave and impassive, rode on, looking straight before them.

"This is easier than walking," thought Tom, "but I would a hundred times rather walk with Scott, or Miles, than ride in my present company."

They rode for three hours, and then dismounted for the midday rest.

Nothing had been seen or heard of his old friends, and that made Tom anxious and thoughtful.

"They have gone on without me, leaving me to my fate," he said to himself, and the reflection gave him a pang. He had been on such pleasant and friendly terms with the whole party, that this cold desertion -- as it appeared -- wounded him. The young are more sensitive in such cases than their elders. As we grow older we cease to expect too much of those whose interests differ from our own.

Tom felt that his fate was more and more bound up with the Indians. If some days should pass before he could escape, he would find himself in an embarrassing condition. Suppose he got away safely, he would find himself in a pathless plain, without provisions, and with no other guide than the sun. If he should meet with no party, he would die of starvation. The prospect seemed by no means bright.

I am bound to say that, for a time, Tom, in spite of his bright, sanguine temperament, was greatly depressed. But his spirits were elastic.

"I won't give up to despair," he said to himself. "Something tells me that I shall come out right. I must wait and watch my chances."

Upon this his face brightened, and his air, which had been listless, became more animated. The Indians glanced at him, with grave approval. They concluded that he was becoming reconciled to living among them.

When the simple midday meal was placed upon the ground, and the Indians gathered around it in a sitting posture, Tom followed their example and did full justice to the meal. In fact, he had taken so much exercise that he felt hungry. Besides, he knew that he must keep up his strength, if he wished to escape. So, instead of keeping aloof in sullen dissatisfaction, he displayed a "healthy appetite."

After resting several hours the Indians resumed their journey but did not travel far. They were in no hurry. They had no long journey to make across the continent. They only wished to go far enough to be safe from attack by a rescuing party of Tom's friends. Again they encamped, and this time, from the preparations made, he understood that it was for the night.

One thing Tom could not help noticing -- the silence of these red children of the plains. They seemed to make no conversation with each other, except on necessary matters, and then their words were few in number, replies being often made in a monosyllable.

"They don't seem very social," thought Tom. "I suppose they have nothing to talk about. I wonder if the squaws ever have sewing-circles. If they have, they can't be much like Yankee women if they don't find plenty to talk about."

The silence became oppressive. Tom would have liked to take a walk, but he knew that this would not be allowed. It would be thought that he wanted to escape. Yet to sit mute hour after hour seemed to Tom intolerably stupid. A bold idea came to him. He would try to afford them some amusement.

Accordingly, he said to the interpreter, "Shall I show you a trick?"

The interpreter communicated the proposal to his comrades, and permission was granted.

Tom took from his pocket a penny. He explained to the interpreter that he would swallow the penny, and make it come out at his nose -- a common boy's trick. The Indians, to whom this also was communicated, looked curious and incredulous, and Tom proceeded.

Now, I am not going to explain how Tom accomplished the illusion. That I leave to the ingenuity of my boy readers to discover. It is enough to say that he succeeded, to the great amazement of his copper-colored spectators. There was a chorus of "Ughs!" and Tom was requested to repeat the trick.

He did so, the Indians being as puzzled as before.

Now, Indians are, in many respects, like children. They displayed, on this occasion, a childish curiosity and wonder that amused Tom. They insisted on his opening his month, to ascertain whether there was any hidden avenue from his mouth to his nose, and found, to their surprise, that his mouth was like their own. Then one of the Indians volunteered to try the experiment and nearly choked himself with the penny, which, it must be remembered, was one of the large, old-fashioned, copper coins, in circulation before the war. It cannot be said that he turned black in the face, but he certainly gasped and rolled his eyes in a manner that alarmed his friends, and they instinctively looked to Tom for help. Tom was equal to the emergency. He rose hastily, slapped the Indian forcibly on the back, and the cent was ejected from his mouth.

There was another chorus of "Ughs!" and it was evident that Tom had risen vastly in their opinion. They looked upon him as a white magician and were even a little afraid that he might work them injury in some way. But Tom's frank, good-humored manner reassured them. They asked him, through the interpreter, if he could perform any other tricks. Tom knew a few that he had learned out of an old tattered book which had fallen in his way at home; and such as he had facilities for, he attempted, to the great delight of his new friends. Tom was becoming popular, and even those who had at first recommended death were glad that his life had been spared.

CHAPTER XXXII

TOM'S ESCAPE

Night came, and the Indian camp was hushed and still. It was long before Tom went to sleep. Generally he was a good sleeper, but his mind at present was too active for slumber. "How long is this strange life going to last?" he asked himself. "How long am I to be exiled from civilization?" This was more easily asked than answered.

When he slept, his sleep was troubled. He dreamed that Lawrence Peabody was a captive, and that the chief was about to scalp him, when suddenly he awoke. He could not at first tell where he was, but a glance revealed the disheartening truth.

He must have slept several hours, for the gray dawn was creeping up the sky, heralding sunrise. He leaned on his elbow and bent a searching glance upon his companions. They were stretched motionless upon the ground, hushed in the insensibility of sleep. "Are they asleep?" Tom asked himself. He satisfied himself that the slumber was genuine, and there sprang up in his heart the wild hope of escape. A few rods distant the horses were fastened. Could he unfasten and mount one before any of them awakened?

Tom's heart beat quick with excitement. He knew that he ran a fearful risk, but he made up his mind that now was his time.

Slowly, and without noise, he raised himself to his feet. As he stood erect, he closely scanned the sleepers. There was not a motion. With stealthy steps he crept to the horses. He selected the one he had ridden the day before and unloosed him. The animal gave a slight whinny, and Tom's heart was in his throat. But no one stirred. He quickly mounted the animal and walked him for a few rods, then gave him a loose rein and was soon speeding away. Just then the sun rose, and this guided him in the direction he was to take.

He had got a mile away when, looking back through the clear air, he saw to his dismay that his flight had been discovered. The Indians were mounting their horses.

**Indians searching for "The Lost Trail"
by Karl Ferdinand, circa 1856**

"I must gallop for life," thought Tom. "They will kill me if they catch me."

He urged on his horse by all the means in his power. Luckily it was one of the two fleetest horses the Indians possessed, the other being ridden by their leader.

Tom's hope was sustained by this fact, which he had proof of the day before.

Rather to his surprise, he did not feel as much frightened as he anticipated. He felt excited, and this was his prominent feeling. Probably he felt like a soldier in the heat of battle.

But the odds against Tom were terrible, and his chance of escape seemed very slender. Behind him was a band of savages, accustomed to the plains and strong, wily, enduring, and persistent. He was new to the plains, and a mere boy. Moreover, he did not know where to find his party. There were no sign-boards upon the prairies, but a vast, uniform expanse stretching farther than the eye could reach.

Inch by inch, foot by foot, the Indians gained upon him, the leader considerably in advance.

Even if he alone were to overtake Tom, our hero would of course be no match for a strong, full-grown warrior, more especially as he had no weapon with him. By some mischance he had left it in the camp.

Tom's heart began to fail him. His horse could not always, perhaps not long, keep up his headlong speed. Then would follow capture and a painful death.

"It's hard," thought Tom sadly, "hard for me and for my dear parents and brothers and sisters. Why did I ever leave home?"

He turned in the saddle and saw the Indian leader, evidently nearer. But he saw something else. He saw a herd of buffaloes, thousands in number, impetuously rushing across the plain from the west. Their speed was great. They seemed to be blindly following their leader.

"Good heavens!" exclaimed Tom in great excitement, "the Indians are in their path. If the herd does not stop, they will be destroyed."

The Indians were fully aware of their great danger. They knew the plains well, and the terrible, resistless power of these wild herds when once on the march. They no longer thought of Tom but of their own safety. But the buffaloes were close at hand. They were sweeping on like a whirlwind. The Indians could only ride on and trust to clear them. But their pathway was wide. It reached to within a furlong of where Tom was riding. They never paused. Some of the animals in the advance might have veered to the right or left on seeing the Indians, but the pressure from behind prevented them. The savages saw their fate, and it inspired them with more dread than an encounter with white foes. Finally, they halted in despair, and their fate overtook them. Riders and steeds were overthrown as by a flash of lightning. The dark, shaggy herd did not stop, but dashed on. Tom, in awe and excitement, halted his horse, and watched the terrible sight. He could not but sympathize with his late companions, though he knew they would have taken his life.

The buffaloes passed on, but left no life behind them. The Indians and their horses were all trampled to death. Tom was alone upon the plains.

He thanked God in his heart for his self-deliverance, though he shuddered at the manner in which it was wrought. He, too, had been near being overwhelmed, but, through God's mercy, had escaped.

But for what had he escaped? Unless he found his own party, or some other, he would starve to death, or might fall into the power of some other tribe of Indians. He must ride on.

An hour later he thought he saw in the distance a solitary horseman. It might be an Indian, but that was not likely, for they generally traveled in numbers. It was more likely to be a white man. Any white man would be a friend and could guide him to safety, unless he were himself lost. At any rate, there seemed but one course to follow and that was to ride toward the stranger.

When Tom drew near his heart was filled with sudden joy, for, in the new arrival, he recognized John Miles. Miles was no less delighted.

"Tom, old boy," he said, "is it you? How did you get away? I was afraid we should never see you again."

"I feared so myself," said Tom, "but I have been saved in a wonderful manner. Has the train moved on?"

"Do you think we would go on without you? Not a man was willing to stir till you were found. Even Peabody, though afraid of falling into the hands of the Indians, and losing his scalp, was in favor of our waiting. The boys are very anxious about you."

Tom heard this with satisfaction. The esteem of our friends and associates is dear to us all, and it is always sad to think that we may be forgotten in absence.

"But you have not told me of your escape, Tom," said Miles. "Where are the Indians who captured you?"

"All dead!" answered Tom solemnly.

"Good heavens! You don't mean to say -- "

"That I killed them? Oh, no! Look over there! Can you see anything?"

Miles looked earnestly.

"I think I see upon the ground some men and horses."

"It is the Indians. They were pursuing me when they were trampled to death by a herd of buffaloes."

"Wonderful!" cried Miles. "I have heard of such things but hardly believed in them."

"It was a terrible sight," said Tom soberly. "I wish I could have been saved in some other way."

"It was you or they," said Miles sententiously. "It is well as it is."

They were warmly welcomed at the camp. Tom was looked upon as one raised from the dead, and the particulars of his wonderful escape were called for again and again.

"You are sure they didn't scalp you, Tom?" asked Mr. Peabody.

143

"Feel and see, Mr. Peabody," said Tom, smiling. "I believe my hair is pretty firm."

"I wouldn't have been in your shoes for all the gold in California," said Peabody fervently.

"I believe you, Mr. Peabody. Indeed, I think I may say that I wouldn't be placed in the same situation again for all the gold in the world."

"Tom," said Scott, "you are bound to succeed."

"What makes you think so?"

"You have shown so much pluck and coolness that you are sure to get along."

"I hope so, I am sure, for my father's sake."

Some weeks later a wagon-train was seen slowly climbing a mountain pass on the crest of the Sierra Nevada Mountains. They reached the summit, and, looking eagerly to the westward, saw the land of gold at their feet. They had spent months in reaching it. Now it lay spread before them, glorious in the sunlight.

"Yonder lies the promised land, my lad," said Ferguson. "It remains to be seen whether we shall be rewarded for our long and toilsome journey."

"If hard work will win success, I mean to succeed," said Tom stoutly.

"I don't see any gold," said Lawrence Peabody, with a disappointed air.

"Did you think it grew on trees, Mr. Peabody?" asked Scott sarcastically.

"I should like to stop a week at a first-class hotel before getting to work," remarked Peabody. "I don't like roughing it."

"We will leave you at the first hotel of that sort we meet. Now, boys, gather about me, and give three rousing cheers for California."

Thus spoke Miles and swung his hat. The cheers were given with a will, and the wagon-train commenced the descent.

THE END

~ ~ ~

TEACHERS GUIDE QUESTIONS FOR THE YOUNG ADVENTURER

1.   Horatio Alger portrays or describes people in ways that were commonplace during his time, but that we would never use today.

    a.   How has the meaning or "appropriateness" of the language that Alger used changed today? What does this teach you about the historical aspect of this time period?

    b.   In what ways, as an individual and as a society, has our choice of words changed?

    c.   In the same way in which Alger's words were considered common language but are now not, how do you think our language will change in the future? What words or phrases commonly used today do you think will one day be considered racist, taboo, crude or inappropriate?

2.   In the opening chapters, how does Mrs. Nelson define happiness? How do you think Tom embodies this concept of happiness throughout the story?

3.   In Chapter II, Tom finds a wallet on the road. What would you do if you had found the wallet? Why would you take this course of action?

4.   Mr. Nelson agrees that Tom is at a pivotal age where he should start to explore life away from the farm.

    a.   Do you agree or disagree that it is important for young men and young women to leave home in order to expand their experiences and opportunities? Why or why not?

    b.   Instead of traveling out west in search of gold, how and at what age do youth sometimes take certain rights of passage away from home today?

5.   Alger refers to Tom as "green." What does the author mean by this word? Support your answer by describing two instances when Tom displays his "greenness."

6.   In Chapter VI, the reader is introduced to Milton Graham. What are the first clues that he is not the person he claims to be? How does he try to swindle Tom in the subsequent chapters?

7.   The reader is first introduced to Mr. Nicholas Waterbury in Pittsburg. How do Tom and Mr. Waterbury become acquainted? How does their relationship develop, and in what ways does Mr. Waterbury help Tom?

8. Tom continues to offer his services during the team's trip out west. In what ways are Mr. Peabody's and Tom's characters and courage different? Give examples to contrast their personalities and abilities.

9. What is Tom's overall outlook on life? How does he confront trying situations during his entire journey out west?

10. Do you think Tom will succeed in his quest for gold and his desire to help his family? Why or why not?

TEACHERS GUIDE ANSWERS FOR THE YOUNG ADVENTURER

1. Some of the words that Alger uses are considered racist or inappropriate today. For example, he refers to Indians as "dirty savages."

    b. When Alger lumps entire groups of people together and makes observations about them, he uses language that reflects how many Americans thought. Alger assumes that all Bostonians, save for Peabody, are strong and hardworking. He writes that all Indians are savages and that Scotsmen, save for Ferguson, like to drink. Today it is generally expected that we steer away from negative and broad generalizations.

2. Mrs. Nelson states that, "Money is not happiness." Though Tom does want to earn gold to help his family, he looks for happiness in other things: through new friendships, through adventure and the unknown and through his desire to help others, including his family.

4. Youth today can take several rights of passage away from home: going away to college, traveling abroad with or without their family, celebrating bar/bat mitzvahs and more.

5. When Alger describes Tom as "green," he implies that he is less experienced and knowledgeable about city life and the outside world because he comes from the country. Tom displays his greenness first when he meets Milton Graham, believes he has good intentions and divulges information about his travels. Later, Graham uses this information to try and swindle Tom. Tom displays his greenness again when he reveals to the clerk at the Pittsburgh house where he keeps his money. Though the clerk does not have ill intentions, he advises Tom to be more prudent and not so trusting of strangers.

6. The first clue that Graham is not who he claims to be is when Tom finds out that Graham lied about the cheaper cost of board by sharing a room. The second clue is when Tom speaks with the clerk at the Pittsburgh house and the clerk advises him to be careful and guard his money. Graham tries to swindle Tom first by searching his belongings for Tom's money and secondly by trying to plant counterfeit money on Tom and blame Tom for Graham's theft.

7.   Tom is walking around Pittsburgh when he bumps into Mr. Waterbury, who is intoxicated. Tom helps the drunken man return safely to the hotel and to his room. The next day, Mr. Waterbury is eternally grateful, and he realizes that Tom is a genuine, honest and trustworthy boy. Mr. Waterbury acts as Tom's guardian for the remainder of their travels together. Mr. Waterbury helps Tom when he confronts Graham regarding the theft of the counterfeit money and warns him to leave Tom alone.

8.   Mr. Peabody's and Tom's characters and courage differ in several ways. Mr. Peabody is constantly complaining about the voyage, his constitution and the prospects ahead. He is so terrified of Indians that he tries numerous ways to escape night watch of camp. His expectations for gold were grand, but he is not realistic or willing to work hard to earn the gold. Tom, on the other hand, is enthusiastic for the journey and the prospects that lie ahead. He is more than willing to help at every opportunity, and he treats the difficulties as forms of new adventure. He is optimistic, hard-working and brave when confronted by Indians and other dangers.

9.   Tom's overall outlook on life is to stay positive, work hard and treat every new situation like an adventure. He confronts trying situations, such as being captured by Indians, with intelligent action and grit.

Stories of Success:

The Young Miner
(Illustrated)

Stories of Success

"Always bear in mind that your own resolution to succeed is more important than any other."
Abraham Lincoln

CHAPTER I

THE GOLD-SEEKERS

A dozen men, provided with gold rocker boxes, were busily engaged in gathering and washing dirt, mingled with gold dust, on the banks of a small stream in California. It was in the early days, and this party was but one of hundreds who were scattered over the new Eldorado, seeking the shining metal which throughout the civilized world exercises a potent and irresistible sway.

I have said there were a dozen men, but this is a mistake. One of the party was a well-grown boy of sixteen with a good-humored and even handsome face. He was something more than good-humored, however. There was an expression on his face which spoke of strength and resolution and patient endurance. The readers of "The Young Adventurer" will at once recognize in our young hero Tom Nelson, the oldest son of a poor New England farmer, who, finding no prospects at home, had joined the tide of immigrants pouring from all parts of the country to the land of which so many marvelous stories were told. Tom had come to work, and, though he doubtless shared to some extent the extravagant anticipations of the great body of Eastern visitors who hoped to make a fortune in a year, he did not expect to succeed without hard toil.

His companions belonged to the same party with whom he had crossed the plains, under the leadership of Phineas Fletcher, a broad-shouldered Illinois farmer, who had his family with him. Next to Tom was Donald Ferguson, a grave Scotchman and Tom's special friend -- a man of excellent principles, thoroughly reliable, and held in high respect by all, though not possessed of popular manners. On the other side was Lawrence Peabody, a young Boston clerk, who had spent several years behind a dry goods counter. He was soft and effeminate, with no talent for "roughing it" and wholly unfitted for the hard work that he had undertaken. He was deeply disappointed in his first work at gold-hunting, having come out with the vague idea that he should pick up a big nugget within a short time that would make his fortune and enable him to go home a rich man. The practical side of gold-seeking--this washing particles of dust from the dirt of the riverbed--was in the highest degree unsatisfactory and discouraging. He was not a bad fellow, and his companions, though they laughed at him, were well disposed towards him.

Among the rest, mention may be made of John Miles, Henry Scott, and Chapman, owner of a refractory donkey named after King Solomon.

Not far away from the river were the tents occupied by the miners. There was but one house, roughly built of logs. This was occupied by Captain Fletcher and his family. He had not had the trouble of building it for he had found it ready for occupation; a previous party, who had wandered farther down the river in search of richer washings, had constructed it. In fact, it was this building in which our party had decided to remain.

"There isn't much difference in places," said Fletcher. "We may as well stay here."

"Then why was it deserted?" suggested John Miles dubiously. "That's rather strange, isn't it, captain?"

"Not necessarily, Miles. You've been on berrying parties, haven't you, when at home?"

"Many a time."

"You've noticed that many of the pickers leave good places, just from love of novelty, and wander about the field, often faring worse than if they remained where they were?"

"That's so, captain."

"Then let us give this place a try. We'll make more working steady in a medium place than wandering here, there and everywhere."

So the whole party agreed to "give the place a try."

There had been no brilliant success as yet but fair luck. In six days Tom had washed out twenty-five dollars' worth of gold dust, in spite of his awkwardness and inexperience. Others had done better, but poor Lawrence Peabody had barely five dollars' worth to show. It must be said, however, that he had not averaged more than two or three hours of real labor in every twenty-four. He spent the rest of the time wandering about aimlessly or sitting down and watching the labors of his companions, while he enlivened them by pathetic lamentations over his unfortunate position, so far away from Boston and the refining influences of civilization.

A little transcript of a conversation between Tom and himself will throw light upon the characters of both.

"This is beastly work," sighed Peabody, resting from his feet by no means arduous labors and looking over to Tom. "I tell you, it isn't fit for a gentleman."

"It is rather hard to keep one's hands clean, Mr. Peabody," said Tom, "but you mustn't think of the present. Think of the time when you will go home, your pockets full of gold."

"I don't see any prospect of it, Tom," sighed Peabody. "Here I've been hard at work for a week, and I haven't got over five dollars' worth of dust."

"I have five times as much," said Tom.

"Some people are lucky," said Peabody.

"You haven't worked like Tom," said the Scotchman plainly. "You haven't averaged over two hours a day, while Tom has worked eight or ten."

"I have worked till my back was likely to break," said the young man from Boston. "I am not accustomed to manual labor, Mr. Ferguson. My friend Tom has worked on a farm, while I have been engaged in mercantile pursuits. Oh, why did I leave Boston?!"

"I am sure I can't guess," said Ferguson dryly.

"I never expected anything like this."

"What did you expect, if I may be so bold as to inquire?"

"I thought I should find the gold in big nuggets worth thousands of dollars apiece. I was always reading in the papers about finding them. I think it's a great shame to deceive people by such stories. I don't believe there are any nuggets."

"Oh, yes, there are, but they are few and far between," said Fletcher. "A neighbor of mine found one worth three thousand dollars. Altogether he brought home five thousand dollars and invested it in a farm and sawmill. He has a good business. When he came to California he had nothing."

"That is what I should like, Captain Fletcher," said Tom. "If I could only manage to carry home five thousand dollars, I could make my father comfortable for life."

"I shouldn't be satisfied with five thousand dollars," said Peabody, whose ideas were lofty.

"How much would satisfy you?"

"About fifty thousand," said the young Bostonian, his face lighting up at the thought of so large a sum.

"And what would you do with it, if I may be so bold?" asked Ferguson.

"I would buy a nice house at the South End, furnish it handsomely, and live in style."

"I suppose you would marry?" suggested Tom smiling.

"I probably should," answered Peabody gravely.

"Perhaps you have already selected the lady."

"I have."

"Who is she?" asked John Miles. "Come, now, Peabody, don't be bashful."

"It is the daughter of a Boston merchant."

"Does the lady love you?"

"We understand each other," answered Peabody loftily. "She would marry me, poor as I am, but for her purse-proud, mercenary sire. It will be a happy day when, with my pockets full of gold, I enter his presence and claim his daughter's hand."

"I wish you success, Mr. Peabody," said Tom. "I hope you have no rivals."

"Yes, there is one."

"Are you not afraid of him?"

"Oh, no. He is a fellow of no style," said Peabody, drawing up his slender form and looking as stylish as a very dirty shirt, muddy boots, and a soiled suit would allow.

"I think I shall wait awhile before getting married," said Tom. "I am afraid I wouldn't stand any chance with an heiress, Mr. Peabody. Do you think I can ever be stylish?"

The Bostonian understood Tom to be in earnest and told him he thought in time, under proper training, he might become fairly stylish.

The conversation was interrupted by the ringing of a bell from the log house. Mrs. Fletcher, by an arrangement with the party, prepared their meals, and thus they fared better than most of the early pioneers. Their labor gave them a good appetite, and they were more solicitous about quantity than quality. Slow as he was at his work, there was no one who exhibited greater alacrity at meal-times, than Lawrence Peabody. At such times he was even cheerful.

CHAPTER II

MISSOURI JACK

At the end of a month the settlement had considerably increased. A large party from Missouri went to work farther up stream, and a few stray immigrants also added themselves to the miners at River Bend, for this was the name selected by Captain Fletcher for the location. The new arrivals were a rougher and more disorderly class than Fletcher and his companions. Already there was a saloon, devoted to the double purpose of gambling and drinking, and the proprietor, Missouri Jack (no one knew his last name), was doing a thriving business. Indeed his income considerably exceeded that of any one in the settlement.

Neither Tom nor any of his party contributed much to Missouri Jack's profits. In consequence, they had to bear the ill-will and sometimes open abuse of Jack and his friends.

"Come in and take a drink, stranger," called out Jack, the day after the opening of the saloon, to Captain Fletcher.

"No, thank you."

"It shan't cost you a cent."

"It would cost me my health," returned Fletcher.

"Do you mean to say I sell bad whiskey?" demanded Jack, angrily, emphasizing the inquiry by an oath.

"I don't know anything about it."

"Then what do you mean?"

"I mean that all whiskey is bad for the health," replied Fletcher.

"Oh, you're a temperance sneak!" exclaimed Missouri Jack, contemptuously.

"I am a temperance man; you may leave out the other word," calmly answered Fletcher.

"You're not a man!" exploded Jack. "A man that's afraid of whiskey is a--a--isn't half a man. He isn't fit to be a woman."

"Have it as you like," said Fletcher, unruffled. "I shall not drink to please any man. I had a younger brother--a bright, promising young man poor Ben was--who drank himself to death. He'd have been alive now but for whiskey."

"Oh, dry up your pious talk! You make me sick!" exclaimed Missouri Jack in deep disgust.

Next he accosted John Miles, who curtly declined and received in return a volley of abuse. Now Miles was a powerful man and not possessed of Fletcher's self-control. He paused and surveyed Jack with a menacing look.

"Look here, stranger," he said sharply, "just have a care how you use that tongue of yours. This is a free country, and if I choose to decline your whiskey, there's no law against it that I know of."

"You're a white-livered sneak!"

Missouri Jack did not proceed with his remarks, for John Miles, seizing him by the shoulder, tripped him up and strode away, leaving him prostrate and pouring out a volley of curses. Being a bully, and cowardly as most bullies are, he did not pursue his broad-shouldered enemy but vowed vengeance whenever a good opportunity came.

In fact, the only one of the original miners who accepted Jack's invitation was Lawrence Peabody.

"Step in, stranger, and have a drink!" said Jack, a little dubiously, having met with such poor luck heretofore.

The young Bostonian paused. He was not a drinker at home, but in his discontent and disappointment he was tempted.

"My dear sir, you are very polite," he said.

"I hope you ain't one of them temperance sneaks," said Jack, his brow clouding in anticipation of a refusal.

"I assure you I am not," Peabody hastened to say. "I have participated in convivial scenes more than once in Boston."

"I don't understand college talk," said Jack, "but if you want a glass of prime whiskey, just say the word."

"I don't care if I do," said Peabody, following his new friend into the saloon.

The draught of prime whiskey scorched his throat as he swallowed it down, but it was followed by a sense of exhilaration, and Peabody's tongue was loosened.

"You're a gentleman!" said Missouri Jack. "You ain't like them fellows you're with. They're sneaks."

"Really, you compliment me, Mr.--, what may I call your name?"

"Missouri Jack--that's the peg I hang on to."

"My dear Mr. Jack, I am glad to know you. You are really quite an accession to our settlement."

"Well, if I ain't, my saloon is. How you've managed to live so long without liquor beats me. Why, it ain't civilized."

"It was pretty dull," admitted Peabody.

"No life, no amusement, for all the world like a parcel of Methodists. What luck have you met with, stranger?"

"Beastly luck!" answered Peabody. "I tell you, Mr. Jack, California's a fraud. Many a time I've regretted leaving Boston, where I lived in style and moved in the first circles, for such a place as this. Positively, Mr. Jack, I feel like a tramp, and I'm afraid I look like one. If my fashionable friends could see me now, they wouldn't know me."

"I ain't got no fashionable friends, and I don't want any," growled Missouri Jack, spitting on the floor. "What I want to meet is gentlemen that ain't afraid to drink like gentlemen. I say, stranger, you'd better leave them Methodist fellers, and join our gang."

"Thank you, Mr. Jack, you're very kind, and I'll think of it," said Peabody, diplomatically. Though a little exhilarated, he was not quite blind to the character of the man with whom he was fraternizing, and he had too much real refinement to enjoy his coarseness.

"Have another drink!"

"Thank you."

Peabody drank again, this time with a friend of Jack's, a man of his own stripe, who straggled into the saloon.

"Do you play euchre?" asked Jack, producing a dirty pack of cards.

"I know little of it," said Peabody, "but I'll try a game."

"Then you and me and Bill here will have a game."

"All right," said Peabody, glad to while away the time.

A Euchre hand consisting of the five highest cards in play

"What'll you put up on your game, stranger?" asked Bill.

"You don't mean to play for money, do you?" asked Peabody, a little startled.

"Sartain I do. What's the good of playin' for nothing?"

So the young Bostonian, out of his modest pile was tempted to stake an ounce of gold dust. Though his head was hardly in a condition to follow the game intelligently, he won, or at least Bill and Jack told him he had, and for the first time Lawrence felt the rapture of the successful gambler, as he gathered in his winnings.

"He plays a steep game, Bill," said Jack.

"Tip-top. A No. 1."

"I believe I do play a pretty good game," said the flattered Peabody. "My friends in Boston used to say so."

"You're hard to beat, and no mistake," said Bill. "Try another game."

"I'm ready, gentlemen," said Peabody, with alacrity.

"It's a great deal easier earning money this way," he reflected, regarding complacently the two ounces of dust which represented his winnings, "than washing dirt out of the river." And the poor dupe congratulated himself that a new way of securing the favors of fortune had been opened to him.

The reader will easily guess that Lawrence Peabody did not win the next game, nor will he be surprised to hear that when he left the saloon his pockets were empty.

"Better luck next time, stranger," said Jack, carelessly. "Take a drink before you go?"

Peabody accepted the invitation, and soon after staggered into the tent occupied by Tom and his friend Ferguson.

"What's the matter, Mr. Peabody?" asked Tom. "Are you sick?"

"Yes," answered Peabody, sinking to the floor. "Something's the matter with my head. I don't feel well."

"Have you been to the saloon, Mr. Peabody?" asked Ferguson.

"Yes," answered the Bostonian.

"And while there you drank some of their vile whiskey, didn't you?"

"I'm a free man, Mr. Ferguson. If I choose to drink, what--what business is it--yours?"

"None, except as a friend I advise you not to go there again."

Further inquiries elicited the facts about the gambling, and Ferguson and Tom seriously remonstrated with Peabody, who, however, insisted that Mr. Jack, as he called him, was a hospitable gentleman.

The dust which Peabody had lost should have been paid to Capt. Fletcher as his share of the expenses that same evening. Of course this was now impossible. Fletcher warned him that any subsequent failure from the same cause would be followed by an exclusion from his table.

CHAPTER III

HOW TOM GOT ON

About this time Tom took account of stock. He had come out to California with the noble and praiseworthy purpose of earning money to help his father pay off the mortgage on his little farm. He was the more anxious to succeed, because two hundred dollars of the amount had been raised to defray his expenses across the continent. The mortgage, amounting now to twenty-two hundred dollars, was held by Squire Hudson, a wealthy resident of the same town, who hoped eventually to find an excuse for foreclosing the mortgage and ejecting Mr. Nelson's family. He was actuated not alone by mercenary motives but also to gratify an ancient grudge. In early life Mrs. Nelson, Tom's mother, had rejected the suit of the wealthy squire, and this insult, as he chose to characterize it, he had never forgotten or forgiven.

Had Tom been aware of the Squire's feelings towards his family, he never would have been willing to have the mortgage increased for his sake, much as he wished to go to California. But neither Tom nor his father dreamed of Squire Hudson's secret animosity, and they regarded his willingness to advance the extra two hundred dollars as an evidence of friendship.

But I have said that Tom took account of stock--in other words, ascertained how much he was worth. First, then, of the money borrowed for his trip--the original two hundred dollars--he had twenty-five dollars left over. Besides this sum, after paying all expenses he had accumulated, by hard work and strict economy, fifty dollars' worth of gold dust.

"I wish father had this money," said Tom to his tentmate, Ferguson. "I am afraid he stands in need of it."

"There may be a way to send it to him, Tom."

"I wish there were."

"There's one of our party going to San Francisco next week. He can buy a draft there, and send it to your father."

"Who is going?" asked Tom, eagerly.

"John Miles. You can trust him with the money, Tom."

"Of course I can. I'd trust John Miles with any sum."

"Who's that taking liberties with my name?" asked a manly voice, and John Miles himself stepped into the tent, bending his head as he entered.

"I hear you are going to San Francisco, John?"

"Yes, I start next week."

"Will you come back again?"

"I intend to. I am going to prospect a little and buy some things for myself and Captain Fletcher."

"Will you do me a favor?"

"Of course I will, if it isn't too large a one," answered Miles.

Tom explained what he wished, and John Miles cordially assented.

"You're a good boy, Tom," he said, "to think of your father so soon."

"I feel anxious about him," said Tom. "He raised money to send me out here, and I don't want him to suffer for it."

"That's the right way to feel, Tom. I wish I had a father and mother to look out for," said Miles, soberly, "but you're in better luck than I. Both died when I was a mere lad. How much do you want to send?"

"Seventy-five dollars."

"Have you saved up so much already?" asked Miles, in surprise.

"Part of it I had left over when I got here."

"Will you have any left?"

"No."

"Isn't it well to reserve a little, then?"

"Oh, I shall have some more soon," answered Tom, sanguine, as most boys are.

"Suppose you are sick?"

"If he is sick he shall suffer for nothing," said the Scotchman. "While I have money, Tom shall not feel the want of it."

"Thank you, Mr. Ferguson," said Tom, gratefully.

"That old fellow has a heart, after all," thought Miles, who had been disposed to look upon Ferguson ever since their first acquaintance as rather miserly.

The Scotchman was certainly frugal and counted his pennies carefully, but he was not mean and had conceived a strong affection for his young companion, whom he regarded much as a son or a nephew.

"Suppose you take the money now, John," said Tom.

"Shall I scribble a receipt, Tom? I am afraid my writing materials have given out."

"I don't want any receipt," said Tom. "I'll trust you without one."

"Nevertheless, lad," said the cautious Scotchman, "it may be well--"

"Yes, Tom, Mr. Ferguson is right. Of course I know that you trust me, but if anything should happen to me--any accident, I mean--the paper may be useful to you."

"Just as you like, Mr. Miles, but I don't ask it, remember that."

"Yes, I will remember it, and I don't mean to meet with any accident if I can help it. Mr. Ferguson, can you oblige me with a pipeful of tobacco? I'll join you in smoking."

Smoking was the Scotchman's solitary extravagance, not a costly one, however, as he never smoked cigars but indulged only in a democratic clay pipe.

John Miles threw himself on the ground between Tom and his Scotch friend and watched complacently the wreaths of smoke as they curled upwards.

"Tom, you ought to smoke," he said. "You don't know how much enjoyment you lose."

"Don't tempt the lad," said Ferguson. "It's a bad habit."

"You smoke yourself."

"That is true, but it isn't well for a growing boy. It can do him no good."

"I smoked before I was as old as Tom."

"So did I, but I wish I had not."

"Well, perhaps you're right, but it's a comfort when a man's tired or out of spirits."

"I am not troubled in that way," said Tom. "I mean with being out of spirits."

"Youth is a hopeful age," said the Scotchman. "When we are young we are always hoping for something good to befall us."

"And when one is older, how is it, Mr. Ferguson?"

"We fear ill more than we hope for good," he replied.

"Then I want to remain young as long as I can."

"A good wish, Tom. Some men are always young in spirit, but those that have seen the evil there is in the world find it harder to be hopeful."

"You speak as if you had had experience of the evil, Mr. Ferguson."

"So I have," answered the Scotchman slowly. Then, after a pause, "I will tell you about it; it's no secret."

"Not if it is going to pain you."

"Oh, the pain is past. It's only a matter of money, and those wounds heal."

"Only a matter of money!" said John Miles to himself. "I must have misjudged Ferguson. I thought money was all in all with him. I did not think he would speak so lightly of it."

"When I was a young man," Ferguson began, "my father died, leaving me a thousand pounds and a small annuity to my mother. With this money I felt rich, but I knew it would not support me, nor was I minded to be idle. So I began to look about me to consider what business I had best go into, when a young man, about my own age, a clerk in a mercantile house, came to me and proposed a partnership. He was to put in five hundred pounds, and contribute his knowledge of business, which was greater than mine. He was a young man of good parts and had a brisk, pleasant way with him, that made him a favorite in business circles. I thought it was a good chance and, after taking a little time for thought, agreed to his proposal. So the firm of McIntire and Ferguson was formed. We went into business, and for a time all seemed to go well. As my partner chose to keep the books, I was not so clear as I wished to be about matters, but we seemed to be prospering. One morning, however, on coming to business, I found that my partner had disappeared after possessing himself of all the money he could collect on the credit of the firm. Of course we were bankrupt, or rather I was, for he left me to bear the brunt of failure."

"Have you ever seen him since, Mr. Ferguson?"

"From that day to this--twenty years--I have never set eyes on Sandy McIntire."

"It was a mean trick to serve you, Ferguson," said Miles.
"Yes," said the Scotchman, soberly. "I minded the loss of money, but the loss of confidence was a sore thought too, after all the trust I had put in that man."

Presently Miles rose to go.

"I'll take care of your money, Tom," he said, "and do my best to get it safely to your father."

"Thank you, John."

As Miles left the tent, he did not observe a crouching figure on the other side of it. It was the figure of Bill Crane, a crony of Missouri Jack, in fact, the man who helped him to fleece poor Peabody of his scanty hoard.

Bill looked after Miles enviously.

"I wonder how much money he's got?" thought Bill. "I'd like some of it, for I'm bust. I must tell Jack. I don't dare to tackle him alone."

CHAPTER IV

A FOILED ROBBER

In the grand rush to the newly discovered gold fields all classes were represented. There were men of education, representatives of all the learned professions, men versed in business, and along with them adventurers and men of doubtful antecedents, graduates of prisons and penitentiaries. Bill Crane, introduced in the last chapter, belonged to the latter undesirable class. He had served a term at Sing-Sing as a housebreaker, and later another term in a Western penitentiary. He had come to California with a prejudice against honest labor and a determination to make a living by the use of the peculiar talents on which he had hitherto relied. He had spent a week at River Bend, chiefly at the saloon of Missouri Jack, whom he found a congenial spirit, and he had picked up a little money from flats like the young Bostonian, but, on the whole, he had found it an unprofitable field for the exercise of his special talents.

"I must make a raise somehow," he thought to himself, "and then I'll make tracks for some other settlement."

Precisely how to raise the fund of which he stood in need was difficult to decide. Moneyed men were not plenty at River Bend. Captain Fletcher and his party had been at work but a short time and were not likely to have collected much.

As we know, Bill Crane overheard a part of the closing conversation between Tom and John Miles. From this he learned that Miles, besides his own money, would be in charge of seventy-five dollars belonging to our young hero. It was not much, but it was something.

"If the whole doesn't come to over two hundred dollars, I can make it do," thought Crane. "It will get me out of this beastly hole and carry me to San Francisco."

John Miles slept by himself under a small tent at the northern end of the small encampment. He looked like a man who ate well and slept well, and this would be favorable to Bill Crane, who proposed to effect the robbery in the night. He had half a mind to secure the aid of Missouri Jack, but then Jack would expect to go shares in the "plunder," and there was likely to be little enough for one. So Bill decided to make the attempt alone.

In a small camp like that at River Bend, the movements and plans of each individual were generally known. So it was generally understood that John Miles intended to start on Thursday for the city.

The previous evening he spent with Tom and Ferguson, with whom he was more intimate than any others of the party. He would not have been drawn to the Scotchman, but for his being Tom's roommate. Through him he came to appreciate and respect the Scot's sterling virtues and to overlook his dry, phlegmatic manner.

"I hope you'll have good luck, Mr. Miles," said Tom.

"Thank you, my boy."

"I would join with my young friend Tom," said Ferguson, "if I were quite clear in my mind whether good luck is the right term to use."

"Don't you think some men are luckier than others, Mr. Ferguson?" asked Tom.

"Some men are more successful, doubtless, but what we call good luck, generally comes from greater industry, good judgment, and, above all, the prompt use of opportunities."

"There is something in that," said Miles, "but when two men work side by side with equal industry and one finds a nugget worth thousands of dollars while the other plods along at a few dollars a day, isn't there some luck there?"

"It may be so," said the Scotchman, cautiously, "but such cases are exceptional."

"So one boy is born to an inheritance of wealth and another to an inheritance of hard work. Isn't there any luck there?"

"The luck may be on the side of the poor boy," was the reply. "He is further removed from temptation."

John Miles laughed.

"Well, at any rate, it seems you believe in luck after all. I am sure you both wish me to be prosperous, whether you call it luck or by some other name. Tom, if I meet with any good opening that I think will suit you, I shall write you. You don't want to stay here, particularly?"

"No, the place is not so pleasant since these new people have come here. Missouri Jack isn't a neighbor that I like."

"He is exerting a bad influence," said Ferguson. "I am afraid Peabody visits him too often for his own good."

"He ought to have stayed in Boston," said Miles. "He is not the man for such a life as ours. He is too delicate to work, or thinks he is, and I see no other reliable road to success."

"I saw Peabody reeling out of the saloon this afternoon," said Tom. "I asked him if he considered it 'high-toned' to drink in a saloon, as that is the word he is always using, but he said it didn't make much difference out here, where he wasn't known."

"Peabody isn't overstocked with brains, though he does come from Boston," said Miles.

Ten o'clock came, and Miles rose to go.

"I must have a good night's rest," he said, "for tomorrow night must see me many miles on my road. Tom, I will attend to that commission of yours just as soon as I have the opportunity."

"Thank you, Mr. Miles."

John Miles walked slowly toward his tent. Arrived there, he threw himself down on his rude couch, and in less than fifteen minutes, he was sound asleep. He had done his usual day's work and made some preparations for his journey besides, and these made slumber sweet and refreshing.

Before settling himself for the night, however, Miles carefully deposited a bag of gold dust under his head, wrapped up in an extra pair of pantaloons. Had he known that Bill Crane had formed a plan to rob him that very night, he would have taken extra precautions, but he was not inclined to be suspicious or to anticipate danger.

Perhaps an hour later, Tom, who found himself unusually restless, got up from his hard couch, leaving Ferguson fast asleep, and went out into the air thinking that a walk would do him good and dispose him to sleep. The night was dark, but not wholly so. There was no moon, but a few stars were shining, and as his eyes became accustomed to the faint light, he could easily distinguish objects at the distance of a few rods.

Tom's thoughts reverted to his humble home, more than three thousand miles away. Probably the fact that he had committed to John Miles a sum of money to send to his father had turned his thoughts in that direction.

"Father will be glad to get the seventy-five dollars," thought Tom, "and I am sure he will need it. I wish it could get there more quickly, but it is a long way off."

Tom was not homesick and was far from wishing himself back, with his object in coming yet unaccomplished, but it did occur to him, that he would like to see his father and mother, and brothers and sisters, if only for a few minutes.

When he came out he had no particular direction in mind in which he wished to walk, but chance directed his steps toward the tent of his friend, John Miles.

When he came near it, his attention was arrested by the sight of a crouching figure which appeared to be entering the tent. His first thought was, that Miles, like himself, had got up from his couch and was just returning. He was on the point of calling out "John," when a sudden doubt and suspicion silenced him.

"Might not it be a robber?"

Tom was determined to find out. He crept nearer, so that he could have a clearer view of the figure.

"It's Bill Crane!" he said to himself, with sudden recognition. "What's he up to?"

Tom could guess. He didn't know the man's antecedents, but he had read his character aright. He was instantly on the alert. Crane evidently was on a thief's errand and was likely to steal not only Miles's money but Tom's. Our hero was alive to the emergency and resolved to foil him. He had his revolver with him, for in the unsettled state of society with no one to enforce the laws, and indeed no laws to enforce, it was the custom for all men to go armed.

Tom was not long left in doubt as to Crane's intentions. He saw him cautiously pulling at something in the tent and felt sure that it was the bag of treasure. He decided that the time had come to act.

"Put that back," he exclaimed in a boyish, but clear, commanding tone.

Bill Crane turned suddenly, panic-stricken.

He saw Tom standing a few feet from him, with a revolver in his hand.

All was not lost. He might, he thought, intimidate the boy.

"Mind your business, you young cub," he growled.

"What are you about?" demanded Tom.

"I am going to sleep with Miles. He invited me. Does that satisfy you?"

"No, it doesn't, for I know that it's a lie. You are here to rob him."

"You'd better not insult me, boy, or I'll have your life."

"Get up this instant and leave the tent, or I'll fire," said Tom resolutely.

"A young cub like you can't frighten me. That shooting iron of yours isn't loaded," said Bill Crane, rather uneasily.

"It'll be rather a bad thing for you to take the risk," said Tom, with a coolness that surprised himself, for the situation was a strange one for a boy brought up in a quiet New England farming town.

"What do you want of me?" growled the desperado, uncomfortably, for he was satisfied that the weapon was loaded, and Tom looked as if he would shoot.

"I want you to leave that tent at once," said Tom.

"Suppose I don't."

"Then I shall fire at you."

"And be hung for attempted murder."

"I think I could explain it," said our hero. "You know very well what will happen to you if you are caught."

Bill Crane did know. Hanging was the penalty for theft in the early days of California, and he had no desire to swing from the branch of a tree.

"You're a young fool!" he said roughly, as he rose from his stooping posture. "I wanted to ask Miles to do a little commission for me in Frisco. I had no thought of robbing him."

"You can see him in the morning about it," said Tom resolutely.

"I'll be even with you for this," said the foiled thief, as he sullenly obeyed the boy, half ashamed to do so.

Tom went back to his tent, aroused Ferguson, and the two took turns in guarding the tent of Miles during the night. Tom did not wish to awaken him, for he needed rest on the eve of a long and fatiguing journey.

CHAPTER V

MILES SETS OUT ON HIS JOURNEY

When Miles woke up in the morning he found Tom beside him.

"Hallo, Tom!" he said, in some surprise. "This is an early call."

"I have been here half the night," said Tom, quietly.

"How is that?"

"I was afraid you would be robbed."

"Did you have any particular reason for fearing it?" asked Miles, quickly.

Thereupon Tom described his chance visit of the evening before and what he saw. As might have been expected, John Miles was indignant.

"The miserable sneak! I'd like to wring his neck," he exclaimed. "Did you say he had his hand upon the bag of gold dust, Tom?"

"Yes; I distinctly saw him attempting to draw it out from under your head."

"If the boys knew of this, Crane's fate would be sealed. A thief in a mining camp has a short shrift."

"You mean he would be hung?" asked Tom, in surprise.

"Yes, he would grace a limb of yonder tree, and I am not sure but it would be the best way to dispose of him."

Tom shuddered.

"It would be a terrible fate," he said. "I should like to see him punished, but I don't want him hanged."

"Then you will have to keep your mouth shut. Once the boys get hold of what happened, nothing will save him."

"Then I shall keep it to myself."

"I will see Crane, and let him understand that I am aware of the attempt he made," said Miles.

After breakfast he came upon Crane within a few rods of Missouri Jack's saloon.

"Look here, Bill Crane," said Miles, "I've got something to say to you."

"What is it?" returned Crane, sullenly, looking ill at ease.

"I understand you favored me with a visit, last night."

"Who told you so?"

"Tom Nelson."

"The young cub had better mind his own business," growled Crane, in a menacing tone.

"He did me a service in preventing your intended theft."

"If he says I meant to rob you, he lies!"

"Nevertheless, if he should make public what he saw, the boys would be likely to believe him rather than you," said Miles, significantly.

"Is he going to tell?" asked Crane, nervously.

"He has told me but is not likely to speak of it to others, being unwilling that you should suffer the punishment you deserve."

"He is very kind," sneered Bill Crane, but he felt very much relieved.

"You probably owe your life to his kindness," said Miles, quietly. "He tells me you wish me to do something for you in Frisco."

"I've changed my mind," said Crane, abruptly. "I may go there myself, soon."

Miles smiled.

"I thought it might be something urgent," he said, "since it led you to come to my tent at midnight."

"I thought you would be starting away early this morning."

"Well thought of, Bill Crane, but it is only fair to tell you that I don't believe a word you say. I have one thing to say to you before I go, and you had better bear it in mind. If you harm a hair of Tom Nelson's head, and I believe you quite capable of it, I will never rest till I have found you out and punished you for it."

"I am not afraid of you, John Miles," retorted Crane, but he looked uncomfortable.

"You will have cause to be, if you injure Tom."

Miles walked off, leaving behind him a bitter enemy.

"I hate him--him and the boy too!" muttered Bill Crane. "If I dared, I would put my mark on him before he leaves the camp."

But Crane did not dare. He knew that he was in a very critical position. His safety depended on the silence of two persons--one of whom would soon be gone. He was not aware that Ferguson also knew of his attempted crime, or the danger would have seemed greater. However much he thirsted for vengeance, it would not do to gratify it now. He must bide his time.

Bill Crane was cunning as well as malignant. He decided to quiet Tom's suspicions if he could, and ensure his continued silence, by an affectation of friendliness. He waited till he saw our hero washing dust beyond earshot of any listeners and strolled up to him.

"How are you getting on, Tom?" he asked, with an appearance of friendliness.

Tom looked up quickly. Considering all that had happened, he was somewhat struck by Crane's effrontery.

"Fairly well," he answered coldly.

"Shan't I relieve you a few minutes?" proposed Crane.

"No, thank you."

"It's pretty hard work and don't pay as well as it might. I think California's a humbug, for my part."

"Have you tried washing for gold?" asked Tom. "I haven't seen you at work."

"Not here. I've tried it elsewhere, but it's slow."

"Then, why do you stay here?" asked Tom, naturally.

Crane shrugged his shoulders.

"Because I haven't money to get away," he said. "I'm waiting for something to turn up. If I could only get to Frisco, I would go into some business. I would like to have gone with Miles."

"Was that what you were going to propose to him, last night?" asked Tom, dryly.

"Yes, I wanted to speak to him on that subject. I had a great mind to ask him to lend me a little money and take me along with him. I would have arranged to pay him soon after we reached Frisco."

Tom knew that the fellow was lying and remained silent.

"You made a little mistake about my intentions," continued Bill Crane, smoothly, "but perhaps it was natural under the circumstances."

Tom thought it was, but still preserved silence, much to Crane's discomfiture.

Bill Crane eyed him sharply and saw his incredulity, but for that he cared little, if only he could secure his silence.

"I think you will see that it isn't fair to me to speak of this matter," he continued.

"I had made up my mind not to speak of it," said Tom. "I don't want to get you into trouble."

"Good morning, Mr. Crane," said Lawrence Peabody, who had just come up.

"Good morning, Peabody. I was watching our friend Tom. How are you getting on?"

"I haven't done anything yet today. It's dirty work. I don't think it's fit for a gentleman. Tom, there, is used to work, and he don't mind."

"Shall we go round to Jack's?"

"All right!"

And the two walked away together.

"I am sorry Peabody doesn't keep better company," Tom said to himself. "Bill Crane won't do him any good."

CHAPTER VI

ROBBED IN HIS SLEEP

Tom was right in concluding that Bill Crane's influence over Peabody was anything but good. The young Bostonian, however, was not long subjected to it. During the night following John Miles's departure, the little settlement at River Bend was called upon to deplore the loss of an eminent member.

In brief, somewhere between midnight and dawn Mr. William Crane took his departure, without the ceremony of leave-taking. Had he gone alone no one perhaps would have felt any violent sorrow, but he took with him a horse belonging to Adam Dietrich, an industrious young German, who had only recently arrived. No one had seen the two go together, but it was only natural to suppose that Crane had spirited away the horse.

Dietrich borrowed a horse, and, accompanied by a friend, set out in search of the thief, but returned at night unsuccessful. Had it been wet weather, it might have been possible to track the fugitive, but it was very dry, and the trail was soon lost. It was almost impossible to tell what direction Crane would choose and continued pursuit would not pay, so Adam sadly returned to his work.

Little doubt was entertained among the miners that Crane was responsible for the loss of the horse. Had he been caught, there would have been small chance for him, so generally was he pronounced guilty. A few of his companions, especially Missouri Jack, defended him.

"Bill Crane wouldn't steal a horse any more than I would," said Jack, and there were those who agreed with him without acquitting Bill. "Bill ain't no saint, but he ain't a thief."

Whether Jack believed what he said is doubtful. Crane needed a different advocate to clear him from suspicion.

It may as well be stated that Crane did steal the horse. He had a decided objection to walking as long as he could ride and, having no animal of his own, annexed the property of his neighbor.

He had two motives which influenced him to leave the settlement. First, he was in Tom's power, and he was by no means certain that our hero would keep silence touching his night attempt at robbery. In the second place, he still coveted the bag of gold dust which John Miles carried away with him. He had been prevented from taking it, but, as Miles was travelling alone, he foresaw a better chance of success if he should follow on his track.

How or under what circumstances he should make the new attempt he left to be decided later. The first thing, obviously, was to overtake him.

Crane experienced the same difficulty in tracking Miles that had led to the failure of his own pursuers. It was only on the fifth day, that, as he halted his steed on the hillside and cast long glances about him, he caught sight, a mile away, of the object of his pursuit. He could not mistake the sturdy, broad-shouldered figure and large, massive head.

"That's Miles, sure enough!" he exclaimed, joyfully. "I thought I had missed him, but I'm in luck. That bag must be mine."

The most direct course was to ride up in the fashion of a highwayman and demand the bag. But Crane did not mean to proceed in this fashion. Physically, though not a weak man, he was not a match for Miles, and he knew it. Cunning must supply the place of strength. He knew that Miles was a sound sleeper, and could think of no better plan than repeating the visit he had made in camp. It was already late in the afternoon when he caught sight of the sturdy miner. It was his policy now to keep him in sight, but not to approach near enough for recognition. Once seen, Miles would be on his guard, and the game would be spoiled. Crane halted, therefore, and drew back within the shadow of the trees, henceforth advancing cautiously.

John Miles did not once turn back. Had he done so, it is quite possible that he might have caught a glimpse of his pursuer. He had travelled since morning, and his faithful horse was beginning to show signs of fatigue.

"You are tired, my poor Dick," he said kindly, stroking the horse. "You deserve supper and rest, and you shall have it."

Dick appeared to understand what his rider said, for he gave a short neigh of satisfaction.

John Miles looked around him. Just ahead was a large tree, under whose broad branches it would be pleasant to recline. Not far away was a slender mountain stream trickling over the rocks. Nothing could have been better.

Miles slid from his horse and made preparations to encamp for the night, first leading his faithful steed to the stream, where he quenched his thirst. Then he brought out his slender stock of provisions and partook of supper.

"It's pleasant to rest after a long day's ride," soliloquized Miles. "I must have made forty miles today. I could easily have gone farther, had it been on the prairies at home, but these mountain roads are hard upon man and beast."

The Beale's Cut at Fremont Pass in Southern California show steep, mountainous roads.

After supper Miles threw himself upon the ground, and his mind became busy with his plans and prospects.

"I shall reach Frisco in three days, according to my calculations," he reflected, "and then, first of all, I must attend to Tom's commission. That's a good boy, Tom. I wish he were here with me tonight. Why didn't I urge him to come with me? He is not doing very well where he is, and there are plenty of chances for a smart boy in the city. If I find any opening for him, I will send for him. I don't know what gives me such an interest in that boy, but I'd sooner do him a good turn than any man I know. I hope that thief Crane won't play any trick upon him. If he does, I swear I'll get even with him."

John Miles little suspected that he himself stood in more peril from the man he denounced than our hero. Had he known that Bill Crane was lurking in the vicinity, he would scarcely have courted slumber so fearlessly.

Physical fatigue and the stillness of outward nature speedily brought on a feeling of drowsiness that was not long in bringing sleep. Twilight had hardly given place to night when our traveller had become "to dumb forgetfulness a prey."

This was what Bill Crane had been waiting for. He rightly calculated that Miles would soon be asleep. He inferred this from his own feelings. He, too, had travelled many miles, and felt drowsy, but, with the object he had in view near accomplishment, he was able to resist the promptings of nature.

Crane rode till he was but a few rods from Miles, then dismounted and tethered his horse. With stealthy step he approached the sleeper. With satisfaction he regarded the upturned face of the man whom, if waking he would have feared, and noted his deep, regular breathing.

"You wouldn't sleep so sound, John Miles," he said to himself, "if you knew I was standing over you. How easily I could put a bullet into you! But then I wouldn't have the satisfaction of anticipating your disappointment when you wake up and find your treasure gone! No, you may live. I have no use for your life, that is, if you don't wake up. In that case, I may have to kill you."

The bag of gold dust lay under the head of Miles. He knew of no better place for it, calculating that any attempt at removal would arouse him. So it might under ordinary circumstances, but unusual fatigue made him sleep like a log. Bill Crane kneeled down, and by delicate manipulation succeeded in drawing the bag from beneath the sleeper's head. Lest the removal of the pillow might awaken Miles, he replaced it by a coat, which he folded up so as to produce about the same elevation above the ground.

The transfer was made, without in the least interfering with the slumbers of the tired traveller.

Bill Crane rose to his feet, triumphant. Not only was he possessed of a sum of which he stood sorely in need, but he had the satisfaction of outwitting his adversary. Moreover, he had obtained

Tom's money in addition, and thus revenged himself upon the boy who had once thwarted him.

"Goodbye, John Miles!" he said, lifting his hat mockingly. "Sorry to inconvenience you, but can't help it. A long sleep, and pleasant dreams!"

Thus speaking, he turned away, unconscious that he had been observed by a third party.

CHAPTER VII

THE HEATHEN CHINEE

This third party belonged to that peculiar race immortalized by Bret Harte. He was a heathen Chinee! His face was smooth and bland, and wore an expression of childlike innocence which was well calculated to deceive. Ah Sin possessed the usual craft of his countrymen, and understood very well how to advance his worldly fortunes. He belonged to the advance guard of immigrants from the Central Flowery Kingdom and with a companion, Ah Jim, was engaged in mining in the immediate neighborhood. His gains had not been great thus far, but then his expenses had amounted to little or nothing. He and his friend had brought two bags of rice from San Francisco, and they were well satisfied with this solitary article of diet.

Ah Sin, from a distance, had seen John Miles encamp for the night and, impelled by curiosity or a more questionable motive, had approached to take a view of the stranger. Before reaching him he caught sight of Bill Crane, and his almond eyes straightway watched the movements of that gentleman, while he himself kept sufficiently in the background to escape observation.

When he saw Crane stealthily remove the bag from under the sleeper's head, he became very much interested and a bland smile overspread his face, while his cue vibrated gently with approval.

"'Melican man very smart," he murmured to himself. "He steal his friend's money while he sleep."

My readers are probably aware that our Mongolian visitors find a difficulty in pronouncing the letter "r", and invariably replace it by "l."

"Suppose other 'Melican man wake up, he make a low," continued Ah Sin, softly.

But the other 'Melican man did not wake up, and Bill Crane got away with his booty, as we already know. Cautiously the Chinaman followed him and ascertained where he intended to pass the night. It was at a moderate distance from the cabin which the two Chinamen had selected for their mining camp.

Bill Crane jumped from his horse, stretched his limbs, and gaped.

"I'm powerful sleepy," he soliloquized. "I can't go any farther tonight. I don't like to rest so near Miles, but I can be on the road before he wakes up. I guess it will be safe enough."

Crane, having made up his mind to rest, rolled himself up in his blanket, and stretched himself out, first tying his horse to a sapling. The place was retired, and he felt moderately confident that, even if he overslept himself, he would not be discovered.

"I'd like to see Miles when he discovers his loss," he said to himself, smiling at the thought. "He'll be ready to tear his hair and won't have the least idea how the gold dust was spirited away. You excel me in brute strength, John Miles, but one thing I am pretty sure of, you haven't got my brains," and he complacently tapped his forehead.

"There must be at least two hundred dollars' worth in that bag," he reflected. "It isn't a great haul, but it will do. It will last me some time and perhaps start me in something in Frisco. Bill Crane, you've done a good stroke of business today. You are entitled to a good night's rest, and you shall have it."

First, however, he concealed the bag. He did not think it safe to place it under his head as Miles had done. He scooped a hole in the earth near by, deposited the bag, replaced the dirt, and spread a few leaves over the top.

"No one will think of searching there," thought Crane. "Even if Miles himself surprises me here, he won't suspect anything."

Bill Crane felt that he was unusually sharp and crafty, and he felt great contempt for the stupidity of the man whom he had overreached. The time was not far off when he had occasion to doubt whether he had not overrated his own artfulness.

A pair of almond eyes, lighted up with mild wonder, followed closely all the movements of William Crane. When the bag was concealed, and Crane lay down to sleep, the Chinaman nodded blandly, and remarked softly, "All light! Me go find Ah Jim."

Ah Sin had to walk but half a mile to find the partner of his toils. Ah Sin and Ah Jim, though not related to each other, were as like as two peas. The same smooth face, the same air of childlike confidence, the same almond eyes, a pigtail of the same length, a blouse and loose pants of the same coarse cloth, were characteristic of both.

When the two met, they straightway plunged into a conversation in which Ah Sin had most to say.

Ah Jim listened attentively and was evidently well pleased with what his companion said. I am afraid my young friends are not well versed in the Chinese tongue and would not understand the conversation, however faithfully reported. They must infer what it was from what followed.

The two Chinamen bent their steps towards the resting place of Bill Crane. Ah Sin carried a bag of about the same size as the one Crane had stolen, which he carefully filled with sandy earth. With stealthy steps these two innocent heathen drew near the spot and looked searchingly at the recumbent form of the eminent representative of American civilization.

Ah Sin turned to Ah Jim with a pleased smile.

"All light!" he said. "'Melican man asleep."

A similar smile lighted up the face of Ah Jim. "'Melican man sleep sound," he said. "No wake up."

Quite unaware of the honor done him by the special Chinese embassy which had taken this early opportunity to call upon him, Bill Crane slept on. There was a smile upon his upturned face as if he were dreaming of something pleasant. He should have been a prey to remorse, if his conscience had done its duty, but Bill's conscience had grown callous, and gave him very little trouble. It was only when he was caught that he became sensible of a kind of mental discomfort which came as near to remorse as he was capable of feeling.

Reassured by the deep, regular breathing of the sleeper, Ah Sin and his friend proceeded to their work. The former drew a slender stiletto-like knife from a fan which protruded above the collar of his blouse, and, stooping down, began skilfully to remove the dirt which covered the bag of gold dust. From time to time he stole a glance at the sleeper to mark the first indications of returning consciousness. It was well for Crane that his sleep continued. A Chinaman does not set a high value upon human life, and the long stiletto would have been plunged into the 'Melican man before he was well aware of what was going on. Bill Crane's good genius saved him from this sudden exit by continuing the profound slumber in which he was repairing the ravages of fatigue.

The Chinamen therefore met with no interruption in their work. They drew out from its place of concealment the buried bag, and emptying the contents of their own poured into it the combined treasures of Miles and poor Tom. Then they filled the first bag with the worthless dust which they had brought with them and carefully reburied it in the ground.

They did their work so carefully and well that no one was likely to suspect that the bag had been tampered with.

Having done their work, Ah Sin and his friend smiled upon each other in bland satisfaction, which was further expressed by a low guttural chuckle.

"All light," said Ah Sin, with a nod.

"All light," chimed in Ah Jim, nodding in return.

A consciousness of lofty virtue could not have produced a happier expression upon any face than appeared on the mild countenance of the Chinamen.

"'Melican man much supplised when he wake up," remarked Ah Jim.

"Chinamen make much money," returned his friend.

The two enterprising visitors returned to their quarters, and concealed their booty in a safe place. Then they too lay down and slept the sleep of confiding innocence.

Bret Harte has not told us whether the heathen Chinee has a conscience, but if he has, neither Ah Sin nor Ah Jim experienced any inconvenience from its possession. Neither they nor Bill perhaps can fairly be taken as fair representatives of the different religious systems under which they were trained. Bill Crane could hardly claim any superiority over the heathen Chinee in point of honesty.

Bret Harte was an American author and poet who captured pioneering life in California.

CHAPTER VIII

BILL CRANE'S DISAGREEABLE DISCOVERY

It was five o'clock in the morning when Bill Crane opened his eyes. He felt refreshed by his night's sleep, yet under ordinary circumstances would have deferred getting up for at least an hour. But the consciousness that he had a treasure to guard, and the knowledge that he was at any moment liable to be called to account by the real owner, whose camp was scarcely more than a mile away, aroused him to exertion.

"I must get away while John Miles is still asleep," he thought to himself. "Let me get to Frisco first, and I can at once dispose of it, and he will never find me out."

Crane did not wait to prepare breakfast. That he could take on the road an hour or two later, when he felt safe from interruption. He rose and shook himself. This was his scanty washing. Next he must take the bag from its place of concealment, and then he could commence his journey.

While uncovering the bag, Crane did not discover that it had been tampered with, partly because it was still there. It was natural to suppose that, if discovered by a third party, it would be carried away. He did not even open the bag, not thinking it necessary.

"John Miles hasn't waked up yet," he said to himself with a smile. "When he does, there'll be some swearing, I'll be bound. You're a good boy, John Miles, but you ain't so smart as you think you are. I think I have got the best of you this time."

Bill Crane rode off smiling.

His course led him by the camp of the Chinamen. Early as it was they were astir. Ah Sin saw the rider, and he at once recognized him as the man he had robbed. How could Crane know that those pleasant-faced barbarians had served him such a trick?

"Hallo, Chinamen!" he said aloud. "Have they got out here already? I'll speak to them. Hallo, John!" he said, halting his horse, for even then every Chinaman was called John.

"How do, John?" replied Ah Sin, smiling blandly.

"My name isn't John, but no matter. What are you two doing?"

"Looking for gold," was the reply.

"Do you find any?"

"Velly little. Bad place."

"Have you been in San Francisco?"

"Yes, John."

"Why didn't you stay there?"

"Too many Chinamen--too little washee--washee."

"What have you got in the way of provisions? Mine are stale. I'd like to buy some from you."

"We have got a little lice, John."

"Got a little what? Oh, I know, you mean rice. Why don't you pronounce your English better?"

"Because Chinamen not 'Melican men."

"Then I suppose I may as well be moving on, as I can't get anything out of you. Oh, have you got any tea, John?"

"Yes, John."

"Got any made?"

Ah Sin produced a cup, for he and his friend had just prepared their breakfast, and being warm, Bill Crane gulped it down with a relish.

"After all, a man needs some warm drink in the morning," he said to himself. "How much to pay, John?"

"Nothing, John. 'Melican man welcome."

"John, you're a gentleman, or rather both of you are gentlemen, even if you are heathens. I'll remember you in my prayers."

The eminent Christian, Bill Crane, rode off from the Chinese camp, calmly confident of his moral superiority to the two benighted heathen whom he left behind him. Whether he remembered his promise to intercede for them in prayer is a little doubtful, or would have been, if he had had occasion to pray himself. It is to be feared that prayer and William Crane had long been strangers.

As Crane rode away, the two Chinamen exchanged glances. A gentle smile lighted up their yellow faces, and they were doubtless thinking of something pleasant. They exchanged a few guttural remarks which I should like to be able to translate, for they doubtless referred to Bill Crane, whom they had kindly supplied with a cup of tea gratis. Yet, perhaps, considering all things, it was the dearest cup of tea Crane had ever drank, since it was the only return he got for a bag of gold dust worth over two hundred dollars. But there is an old saying, "Where ignorance is bliss, 'tis folly to be wise." Crane was just as happy as if the bag really contained gold dust. But this happy ignorance was not to last long.

After riding five or six miles our traveller thought he might venture to dismount for rest and refreshment. He selected as his breakfast table the green sward beside a sparkling mountain streamlet. He dismounted, permitting his horse to graze while he took out the stale provisions which must constitute his morning meal. They were not very palatable, and Crane sighed for the breakfasts of old, the memory of which at this moment was very tantalizing. But he comforted himself with the thought that he had the means of making up for his enforced self-denial when he reached San Francisco.

This naturally led him to open the bag, and feast his eyes over his easily obtained wealth. He untied the string and with a smile of pleased anticipation peered at the contents.

His face changed suddenly.

Was he dreaming? In place of the shining dust, his eyes rested on--sand.

He hastily thrust in his finger, and stirred the grains. But nothing else was to be discovered. The bag contained nothing but worthless sand.

Crane stared at the deceptive bag in the most lugubrious astonishment. Surely the bag contained gold dust when he concealed it. There could be no doubt on that point, for he had opened it and seen the contents for himself. But in that case, how could such a change have been effected in one night? It had not been touched; so, at any rate, he believed. He had found it in the morning in the exact spot where he had placed it overnight, and yet--

Bill Crane took another look at the contents of the bag, hoping that he had been deceived by some ocular delusion, but the second examination brought him no comfort. He sank back, feeling in a state of mental and bodily collapse.

Never was poor thief so utterly bewildered as Bill Crane. He could almost believe that some magical transformation had been practiced at his expense. Was it possible, he thought, that John Miles, discovering his loss, had visited him and played this trick upon him? He could not believe this. It was not in accordance with John's direct, straightforward nature. Instead of acting in this secret manner, he would have sternly charged Crane with the robbery and punished him on the spot. Leaving him out of the account, then, the mystery deepened. It never occurred to Crane to suspect the Chinamen who had so hospitably furnished him with a cup of tea. Even if they had come into his mind, he would have been puzzled to account for their knowledge of his having the bag in his possession.

Bill Crane was decidedly unhappy. His glowing anticipations of prosperity, based upon the capital contained in the bag, were rudely broken in upon, and the airy fabric of his hopes dashed to the ground. He felt that fortune had been unkind--that he was a deeply injured man. Had his claim to the stolen property been the best possible, he could not have felt the injustice of fate more keenly.

"It's always the way!" he exclaimed in deep dejection. "I always was unlucky. Just as I thought I was on my feet again, this cursed gold dust turns to sand. Here am I out in the wilderness without an ounce to my name. I don't know what to do. I'd give a good deal, if I had it, to find out what became of the gold dust."

As he spoke, Crane, in a fit of ill-temper, kicked the unlucky bag to a distance and, slowly and disconsolately mounting his horse, plodded on his way. All his cheerfulness was gone. It was some comfort, but still scant, to think that John Miles was as unlucky as himself. Both had become penniless tramps, and were alike the sport of Fortune. There was a difference in respect to their desert, however. John Miles may rightly claim the reader's sympathy, while Bill Crane must be considered to have met with a disaster which he richly deserved.

CHAPTER IX

CLEANED OUT

John Miles slept long and awoke feeling refreshed and cheerful. He had a healthy organization and never failed to eat and sleep well. Like Crane, he had no washing to do, but sprang to his feet already dressed.

His first thought was naturally of his treasure. His heart gave a quick bound when he failed to discover it in the place where he remembered to have put it. In dismay he instituted a search, which, of course, proved unavailing.

"Who could have taken it?" thought Miles, large drops of perspiration gathering upon his forehead.

All about him was loneliness. He could see no signs of life. Yet the bag could not have gone away by itself. There was certainly human agency in the matter.

Miles confessed to himself with sadness that he had been imprudent to leave the bag where it would naturally excite the cupidity of any passing adventurer. That it must have been taken by such a one seemed evident. In that case, the chance of recovering it seemed slender enough. Nevertheless, John Miles decided to make an effort, hopeless as it was, to discover the whereabouts of his lost property.

"If it had been mine, I wouldn't have cared so much," he said to himself, with a sigh, "but poor Tom's money is gone too. I will make it up to him if I live, but I am afraid his father will be inconvenienced by the delay."

Miles made preparations for his departure, and strode away, looking searchingly to the right and left in search of something that might throw light upon his loss. Presently he espied the two Chinamen. Could they have taken it? He would at any rate speak to them.

"Good morning, John," he said, when he came within hearing distance.

Ah Sin bobbed his head, and repeated "Good morning, John."

"Do you live here?"

"Yes, we washee-washee for gold."

"Does anyone else live near by?"

The two inclined their heads and answered in the negative.

"Have you seen anyone pass last night or this morning?"

"Yes," answered Ah Sin. "'Melican man stay all nightee--over there. Chinaman give him a cup of tea this morning."

"How long ago?" asked Miles, eagerly.

"Two hours," answered Ah Jim.

"In what direction did he go?"

The two Chinamen readily told him.

Miles decided to tell them of the loss of his bag of gold dust. Possibly they could throw some light upon his loss.

"Someone stole a small bag of gold from me last night," he said. "I suspect it was the man you describe. Did he appear to have any such article with him?"

"Yes," answered Ah Sin, who, with natural cunning, saw that this information would divert suspicion from them. "It was so large," indicating the size with his hands.

Of course his description was accurate, for he had very good reason to know the size of the bag.

"He must have been the thief," said Miles, eagerly. "In what direction did you say he went?"

Ah Sin pointed to the west.

"I will follow him. It is on my way. If I catch the villain, it will be the worse for him."

"He velly bad man," said Ah Sin, sympathetically.

"That's where you are right, my heathen friend. Well, good morning, John. I am much obliged to you for your information."

"Velly welcome, John."

As John Miles rode away, Ah Sin turned to his friend Ah Jim, and remarked, "S'pose he catch him, he kill him."

"All lightee!" returned Ah Jim. "He velly bad man, he thief."

The two Chinamen exchanged glances. If they had been white men, there would have been a smile or a wink, but these children of Confucius looked so serenely virtuous, so innocent of guile, that the most experienced detective would have seen nothing in their faces indicating any guilty knowledge of the lost treasure. But, guileless as they seemed, they had proved more than a match for Bill Crane and his victim.

*****

189

John Miles rode away with a faint hope that he might overtake the man, whoever he might be, who had stolen his precious bag. In due time he reached the spot where Crane had examined the bag, and on discovering its worthless contents, had thrown it away. The thief had not taken the trouble to empty it.

When Miles saw it he hurried to it, hoping he might find some of the treasure inside. Of course he was disappointed and at the same time bewildered.

"This is certainly my bag," he said to himself. "Here are my initials, J. M. Then there are other marks well known to me. I could swear to it anywhere. But how does it happen that it is full of sand, and why has the thief thrown it away? That beats me!"

Miles decided that for some unknown reason the thief had transferred its contents to some other bag--perhaps his own--and then had discarded the original one, in wanton humor filling it instead with sand.

"He may have been afraid it would be found on him," thought Miles. "The marks on the bag would have been evidence enough to condemn him. By throwing away my bag he thinks himself safe."

His solution of the puzzle was ingenious, but as we know he erred in two respects. Bill Crane had not filled the bag with sand and thrown it away from prudential considerations, nor had he profited by the theft he had committed. He had been as badly outwitted as his victim, and the profit had gone to the bland and obliging Chinamen, who had thus far escaped suspicion.

John Miles slackened his rein and thought seriously and sadly of the position to which he was reduced. What was he to do? He was, in the expressive language of the country, "cleaned out," and brought to a pass where he must begin life over again, with the disadvantage of being seventy-five dollars in debt, for he was resolved that Tom's loss should be paid back to the uttermost penny.

Presently philosophy came to his aid.

"It might have been worse," he reflected. "Two hundred dollars is too large a sum to lose, but it won't take long to make up if I have any sort of luck. I wish I were in San Francisco. It may trouble me to get there without means."

When misfortune comes it is always best to look it manfully in the face and not to shrink from or over estimate it. John Miles had a strong, healthy nature, with a good deal of confidence in his own resources, and in an hour or two he was again looking hopefully forward to the future. Not that he cherished a hope of recovering his lost money. There seemed to be no way of identifying it, even if he should track the thief. One ounce of gold dust looks like another, and there is no way of distinguishing individual property in that form.

John Miles pushed on slowly. About noon he found himself threading a narrow canyon, shaded by gigantic redwood trees, with steep, almost perpendicular sides, with here and there a narrow streamlet descending in a cascade, and lighting up the darkened scene with its silvery reflections.

"This is a pretty spot, but it would be lonely to live here," thought Miles. "Yet," shading his eyes, "there seems to be a cabin of some sort. Is it possible that anybody lives in this canyon?"

Ten minutes' ride brought him to a rude cabin, with a gigantic tree spreading at a great height protecting branches over it. That it was inhabited was clear, for in front of it stood a strongly built, robust woman, who seemed to be nearing forty.

She bent a searching look upon the intruder, who bent his head courteously.

"Good morning, ma'am," said Miles.

"Good morning, stranger," was the reply. "Where might you be going?"

"I am on my way to the city. Am I on the right track?"

"I reckon so."

"Do you live here--alone?" asked John Miles, in some curiosity.

"It looks like it, doesn't it?" returned the woman. "I've been alone since my man pegged out."

"Is that long?"

"A matter of three weeks."

"I sympathize with you," said Miles. "You must be very lonely."

"Yes," said the widow. "Jim was good company, and I feel kind of lonesome without him, you better believe."

"There isn't much sentiment there," thought Miles. "She doesn't appear to be heart-broken. Do you mean to stay here alone?" he inquired. "Are you not afraid?"

"What's there to be afraid of?"

———

"Some tramp or adventurer might attack and injure, or at least rob you."

"Look here, stranger! Do you see that?" and the woman produced a revolver. "Do you see that shooting iron?"

A revolver from the 1850s.

"It looks as if it might be a good one," said Miles, who began to think the woman better able to take care of herself than he had at first supposed.

"You bet it is! I know how to use it, too. If one of them tramps gets in front of it, and sasses me, he'd better say his prayers mighty quick, for he'll need 'em. He needn't reckon much on my being a woman. I can shoot jest as true as my man could when he was alive."

CHAPTER X

A CALIFORNIA WIDOW

John Miles eyed the woman curiously. There did not seem much that was feminine left in her. Life in the wilderness had made her as bold and self-reliant as a man. She was not compelled to plead for women's rights. She resolutely took a man's rights, and was prepared to maintain them against all comers.

"I rather think you can take care of yourself, ma'am," he said.

"You can bet your bottom dollar on that, stranger," said the woman, cheerfully. "Brown--that's my husband--knew what I was. We was ekal partners--Brown and me--and he knew too much to tread on me."

"I'm glad I wasn't Brown," thought John Miles. "When I marry, it'll be a woman, and not a man in petticoats."

"If you're hungry, stranger," said the woman, "just jump off that horse of yours, and come in. I can give you a square meal, and I reckon you haven't had one lately."

"You are right, Mrs. Brown," said Miles, dismounting with alacrity. "My provisions are dry and stale, and I shall enjoy a square meal amazingly. But I ought to tell you that last night I was robbed of a bag of gold dust, and I have nothing to pay you."

"Who asks for pay?" returned the woman. "I don't keep a hotel, but I'm tired of eating alone. I want to see how it seems to have a man setting opposite me agin. So come in, and I won't keep you waiting long."

"Thank you, Mrs. Brown. If you don't mind, I'll light my pipe, and sit out here till I've had a smoke."

"You can smoke inside if you want to. I always let Brown. It makes me feel better, now that he's pegged out, that I didn't deny him any of his little comforts."

"Clearly Mrs. Brown was a considerate wife," thought Miles, "but she doesn't look like a woman to fall in love with."

Tying his horse, he threw himself down on the grass and enjoyed the luxury of a smoke while Mrs. Brown was heard bustling about inside, preparing the square meal which she had promised to her unexpected guest.

Presently she reappeared.

"The victuals is ready, if you are, stranger," she said.

"I am ready, Mrs. Brown," said Miles, rising at once, and entering the cabin.

The cabin was rough and ill-adapted to a fastidious tenant, but it looked comfortable. What attracted Miles most, however, was a table set in the middle of the floor, covered with a substantial and appetizing meal. Mrs. Brown was a fair cook--perhaps her only feminine accomplishment. She placed Miles at the head of the table and seated herself opposite him. She watched his attacks upon the fare she had provided with evident satisfaction.

"I hope you like it," she said.

"Mrs. Brown, I haven't tasted anything so good for a long time."

She nodded, with a pleased look.

"Brown allus liked my cookin'," she said. "He had a good appetite most generally, and it was a pleasure to see him eat. It's kinder lonesome cookin' for yourself. Then, too, it takes away my appetite sittin' down alone to eat."

"You must be very lonely, Mrs. Brown."

"Yes, its lonesome like bein' a widder. I'm kinder used to seein' a man about the house."

"So I suppose."

"Be you a married man?" asked the lady, pointedly.

"No, ma'am."

"How old be you?"

"Twenty-eight," answered Miles, rather amused.

"Then you're old enough to get married?"

"Oh yes, I am old enough."

"Be you in love with any girl?"

"The old woman's getting curious," thought Miles. "However, I don't mind gratifying her curiosity."

"No, I'm not in love," he replied.

Mrs. Brown eyed him thoughtfully. She seemed to be revolving some plan in her mind.

"Take a good look at me, stranger," she said, bracing herself up, as if on exhibition.

"Certainly," said John Miles, considerably astonished.

"I want to ask you a few questions."

"Go ahead, Mrs. Brown."

"Am I hump-backed?"

"Certainly not. Who said you were?"

"Just attend to my questions, if you please, stranger. Am I squint-eyed?"

"Mrs. Brown must be crazy," thought Miles. However, he answered in the negative.

"Am I as homely as a hedge-fence?" pursued the widow.

"Has anybody been calling you so? If so, tell me who it is."

"Never you mind, stranger. Am I old and wrinkled?"

"Certainly she's out of her mind," thought Miles. "I must humor her."

"I think you are a very good-looking woman," he said, soothingly.

"No, I'm not," said the strong-minded lady, "but at the same time I ain't a scarecrow."

"Certainly not."

"Don't talk too much, stranger. I expect you're surprised at my questions, but I'll come to the p'int at once. I'm tired of livin' here alone. I didn't think I'd miss Brown so much. He wasn't any great shakes of a man, but he was better than nothing. He was company for me, Brown was, in the long evenin's, and I miss him. I've made up my mind to take on somebody in his place, and I reckon I'd like to engage you, stranger. Will you marry me?"

Mrs. Brown did not blush when she asked this extraordinary question. She was entirely self-possessed, and she could not have been cooler if she had been transacting an ordinary piece of business.

John Miles had never before received a proposal of marriage. He felt as awkward and confused as a young girl, and he began to hesitate and stammer.

"Really, Mrs. Brown," he began, "you have taken me by surprise."

"I expect I have," said the widow, "but I'll give you time to think it over. Brown left me I pretty comfortable, though I did more to get the property together than he. You wouldn't think it, perhaps, but I've got five thousand dollars in gold hid away somewheres near, and there's a claim not far away, that belongs to me, and will pay for workin'."

"I am glad you are so well off, Mrs. Brown," said Miles.

"If you marry me," continued the widow, "you can work that claim. You're a strong, able-bodied man, and a year from now, if you want to, we'll go to the city and settle down. I'm older than you, but a matter of a few years don't make much difference. You were robbed, you told me?"

"Yes, of all that I had."

"How much was it?"

"About two hundred dollars."

"That ain't much."

"It's a good deal when it's all you have," answered Miles.

"If you marry me you won't miss it," said Mrs. Brown. "I won't give you my money right off, for you might run off with it, but at the end of the first year you shall have half of it. There's a parson a few miles up the canyon, at Dirt Hole, that will marry us any time we ride over. What do you say, stranger?"

It was an embarrassing moment for John Miles. He had no desire to succeed the deceased Brown, notwithstanding the little property he had left behind him. Mrs. Brown did not in the least resemble the wife of whom he had sometimes dreamed. But how could he decline without exciting the resentment of that singular female? He bore in mind that Mrs. Brown carried a revolver, and she might take a notion to shoot him down. He must temporize.

"Your proposal is a very kind and flattering one, Mrs. Brown, but I don't care to marry just at present. I want to go to the city and try my fortune. I've only lately arrived in California, and I am not ready to settle down yet."

To his relief Mrs. Brown accepted his objection in good part.

"No offence, stranger," she said. "I didn't know how you might feel about it. I've made you a fair offer."

"Indeed you have. The time may come when I shall return, and- _"

"I won't promise to wait for you, stranger. Somebody else may happen along that'll take the offer."

"It would be too much to expect you to wait for me, I admit."

"All right, stranger. You've answered fair, and now we'll let the matter drop."

When Miles left the cabin he carried with him an addition to his stock of provisions, for which he was indebted to Mrs. Brown's generoristy. It was evident that she bore no malice, notwithstanding her suit had been rejected.

196

CHAPTER XI

BILL CRANE'S GOOD LUCK

About an hour after John Miles rode away from the widow's door Mr. William Crane came in sight of the cabin. He had strayed from the direct course and that had delayed him. Otherwise he would not have fallen behind Miles.

Bill Crane was in rather a melancholy mood. He had not got over his disappointment of the morning. He was exhausted and hungry, and he felt that luck was against him. When he saw the cabin, and the widow Brown sitting in the doorway, it instantly occurred to him that here was a chance to get a dinner. He had nothing to pay, to be sure, but he need say nothing about it till after the dinner was eaten.

As he rode up, he removed his hat, and said, "Good day, ma'am."

Mrs. Brown scrutinized the new-comer with critical eyes. She decided that he was not as good-looking as John Miles. Indeed Bill Crane never could have been accounted handsome, but on this point the widow was not exacting. She was looking for somebody to fill the place of her lamented Brown, and relieve her loneliness, and it was Crane's eligibility in this respect that she was considering. Beauty was but skin deep, as Mrs. Brown was practical enough to admit, and she was not overstocked with that attractive quality herself. Though Crane did not know it, the resolute, middle-aged female, from whom he hoped to obtain a gratuitous dinner, was making up her mind to offer him the position of husband.

"Good day, stranger," she answered composedly. "Are you travelin' fur?"

"I'm thinkin' of goin' to Frisco," he said, "but it's a long journey and I'm exhausted. If you have no objection, I'll stop at your place and see if I can rest a few minutes."

"You can stop if you want to," she said. "I don't see much company, and I like to see a new face now and then."

"So do I," said Crane, thinking a little flattery might help him, "especially when it's the face of a good-looking woman."

"I ain't good-lookin' enough to hurt me," returned Mrs. Brown, with a frankness which rather disconcerted and puzzled Crane, "but I don't mind you callin' me so. If you are anyways hungry, I haven't cleared away the dinner, and--"

"You are very kind," broke in Crane, eagerly. "I don't mind saying I am a little bit hungry."

"All right, stranger. If you'll wait long enough for me to make some hot tea and warm the victuals, you shall have a chance to judge of my cookin'."

Bill Crane was quite elated. He decided that the widow would not ask him for payment, thus saving him from embarrassing excuses. In due time he was called in and seated in the chair not long since occupied by John Miles.

"You're the second man that's dined with me today," said the widow.

"And who was the first lucky man?" inquired Crane, suspecting at once that it might have been Miles.

"I don't know his name, but he was a good-looking young man, who said he had had a bag of gold dust stolen from him."

"That's Miles," thought Crane, and he at once decided not to betray any knowledge of him.

"He was in bad luck," said Bill. "Did he know who stole it?"

"He didn't tell me. I don't think he knew."

"That's well," thought Crane.

"Did he say where he was going?"

"To the city."

"Do you live here all the year round, Mrs.----?"

"My name's Brown, stranger."

"All I can say is that Brown is a lucky man. Another cup of tea if you please, Mrs. Brown."

"You might not like to exchange places with him, for all his luck, stranger," remarked the widow.

"Indeed I would," said Bill, with a languishing look.

"He's six feet under ground!" explained Mrs. Brown, dryly.

"Dead?" cried Crane.

"Yes, he's been dead these three weeks."

"And you are a widow?"

"That's so, stranger."

"But you don't mean to stay a widow?" interrogated Crane.

"Well, it is kinder lonesome. It seems natural like to have a man round."

"I wonder if she's got any money," thought Crane. "I'll find out if I can."

"Yes, Mrs. Brown, I feel for you," he said. "A woman can't struggle with the world as a man can."

"I don't know about that, stranger. I can take care of myself, if that's what you mean."

"But a woman needs a man to protect and work for her," insinuated Crane.

"I don't need any one to protect me," said the widow, "and, as for support, I've got a matter of five thousand dollars laid by and a good claim that'll pay for the workin'. I don't think I shall need to go to the poor-house yet awhile."

Bill Crane's eyes sparkled. The widow Brown seemed wonderfully attractive in his eyes. He was willing to barter his young affections for five thousand dollars and a claim, even if the widow had been thrice as homely as she was. If he had known that Mrs. Brown was bent on marriage his way would have been clearer. His mind was made up. He would woo and win his fair hostess if he could.

"When did Brown die?" he inquired.

"Three weeks ago, stranger."

"You must miss him."

"Yes, he was a quiet man, Brown was. He never gave me any trouble, and it was natural to see him round."

"You must not mourn for him too much, Mrs. Brown."

"I shan't make a fool of myself," said the widow. "He's gone, and he won't come back. There's no use cryin'."

"She's rather a queer specimen," thought Crane. "She hasn't broken her heart, it seems."

"You ought to marry again," he said.

"I mean to," said Mrs. Brown.

"Well, that's frank," thought Crane. "There ain't any nonsense about her."

"Your second husband will be a lucky man, Mrs. Brown."

"Well, he'll have a good livin', and, if he treats me right, he'll get treated right too."

"This is a cold world, Mrs. Brown. I've been drifting about till I'm tired. I'd like to settle down with a good wife."

"If you want to take Brown's place, say so," remarked the widow, in a business-like tone.

Bill Crane was staggered by the promptness with which his hint was taken, but did not hesitate to follow it up.

"That's what I mean," he said.

"What's your name, stranger?"

"William Crane."

"You haven't got another wife anywhere, have you?"

"Of course not."

"I've got to take your word for it, I s'pose. I guess I'll take the risk. I'll marry you if you say so."

"How soon?" asked Crane, eagerly.

"Well, there's a parson a few miles from here. We can ride right over and be back by sundown, if that will suit you."

"A capital idea, Mrs. Brown. You won't be Brown long," he added, sportively. "How will you like to be called Mrs. Crane?"

"One name will do as well as another," said the widow, philosophically.

Crane wanted to make inquiries about the five thousand dollars and the claim, but he reflected that it might be inferred that his views were mercenary. It would be more politic to wait till after marriage. He did not understand the character of the woman he was going to marry. She understood very well that Crane was marrying her for her money, but she felt lonesome, and it suited her to have a husband, and she was willing to overlook such a trifle.

The widow had a horse of her own. Directly after dinner it was harnessed, and the two rode over to Dirt Hole, a small mining settlement, where the Rev. Pelatiah Pond, a Methodist minister, united them in the bonds of matrimony.

When Mr. and Mrs. Crane reached home, Bill ventured to inquire, "Have you got the money in the house, Mrs. Crane--the five thousand dollars, I mean?"

"It's put away in a safe place."

"You'd better let me take care of it for you, my dear."

"Not at present, Mr. Crane. A year from now I will let you have half of it, if you behave yourself."

"As your husband, madam, I insist."

"Stop right there, stranger--Mr. Crane, I mean," said the bride, decidedly. "Do you see that?" and she whipped out a revolver.

"Good gracious, Mrs. Crane! Do you want to murder me?"

"No, I didn't marry you for that, but I want you to understand that the money is in my hands, and I don't allow any man to insist. I may let you have some of it when I get ready. Do you understand?"

"I believe I do," murmured Crane. "I'm regularly taken in and done for," he reflected sadly.

But directly after their return Mrs. Crane prepared a nice supper, and Crane, as he ate it and smoked a pipe later, began to be reconciled to his new situation.

CHAPTER XII

TOM RECEIVES NEWS FROM HOME

Meanwhile Tom, happily unconscious that the money entrusted to John Miles had been lost, continued to work diligently at his claim. His success varied from day to day, but, on the whole, he was gaining. He spent nothing except for absolute necessities, and in spite of all temptations, he gave a wide berth to Missouri Jack's saloon. In this way he gained the ill-will of the saloon-keeper, who felt a certain portion of every miner's gains ought to find its way into his till.

One evening Tom met the saloon-keeper when out walking. The latter had not at that time given up securing Tom's patronage.

"Good evening, young feller," said Jack.

Tom answered the greeting politely.

"Why don't you come round to the saloon in the evenings? We always have a jolly crowd there. After a hard day's work it'll do you good to take a social glass."

"I would rather not drink, thank you," said Tom.

"You ain't afraid of a little drink, I hope, are you?"

"Yes, I would rather let it alone."

"Oh, you're too good to live," said Jack, in deep disgust.

"I hope not," answered Tom, smiling, "for I hope to live a good many years."

That was the last attempt Missouri Jack made to secure Tom as a patron. Our hero spoke in so decided a tone that he understood the uselessness of the attempt.

The interior of a saloon in California in the late 1800s

Two months passed, and Tom heard nothing from John Miles. He was not surprised or disquieted, for he knew that mails to the interior were very irregular, and, besides, Miles might not be fond of letter-writing. He took it for granted that the seventy-five dollars had been forwarded home and were now in his father's hands. He had saved as much more and would like to have sent that too, for its possession gave him anxiety, but there seemed to be no opportunity.

About this time he received two letters. The first was from John Miles, written from San Francisco. After acquainting Tom with his loss of the bag of gold dust, he proceeded:

"I should not have cared so much, Tom, had the loss been mine only, but it was hard to think that I had lost your money too and was unable to pay it back. I know, from what you said, that your father needed the money and that the delay would put him to a good deal of inconvenience. You shall have it all back, Tom, every cent, but you will have to wait awhile. On reaching Frisco I got work and soon saved up enough to pay the debt, when, as bad luck would have it, I fell sick, and before I got well all my money had been used up. Now I am well again, and at work, and if I have good luck I will be able soon to send on the money to your father. I know you will, understand the circumstances, excuse the delay.

"The very day I discovered my loss I had a chance to marry a fortune. You will stare at that and wonder how it happened. At a lonely cabin I made the acquaintance of a widow, who was looking out for a second husband. She was left with a comfortable property, which, with her hand, she was willing to bestow upon your friend, but she didn't tempt me much. I believe her fortune amounted to five thousand dollars and a claim. It would be a good chance for you, if you were old enough, Tom.

"I don't know when this letter will reach you, for the country mails--at least to such out-of-the-way places as River Bend--go quite irregularly. However, I hope you will get it after a while and won't be too much troubled about the money. If I live it shall be repaid."

Tom showed this letter to Ferguson.

"It's a pity, my lad, that the money was stolen," said the Scotchman, "but you'll get it again. John Miles is an honest man."

"I am sure of that, Mr. Ferguson. I don't know that I ought to make him pay it back, though. It isn't his fault that it was lost."

"That's true, my lad, and you might offer to share the loss with him, but I doubt if he would accept your offer. He will feel better to pay it all back."

"At any rate I will write him and make him the offer."

"That's fair, Tom, but you'll see what he'll say."

It may be stated here that Miles utterly declined to accept any abatement of the debt.

"I ought to have taken better care of the money," he said. "It's my fault, and I shall pay it in full."

The next letter was from home. Tom opened and read it eagerly. It was mainly from his father, but there was a note from each member of the family.

His father wrote:

My dear Tom,

We are glad to hear that you have reached California after a wearisome journey and are now at work. We have travelled so little that we can hardly realize that you are more than three thousand miles away from us, with so many mountains, plains and valleys between. Of course you cannot tell us much in your letters of your various experiences. I wish we could have you with us this evening and hear some of them from your own lips.

I am anxious to hear that you are succeeding in the object of your journey and that you will not find the stories of the rich gold fields greatly exaggerated. I do not myself believe all I hear, yet I think there must be gold enough to pay those who search for it diligently. You must remember, my dear boy, that hard work is better than luck, and more to be relied upon. Don't expect to make your fortune all at once by finding a big nugget, but work steadily, and you will meet with more or less success.

If you succeed moderately, I shall be glad you went away, for here prospects are not very good. Our little farm seems to be less productive every year. The soil is not very good, as you know, and I cannot afford fertilizers. This year the crops were not as good as usual, and we have felt the decrease sensibly. If there were not a mortgage on the farm, I could get along very well, but the interest now amounts to one hundred and thirty-two dollars annually, and it is hard to get that amount together. Next month sixty-six dollars come due, and I don't know how I am to find the money. Squire Hudson could afford to wait, but I am afraid he won't. The older and richer he gets, the more grasping he becomes, I sometimes think. However, I don't want to borrow trouble. If it is absolutely necessary I can sell off one of the cows to raise the money, and before the year comes round I think you will be able to help me.

Walter, though only twelve years old--his thirteenth birthday comes next month--helps me about the farm and is very useful in doing chores. He likes farm work and will be ready to succeed me in time. As for Sarah, she is a good, sensible girl, and she helps her mother in a good many ways. Though I am a poor man, and always expect to remain so, I feel that I am blessed in having good, industrious children, who promise to grow up and do me credit. I should not be willing to exchange one of my boys for Squire Hudson's son Sinclair. He is, to my mind, a very disagreeable boy, who makes himself ridiculous by the airs he puts on. I have seen him once or twice lately when he appeared to have been drinking, but I hope I am mistaken in this. He is an only son, and it would be a pity that he should go astray.

Tom looked thoughtful after reading this letter.

"Is it bad news, Tom, lad?" asked Ferguson.

"Times are hard at home, Mr. Ferguson," answered Tom. "Father is very much in need of money. It would have been a great help to him if he had received that seventy-five dollars."

"You have as much as that on hand now, Tom. If it isn't enough, I will lend you some."

"Thank you, Mr. Ferguson. You are a good friend, and I wouldn't mind accepting your offer, if I needed it. But father won't need any more than I can send him. Only I don't know how to get it to him."

"If you were in San Francisco, you would have no difficulty in sending the money."

"No."

"I've been thinking, Tom," said Ferguson, after a while, "that it might be a good plan for us to take a little vacation and visit the city. We have been working steadily here over three months, and the change would do us good. Besides, we might on the way come across some better place. This isn't as good now as when we began to work it."

"That is true," said Tom.

"Suppose, then, we stay a week longer, sell out our claim if we can, and start in the direction of the city."

"You and I?"

"Yes; we shall be better off without company."

"We had better not let Peabody know we are going, or he will want to accompany us."

"I could almost be willing to take him, poor creature, to get him away from that Missouri Jack, but, as you say, he would not be a help to us."

So it was decided that, in a few days, as soon as they were ready, Tom and Ferguson should leave River Bend.

CHAPTER XIII

A SPECULATIVE INVESTMENT

It leaked out after a while that Tom and Ferguson were intending to leave River Bend and considerable regret was expressed by the other members of the party. Tom was a general favorite. His youth and his obliging disposition made him liked by all except Missouri Jack and his set. It cannot be said that his Scotch friend was popular, but he was, at all events, highly respected as a man of high principle and rigid honesty. This was not the way the miners expressed it. They called him a "square" man, and that word expressed high moral praise. They all felt that Tom was going off in good company.

Before they went, the two had a chance for a speculation. Two weeks before, a man came to River Bend, across the country, with a horse and wagon, the latter an old express wagon, which he had brought round the Horn from some one of the Eastern States. What had induced him to take so much trouble to convey such bulky articles was not quite clear. Now that he was a miner he had no use for them, and at River Bend they were not saleable. This man, Abner Kent, came to Ferguson's tent, where he and Tom were resting after the labors of the day. He was a tall man, with a shambling gait and an angular face.

"Good evening," he said. "If you ain't busy I'll sit down a few minutes."

"We are glad to see you Mr. Kent," said Ferguson. "Tom and I were discussing our plans, but we've plenty of time for that. Come in. Here's a place for you."

"I hear that you are going to leave us, you two?"

"Yes, Tom has some business in San Francisco, and I want to see a little more of the country."

"How are you going?"

"We'll take the cars if we can find any," answered Tom. "If we can't we'll foot it."

"That's what I came to see you about. You know I've got a horse and wagon."

"Yes."

"Why don't you buy it? You'll go easier and quicker."

"We can't afford it," said Ferguson. "Poor men must walk."

"You don't see the point. When you get through with the team, you can easily sell them for more than you gave. It will be a good speculation."

"That will depend on how much we give," said the Scotchman, shrewdly.

"To be sure, Mr. Ferguson. Now about that, I'll be easy. They ain't any good to me here. I'll take--let me see--four hundred dollars cash. You'll maybe double your money inside of a month."

The team did seem cheap at this price, as prices of all articles in a new country are very much enhanced.

"Tom and I will talk it over and let you know tomorrow morning," said Ferguson.

"That's all right. It's a good chance for you."

When Kent was gone Tom asked, "What do you think of his offer, Mr. Ferguson?"

"I think it will be a good investment, Tom, and one that will make it less likely to be robbed than if we carried gold dust with us. You know how John Miles got robbed."

"I have only a hundred dollars," said Tom, doubtfully.

"I have enough to add to it, but I think we can get the team cheaper. I don't want to beat the man down, but a bargain is a bargain, and we must look out for our own interest."

"You know more about such things than I do, Mr. Ferguson; I will agree to anything you say."

"Very well, my lad, I shall be sure to consult your interest as well as my own. It will be very comfortable for us to have a team of our own."

"It will seem strange to me," said Tom, laughing. "What will they think at home when they hear that I have set up a carriage?"

"They might think it imprudent to invest all you had in that way, but we'll make money out of it yet, or I am sorely mistaken."

The next morning, while Tom and Ferguson were at work, Kent came up to them.

"What have you decided about the team?" he asked.

"We are not willing to pay four hundred dollars," said Ferguson.

"That's a fair price."

"It may be, but it will take all the money Tom and I can raise. You know it wouldn't be quite prudent for us to part with all our funds."

"I will take a note for part of the money," said Kent.

"That's very considerate of you, but scarcely prudent."

"Then don't you want it at all?" asked Kent, disappointed.

"Yes; we are prepared with an offer. We'll give you three hundred dollars."

Kent shook his head.

"That's too little," he said.

Ferguson remained silent. He wished to give Kent time to reflect upon his offer.

"Have you sold these claims of yours?" asked Kent, after a pause.

"No."

"Then add them to your offer, and I accept it."

This proposal struck Ferguson favorably. They could not carry away their claims, and very possibly no other purchaser might offer, as, except as regards to location, other places along the river-bank could be had without cost.

"What do you say, Tom?" asked Ferguson.

"I agree if you do, Mr. Ferguson."

"Then it's a bargain, Mr. Kent. I hope it'll prove satisfactory to both of us."

"I don't think you'll regret it. It's a good speculation."

A restored wooden wagon from a mid-1800s mining camp.

When the two friends had settled for their purchase, Tom paying one hundred and Ferguson two hundred dollars, our hero found himself left with twenty dollars, or its equivalent in gold dust, while his companion had about one hundred and fifty left over.

"We shall go off in style," said Tom, "riding in our own carriage. But there's one thing I have been thinking of. I want to send a hundred dollars home as soon as I get the chance. Suppose we can't sell the team?"

"Have no fears about that, Tom. I'll lend you the money if that is the case, but, mark my word, we shan't have it left on our hands, of that you may be sure."

The night before they were to start Lawrence Peabody dropped in. He was looking down in the mouth.

"How does the world use you, Mr. Peabody?" inquired Tom.

"Fortune is against me," said Peabody. "I'm tired of River Bend."

Tom glanced at his companion. He could guess what was coming.

"Won't you take me with you, Tom?" entreated the young Bostonian.

"You must ask Mr. Ferguson. He is the head of our party."

Peabody looked appealingly towards Ferguson, but the Scotchman shook his head.

"You mustn't be offended, Mr. Peabody," he said, "when I tell you that you are responsible for your own bad luck. You have had just as good a chance as Tom or I."

"Your claim was better."

"There was no difference that I can see, except that we worked, and you didn't. You don't expect gold to come to you?"

"You and Tom are more used to hard work than I," murmured Peabody.

"If you did not feel able to work, you should not have come to California. A man must work harder here than at home, and then he stands a chance of succeeding better."

"Then you won't take me?" asked Peabody, sadly.

"Are you in debt to Captain Fletcher for board?"

Peabody reluctantly admitted that he was but had no idea how much he owed.

"Fletcher tells me that he shall not trust you any longer."

Lawrence Peabody looked frightened.

"What shall I do?" he faltered. "I shall starve."

"You can't blame the captain; he knows that you spend the little money you do earn at the saloon. But he will give you a chance. There is no one to wash clothes in the camp, and we have all observed that you keep yours looking well. If you will set up a laundry, you can make more money than in any other way."

"But then I should be a common washer-woman," objected Peabody. "What would my friends in Boston say?"

"They won't hear of it. Besides, a man can do here what he would not do at home."

It may be stated here that Peabody, finding work absolutely needful, went into partnership with a Chinaman, who arrived at the camp a day or two later, and succeeded in making a fair living, which hitherto he had been unable to do. After he was employed, his visits to the saloon became less frequent. At times he was disturbed by the fear that his friends at home might learn the character of his employment. Apart from this he found his new business, with the income it yielded, not distasteful.

CHAPTER XIV

A NEW ACQUAINTANCE

Having made all necessary preparations, Ferguson and Tom set out on their way. They took a course differing somewhat from that chosen by John Miles, one object being to survey the country and find, if possible, a suitable place for continuing their search for gold. After their three months' steady work both of our travellers were prepared to enjoy the journey. Their road was difficult at times, from its steepness, and more than once they found it necessary, out of consideration for the horse, to get out and walk. But this only added to the romantic charm of the trip.

"It's like a constant picnic," said Tom. "I should like to travel this way for a year, if I did not feel the need of working."

"We might tire of it after a while," suggested Ferguson--"in the rainy season, for example."

"That would not be so pleasant, to be sure," Tom admitted. "Do you have such fine scenery in Scotland, Mr. Ferguson?"

"Our mountains are not so high, my lad, nor our trees so gigantic, but it's the associations that make them interesting. Every hill has a legend connected with it, and our great novelist, Walter Scott, has invested them with a charm that draws pilgrims from all parts of the world to see them. Now this is a new country--beautiful, I grant, but without a history. Look around you, and you will see nothing to remind you of man. It is nature on a grand scale, I admit, but the soul is wanting."

"I like mountains," said Tom, thoughtfully. "There is something grand about them."

"There are some famous mountains in your native state, New Hampshire, are there not, Tom?"

"Yes, but I have only seen them from a distance. They are not above thirty miles away from where I was born, but poor people don't travel in search of scenery, Mr. Ferguson."

"No, my lad, and there's another thing I have noticed. We don't care much for the curiosities that are near us. The people about here, if there are any settled inhabitants, care nothing about the mountains, I doubt."

"That is true. In our village at home there is an old man nearly eighty years old who has never visited the mountains, though he has lived near them all his life."

"I can well believe it, my lad. But what is that?"

The sound which elicited this exclamation was a loud "Hollo!" evidently proceeding from someone in their rear.

Both Tom and the Scotchman turned, and their eyes rested on a horseman evidently spurring forward to overtake them. Tom, who was driving, reined in the horse and brought him to a stop. The horseman was soon even with them.

He was evidently a Yankee. All Yankees do not carry about with them an unmistakable certificate of their origin, but Ebenezer Onthank was a typical New Englander. His face was long and thin, his expression shrewd and good-natured, his limbs were long and ungainly. In later life, with the addition of forty or fifty pounds of flesh, he would be much improved in appearance.

"Good morning, gentlemen," said he. "It seems kinder good to see a human face again. It ain't very populous round here, is it?"

"We haven't seen any large towns," said Tom, smiling.

"Where are you steerin'?" inquired the Yankee. "I'm expectin' to fetch up at San Francisco some time, if I don't get lost in the woods."

"That is our destination, my friend," returned Ferguson.

"Would you mind my joining your party?" asked Onthank. "It's lonesome travelin' by one's self without a soul to speak to."

"We shall be glad of your company," said the Scotchman, sincerely, for, though naturally cautious, he could not suspect the new-comer of anything which would make him an undesirable companion.

"Perhaps you'd like to know who I am," said the new acquaintance. "My name is Ebenezer Onthank, from Green Mountain Mills in Vermont. My father is deacon of the Baptist Church at home."

"I suppose you will take his place when you get older," said Tom, gravely.

"No, I guess not. I wonder what Susan Jones would say to my bein' a deacon!" and Ebenezer burst into a loud laugh.

"Is Miss Jones a particular friend of yours?" asked Tom, slyly.

"I should say she was. Why, I expect to marry her when I get home."

"I congratulate you."

"Don't be too fast. We ain't hitched yet. Say, boy, where do you come from?"

"From Vernon in New Hampshire."

"You don't say! Why, that ain't more'n fifty miles from Green Mountain Mills. Cu'rus we should meet so fur away from hum, ain't it? When did you start?"

"Seven or eight months ago."

"I've been in California six months. Does that gentleman come from your town?"

"My friend," answered the Scotchman, not without a touch of pride, "I am not an American. I am from the Highlands of Scotland."

"You be? Sho! Well, of course you can't help that."

"Help it, sir? I am proud of hailing from the land of Scott and Burns."

"Well, I guess it's a pretty nice sort of country," said Mr. Onthank, patronizingly. "I guess you'll like America best, though."

"I am by no means sure of that, my friend," said Ferguson, a little nettled. "America's all very well, but--"

"Why, you could put Scotland into its waist-coat pocket, and there'd be plenty of room left," said Ebenezer, energetically.

"I admit that, as regards to size, Scotland cannot compare with this country."

"Say, have you got mountains as high as them, or trees as high as that?" pointing to a gigantic redwood.

"No, but size is not everything."

"That's so. Vermont is a little State, but she's smart, I tell you. But you haven't told me your names yet."

"I am called Donald Ferguson, Mr. Onthank. My young friend here answers to the name of Thomas Nelson."

"Commonly called Tom," added our hero, smiling.

"Why, I've got a brother Tom," said Mr. Onthank. "Cu'rus, isn't it?"

Considering that Tom is by no means an uncommon name, it could hardly be called very remarkable, but Tom politely assented.

"Is he older than I am?" he inquired.

"Yes, my brother Tom is twenty-one years old. I expect he voted at the last town-meeting. I'm four years older than Tom."

"Have you been fortunate so far in California, Mr. Onthank?"

"Can't say I have. I guess I've wandered round too much. Been a sort of rollin' stone, and my granny used to say that a rollin' stone gathers no moss. I've got about enough money to get me to San Francisco, and I own this animal, but I haven't made a fortune yet. What luck have you two had?"

"Pretty fair, but it will take a good while to make our fortunes. We own this team, and that's about all we do own."

"A sort of an express wagon, isn't it?"

"Yes."

"Ain't goin' into the express business, be you?"

"Probably not. We bought it on speculation."

"That reminds me of old Sam Bailey in our town. He was always tradin' horses. Sometimes he made money, and then again he didn't. How much did you give?"

Tom told him.

"That was a pretty stiff price, wasn't it?"

"It would be considered so at home, but we hope to get a good deal more, when we come to sell it."

Their new friend kept on with them, amusing them with his homely sayings and original views of things. His conversation beguiled the tedium of the journey, so that all were surprised when the shadows deepened and suppertime came. Selecting a favorable place they encamped for the night.

CHAPTER XV

A GRIZZLY BEAR

Ebenezer Onthank was an early riser. He had been brought up on a farm, where, during a part of the year it was the custom for the "menfolks" to rise between four and five o'clock in the morning to begin the labors of the day. His old habit clung to him, and at five o'clock, when Tom and Ferguson were yet asleep, Mr. Onthank sprang from his leafy couch refreshed and vigorous.

Seeing his companions yet sleeping, he concluded to take a walk.

"It'll give me an appetite for breakfast," thought he, "and a chance to see something of the country."

As to the appetite, Ebenezer was generally well provided. Indeed, latterly his appetite had exceeded his means of gratifying it, and more than once he had longed to be back at his old home in the Vermont farmhouse, where the table was always generously, if not elegantly, furnished. If Ebenezer had a special weakness it was for doughnuts, which he called nut-cakes.

"If I only had a few of marm's nut-cakes," he had said the night before to his new-found friends, "I'd be a happy man."

"What are nut-cakes?" asked the Scotchman, puzzled.

"Don't you know what nut-cakes are?" inquired Ebenezer, astonished at Ferguson's ignorance.

"I never heard of them before," said Ferguson.

"Well, I declare! I thought everybody knew what nut-cakes are," cried the Yankee. "Don't you ever make 'em in Scotland?"

"Not that I ever heard."

"Then you don't know what is good. You know what they are, Tom?"

"Oh, yes," said Tom, smiling. "We often have them at home. Perhaps Mr. Ferguson would understand better if he heard them called doughnuts or crullers."

Thus defined Mr. Ferguson acknowledged that he had heard of them, and he thought he had once tasted one. Scotland, however, fell considerably in the estimation of Mr. Onthank, when he learned that his favorite article of food was almost unknown in that distant country.

"You Scotchmen don't know what is good," he said. "If you ever come to Green Mountain Mills, I'll get marm to fry a batch of nut-cakes, and you'll say they're goluptious."

This last word was not familiar to Ferguson, but the smack of the lips with which it was accompanied made it sufficiently intelligible. He assured Ebenezer politely that he hoped some day to accept his kind invitation.

When Ebenezer left the camp he had no definite plan of exploration. Everything was alike new to him, and it mattered little in what direction his steps led him. It was a charming morning. The sun had risen, and hill and valley were glorified by its slanting rays. The air was bracing, and Ebenezer, though neither a poet nor a sentimentalist, felt his spirits rise, as with vigorous steps he strode on, letting his eyes wander at will over the landscape.

"Looks kinder han'some," he said to himself. "I wish Susan Jones was with me now. Gals like to walk round and look at scenery and pick flowers and so on. As for me, a good field of corn suits me better than all the flowers in the world. They're only good to smell of; out here though I'd like a good 'claim' best. It seems cu'rus to think how much money you can get sometimes from a hole in the ground. Beats cornfields for profit, by a great sight, if you only get hold of the right place. I just wish I could find a big nugget, as big as my head. I guess it would make me the richest man in Green Mountain Mills. I'd be a bigger man than the old deacon. They'd be glad to make me selectman, and perhaps send me to Montpelier after a while to make laws. Well, there's no knowin' what may turn up. Why shouldn't I light on a nugget as well as the next man?"

In this pleasant channel the thoughts of our Yankee adventurer were running as he strode over the uneven ground, with all the vigor gained by his hardy training. But his walk was destined to be interrupted in a decidedly unpleasant manner. All at once he became conscious of a huge object, scarcely thirty yards away, whose attention he had already attracted. Mr. Onthank had been long enough in California to recognize in the huge, unwieldy figure--a grizzly bear!

Ebenezer Onthank was no coward, but it must be admitted that when he saw the eyes of the grizzly fixed upon him he turned pale, and his limbs trembled. He had heard from fellow-miners stories of the great strength and ferocity of this most formidable beast. The grizzly bear shows no fear of man. He is always ready to make an attack, even when not stimulated by hunger. Even the lion is crafty and cunning and likes to attack his enemy unawares, but the grizzly boldly advances to the attack without seeking to surprise his adversary. If out of humor it makes no account of odds, but will as readily attack a party as a single foe. Col. Albert S. Evans, the author of an interesting volume, containing sketches of life in California, says, "I am satisfied that an average grizzly could at any time whip the strongest African lion in a fair stand-up fight, while a full-grown bull is no more to him than a rat is to the largest house-cats."

Twenty-five years ago the grizzly was to be found in various parts of California. As the State has become settled his haunts have become contracted, but even now, as the writer just quoted assures us, he is still found in great numbers in the Coast Range Mountains from San Diego to Del Norte. In describing Samson, a famous specimen once on exhibition in San Francisco, we are told that "his strength was that of an elephant, and his claws, eight inches in length, curved like a rainbow and sharp as a knife, would enable him to tear open anything made of flesh and blood as you or I would open a banana."

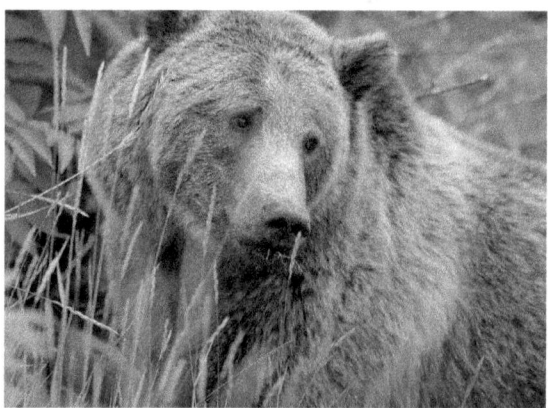

The large and strong grizzly bear

Such was the new acquaintance who confronted Mr. Onthank and barred his progress.

"Jerusalem!" exclaimed the surprised and dismayed Yankee, and he instinctively felt for his rifle. But, alas! He had left it in the camp. It was thoughtless and imprudent to venture out unarmed, but the scene was so quiet and peaceful that no thought of danger had entered the mind of our unlucky friend.

The bear sat upon his haunches and stared at the intruder. Ebenezer, brought to a stand-still, returned his gaze. They were less than a hundred feet apart, and the situation was decidedly critical.

"I guess he wants to chaw me up for his breakfast," thought Ebenezer, despairingly, "and I don't see what I can do to prevent it."

The bear, however, seemed in no hurry to commence the attack. He surveyed our Yankee with dignified gravity, conscious that he had him at advantage. When Ebenezer felt for his rifle he uttered a low growl, being possibly aware of his purpose. Possibly he laughed in his sleeve (some of my young critics may suggest that bears have no sleeves) at his failure.

Ebenezer looked about him despairingly. No man will surrender at discretion to a grizzly, for he can hope for no mercy. But what could be done? Once subjected to the terrible hug, the life would be crushed out of him in less than a minute.

"If Ferguson and Tom were only here!" thought poor Ebenezer.

But the camp was at least two miles away, and his two companions, unconscious of his terrible peril, were calmly sleeping and not likely to awaken till he was a crushed and bleeding corpse.

In great crises the mind travels rapidly. I shall not attempt to record the thoughts that chased one another through the mind of the luckless adventurer. But they were by no means pleasant.

"I shall never see Green Mountain Mills again," he thought, with an inward groan. "I shall never marry Susan Jones or eat any of marm's nut-cakes. If I only had my rifle here, I'd make one effort for my life. I'd spoil the beauty of that ugly devil anyhow."

Still, as if charmed, he stood staring open-eyed at the grizzly.

Bruin, deciding that this had lasted long enough, began in a slow and dignified manner to approach the intruder upon his solitude.

This broke the charm. With a wild shout Ebenezer Onthank took to his heels and flew over the ground at a rate of speed which Weston, the champion runner, would scarcely be able to equal.

The grizzly accepted the challenge and increased his own speed, developing an activity hardly to be expected of his huge and unwieldy form.

It was man against beast, with the odds decidedly in the favor of the latter.

CHAPTER XVI

UP A TREE

The race between the Yankee and the bear was an exciting one, to the former at least. He was fleet of foot, and in a hundred yards' dash would have won without great difficulty, but in wind and endurance the grizzly excelled him. So, as the race continued, Mr. Onthank, looking back from time to time, was painfully conscious that his enemy was gaining upon him. The perspiration came out upon his face in large drops, and he panted painfully. He felt that the chances were against him, and he could almost feel in advance the fatal hug which would slowly press the life out of him. As he felt his strength failing he looked around him despairingly. Just before him was a moderate-sized tree. Though he knew that bears can climb, he gathered his remaining strength, seized a low hanging branch, and swung himself up just in time to avoid his persistent foe, who was close upon his heels. He did not tarry where he was but climbed higher up, until from a height of twenty feet he could look down upon the bear.

Bruin looked up placidly but did not begin to climb at once. Probably he was fatigued with his race. Moreover he knew that his intended victim could not get away. The latter was emphatically and literally "treed." The bear sat upon his haunches and complacently regarded the Yankee.

Ebenezer Onthank made himself as comfortable as he could under the circumstances. He was by no means easy in mind, however. He was "holding the fort," it is true, but the enemy was in force outside and evidently intended to remain. Worse still, he would probably after a while climb the tree, and this would bring matters to a crisis.

"You pesky critter! Why don't you go along about your business?" exclaimed the unhappy adventurer, shaking his fist at the foe.

Bruin deigned no reply, but continued to survey him with steady, unwinking eyes.

"If I only had a gun, I'd pepper you," continued Ebenezer. "I should like to put a bullet into that impudent eye of yours."

Though the bear had never received an English education, his instinct probably enabled him to understand the feelings of his intended victim, but he remained as placid as ever.

So an hour passed. At the end of that time the situation remained unchanged. The unfortunate Yankee was getting hungry, as well as tired of his somewhat constrained position. Bears probably have more patience than the human family, for Bruin had scarcely moved, except occasionally to wag his great head. He felt that in the game that was being played it was his adversary's turn to make the next move.

"I wish Tom and the Scotchman would find me out," thought Onthank. "What on earth makes them sleep so late?" he continued, irritably. "They must be naturally lazy."

He may be excused for feeling irritated, though there was no particular reason to expect his two friends to curtail their hours of slumber because he had done so. But he was not in a position where it is easy to be reasonable, and in his situation every minute seemed to him as long as five.

Meanwhile, in the camp, a mile away, Tom and Ferguson had awakened.

"How did you sleep, Tom?" asked the Scotchman.

"Tip-top. Did you rest well?"

"I have a gift of sleep," replied Ferguson. "But where is our Yankee friend?"

"I suppose he has taken an early walk," said Tom. "He will be back before long, I guess. We'd better not wait for breakfast for him. I'm hungry for one."

The two friends proceeded to break their fast, washing down the rather stale provisions with water from a spring near by.

"I wish it were coffee," said Tom. "I'm tired of cold water."

"Doubtless the coffee would be more gratifying to the palate, Tom, but it's likely the water is better for the health."

"I suppose you would refuse a cup of hot coffee, Mr. Ferguson, if it were offered you," said Tom, smiling.

"I don't say that, Tom. I would risk its effect upon my health for once. But, as we haven't got it, we may as well make the best of what we have."

Soon after their simple meal, which did not consume much time, Tom suggested to his companion that they set out in search of Mr. Onthank. He did not suspect that their missing companion was in trouble, but he thought that it would be pleasant to take a walk.

"You can go, if you like, Tom," said Ferguson, with characteristic caution. "I will remain behind to look after the camp."

"All right, Mr. Ferguson. I'll soon be back."

"Don't go too far away, my lad, and mind your bearings, so that you can find your way back."

"Never fear, Mr. Ferguson. It wouldn't be very easy to be lost here. I'll keep my eyes open and bring Mr. Onthank back with me if I see him anywhere."

Ferguson sat down and indulged himself in reading, probably for the hundredth time, Walter Scott's Marmion, of which he had a small pocket edition, while Tom went on his way.

A fortunate chance directed our hero by an almost straight course to the very tree where Ebenezer Onthank was still perched with the grizzly standing guard beneath. From time to time he looked about him anxiously, in the hope of seeing the approach of one of his travelling companions.

It was with a feeling of joy, not wholly unmingled with anxiety, that he descried Tom descending a hillock not many rods away. As yet it was evident that our hero had not caught sight of the bear and his prisoner. It was very necessary to put him on his guard.

"Tom!" shouted Mr. Onthank, at the top of his voice.

Tom heard the call in spite of the distance and looked about him, but he did not immediately catch sight of the speaker. It did not occur to him to look upwards.

"Tom!" shouted the Yankee again. "Here I am. Look up in the tree."

That time Tom's glance detected his companion, and, not yet having discovered the bear, he was led to wonder why Mr. Onthank had climbed the tree. As he was advancing incautiously, Onthank shouted again, "There's a cursed grizzly under the tree. Don't come too near."

Tom saw the bear, and he paused suddenly. He was startled in truth, for he had been long enough in California to be aware that it was a dangerous beast.

"Isn't Ferguson with you?" asked Onthank, anxiously, for he knew that a boy of sixteen, even if armed, was no match for the king of the California sierras.

"No, he's behind in the camp," shouted Tom, in reply.

By this time the bear became aware that there was a second intruder within his precincts. He turned his head deliberately and surveyed our hero. It is not within the range of the author to read the thoughts of a grizzly, but, from the indifference with which he turned away and resumed his watch, it may be inferred that he considered Tom too small game to merit his attention. This was rather satisfactory to our young hero, who was not ambitious to come in close quarters with so formidable an antagonist.

Startled as he was, Tom maintained his ground. He wanted to help Onthank, but he did not know how to do it.

"What can I do to help you, Mr. Onthank?" shouted Tom.

"Blamed if I know," answered the Yankee, helplessly. "I wish Ferguson were here. It won't do for you to attack the beast single-handed."

"Shall I go back for Ferguson?" asked Tom.

"I don't know. How far away is the camp?"

"It must be as much as a mile."

"While you are away the brute may take it into his head to climb the tree, and then I am gone up."

"Haven't you any weapon?"

"No."

"I'll fire at the bear if you say so."

"It would be of no use. If you missed, or only grazed him, he would make for you."

"I wish you had my rifle," said Tom.

"So do I. I'd let him have it straight in the eye. Have you had breakfast?"

"Yes."

"I'm as hungry as a bear--as this bear who probably wants me for his breakfast. Oh Tom, if I was only back at Green Mountain Mills once more, I'd be content to live and die there, and all the gold in California wouldn't bring me out here again."

Tom stood silent and perplexed. While he was considering whether he could do anything to help his friend, the bear slowly rose, approached the tree, and, grasping it between his paws, prepared to climb. He was evidently tired of waiting.

"He's coming, Tom!" shouted Onthank. "Oh Lord, what shall I do?"

CHAPTER XVII

AN EXCITING PURSUIT

Mr Onthank's reflections when the grizzly was slowly but steadily climbing the tree were by no means pleasant.

"If he once grips me, I am gone," he said, despairingly.

"Shall I shoot?" asked Tom, looking on in excitement.

"You might hit me," said Ebenezer, who knew nothing of Tom's skill as a marksman.

"No, I won't."

"I think I'll swing off," said the Yankee, "and join you."

Whether this was or was not a wise thing to do Tom did not feel qualified to decide. It was evident that Onthank must do something speedily, or he would be in the power of the bear. He waited nervously till Bruin was uncomfortably near, and then, seizing the branch with his hands, swung to the ground. The height was considerable, and the fall jarred him, but, quickly recovering himself, he ran towards Tom.

"Now we must run for our lives, Tom," he said, suiting the action to the word.

Tom fully understood the necessity, and followed suit, first hazarding a glance at the discomfited bear.

When the grizzly witnessed the escape of his victim he showed no excitement, nor did he accelerate his motions. He began deliberately to back down the tree. This required some little time, which Tom and his friend made the most of.

"Give me your rifle," said Onthank.

"I'd rather keep it," said Tom.

"I can make better use of it," said the Yankee.

"I don't know about that," said Tom. "At any rate I will keep it."

He felt that it was hardly reasonable to expect him, in the presence of such a danger, to give up his only instrument of defence.

"You are only a boy," said his companion, discontented.

"I can shoot," answered Tom, briefly.

Onthank was not in general an unreasonable man, but danger makes men selfish.

"Give it to me," he said, in a tone of authority, and he tried to wrest it from Tom's hands.

"You shall not have it," exclaimed Tom, indignantly. "Take away your hand, or I'll shoot you!"

Of course Tom was excited and would not have carried out his threat, but he was fully resolved to stand up for his rights.

Whether Ebenezer would have yielded the point, being stronger than Tom, is uncertain, but our hero shouted "Look out for the bear!" and the Yankee, in alarm, released his hold, and the two entered upon a race, in which the Yankee's superior length of limb enabled him to keep the first place.

Bruin was now on terra firma and was on his way, wagging his great head, developing an alarming rate of speed. Tom was somewhat hampered by the weapon which he carried, and he was getting out of breath. Onthank was three or four rods ahead of him. The situation had changed, and it was now Tom that was in the greater peril.

"Don't give out, Tom!" called out Ebenezer, encouragingly.

"I won't," gasped Tom, "if I can help it."

"Is he gaining on us?"

"Yes," returned our hero.

"Then I'll try another tree," said Onthank, and he caught a branch, and clambered up into a tree quite similar to the other in which he had been besieged.

Tom would gladly have followed his example, but the branch was too high for him to reach readily, and the grizzly was too near to give him adequate time. Poor boy! He began to despair and was at an utter loss what to do. To face round and fire at the foe seemed about all that was left him, but he wanted to reserve his fire to the last. He caught sight of another tree, of a larger trunk than the one which Onthank had ascended, and ran towards it, pursued by the grizzly. Then commenced a dodging game, which seemed to afford but a brief respite from destruction.

"This can't last long," thought poor Tom. "I suppose I must die."

In that brief time of peril many thoughts passed through his mind. To die at his age would be sad enough, but the thought that his expedition would be a failure, only involving his father deeper in difficulty and debt chiefly troubled him. The mortgage would be foreclosed, and his father and whole family deprived of their humble home. Onthank watched the boy's peril, unable to give him assistance. To do him justice he almost forgot his own danger in the more apparent and immediate peril of his young companion.

226

"Be careful!" he shouted, quite needlessly. "Don't let him grip you. Give it to him right in the eye."

Tom was so absorbed, and his mind so painfully occupied by his efforts to keep out of his enemy's clutches, that he was not conscious of the warning.

Active and alert as he was, the result was hardly a matter of doubt. He would tire sooner than the bear, and if he ran again he was sure to be overtaken. This, however, was what he did. Of course the grizzly instantly pursued him. Poor Tom breathed a prayer for help, though there seemed no chance of his prayer being answered, but sometimes God sends assistance when there seems no chance of escape.

The galloping of a horse was heard. There was a whirling sound, and Bruin, already within two yards of Tom, was jerked back, and brought to a standstill by a lasso which wound about his neck. A shout caused Tom suddenly to turn his head, and to his joy he saw a mounted Mexican vaquero, who had brought him timely relief.

Bruin growled angrily on finding himself balked of his prey. He was not disposed to yield to his new antagonist. Rising and sitting on his haunches he began coolly to draw in the lasso, against the combined strength of man and horse. The muscular force of a big grizzly is simply enormous. Usually he is attacked from two sides, two lassos being thrown around him. For a single antagonist he is sometimes more than a match, as seemed likely in the present case. The rieta was attached to the pommel of the saddle, and of course the bear, in pulling as he did, hand over hand, steadily brought the vaquero and his steed nearer. The horse, terrified, trembled in every limb, and tried to rear, but his strength was as nothing when opposed to the steady power of his massive antagonist.

elieved from the immediate attentions of the grizzly, Tom did not continue to run, but stood still, and, forgetting his own peril, remained an excited spectator of the struggle between the bear and the vaquero.

The Mexican, in an excited manner, shouted to him to shoot. This brought Tom to a sense of his duty. A third person had been brought into danger by an effort to give him assistance, and he was too manly to leave him to his fate. He raised his rifle, and, taking quick aim, fired. Our young hero was of course inexperienced, and it was only by a piece of good fortune that his bullet inflicted a serious wound, striking the bear in the throat. The blood began to flow and the grizzly, growling fiercely, slackened his hold on the lasso. The vaquero followed up Tom's shot by another, equally effective, and the powerful animal dropped to the ground, dangerous still if approached, but unfitted for pursuit.

The vaquero reined his horse back, and his dark face became illumined with a smile of satisfaction.

"He will do no more harm," he said in good English, but with a foreign accent. "The danger is over."

"Is the critter used up?" shouted Onthank, cautiously, from his elevated perch. "Is he defunct?"

"He soon will be," answered Tom. "I guess it will be safe to come down."

Ebenezer Onthank needed no second invitation. He "shinned" down the tree in a manner not unlike the grizzly and approached the spot where the huge foe was lying, the life-blood flowing from his throat.

"I'd like to kick you, you big brute!" said Mr. Onthank.

The bear slowly turned upon him his glazing eyes, and they expressed so much ferocity that almost involuntarily the Yankee drew back. The bear partly raised himself, and tried to drag himself towards his adversaries, but the effort was vain.

"He is one of the largest I have seen," said the vaquero. "See how strong he is!"

"It was lucky for me that you came up," said Tom. "He was almost upon me."

"I had about given you up, Tom," said Onthank, "and I thought my turn was coming next."

"We are much indebted to you, sir," said Tom, gratefully, to the Mexican. "You have saved my life."

The vaquero courteously expressed his satisfaction, and, remounting his horse, resumed his journey.

A vaquero in the early 1800s who has just lassoed an animal

"I never want to see another grizzly," said Onthank. "This one is enough for me, darn his ugly pictur'!"

"I quite agree with you, Mr. Onthank," said Tom.

CHAPTER XVIII

TOM'S OLD HOME

Leaving Tom for a time, we will cross the continent, and, a little earlier in point of time, look in upon Mark Nelson and his family at their humble home in New Hampshire.

For years Mr. Nelson had been struggling to provide a comfortable living for his wife and children. The struggle was not an easy one. His small farm was sterile, and yielded grudgingly its annual crops. Then the mortgage held by Squire Hudson imposed a burden of interest very hard to meet. Each half year sixty-six dollars must be raised somehow to satisfy the squire's demand. Though a rich man, with ready money in plenty, he never failed to call for his money on the very day it was due. Once or twice he had granted a delay of a day or two, but his manner was so unpleasant that the farmer, except from dire necessity, was hardly likely to ask a renewal of the favor.

The six months immediately following Tom's departure from home were not favorable to his father. There was a drought of considerable duration, which made the crops smaller than usual, and thus materially decreased the farmer's income. When the semi-annual interest became due, with the most energetic effort Mark Nelson had got together only thirty-six dollars towards it, leaving a deficit of thirty dollars.

"I feel anxious about tomorrow, Mary," he said, as the little family sat together the night before in the plain sitting room. "I have never been so much behind before with the interest."

"How much do you lack, Mark?" asked Mrs. Nelson.

"Thirty dollars."

"That is a good deal of money," said his wife, gravely.

"Yes, I don't know where to raise it. If Squire Hudson were only a little considerate. But he isn't, and, even if he were, I am afraid there is no prospect of my raising the money at present."

"You may get some money from Tom soon," suggested Sarah.

"I can't rely upon that. Tom will doubtless send when he is able, for he understands my circumstances and is a thoughtful boy, but it is going to take time for him to earn a surplus--enough to send on."

"He may find a big nugget," said Walter, the second boy, who eagerly read the letters from California which from time to time appeared in the weekly paper.

"He may, but the chances are against it."

"I was reading in last week's paper about a man finding a nugget worth over two thousand dollars."

"Such nuggets are as rare as large prizes in a lottery, I suspect," said Mark Nelson, who had a large share of plain common sense.

Walter looked rather disappointed, having made up his mind that Tom would certainly find a big lump of gold and come home rich.

"Don't you think Tom will find some gold?" he asked.

"Yes, I have no doubt he will gather some gold dust. I have no doubt, too, that he will earn more than he or I can do at home, but I haven't much faith in these extraordinary pieces of good luck."

"Still, Tom may find a nugget," persisted Walter.

"Yes, he may, and I shall be very glad if he does, but we must not build too many air-castles on that chance."

"I wish I could see the dear boy again," sighed his mother, looking up from the stocking she was laboriously darning.

"So do I," said Walter. "He would have a lot to tell us."

"California seems so far away," resumed Mrs. Nelson, "and he has no one there to look after him and mend his clothes--"

"And darn his stockings," said Walter, smiling.

"If he walked all the way across the continent," said Sarah, "I don't believe he would have larger holes in his stockings than you have, Walter."

"Oh, well, I exercise a good deal," said Walter. "Ask father if I don't."

"Walter will be more successful as a farmer than as a scholar," said Mr. Nelson. "He helps me a good deal."

"Tom was a good scholar," said Sarah, "and he was always ready to work, too. Walter will never astonish or electrify the world by his learning."

"I don't want to," said her brother. "It isn't in my line."

"That's true enough."

"Don't tease Walter," said Mrs. Nelson. "He helps your father a good deal, and he is not a dunce."

"Thank you, mother, for taking my part. Sarah is going to be a strong-minded woman. I should not wonder if she came out as a lecturer on 'Woman's Rights' some time. I think I see her, with a pair of iron-bowed spectacles on her nose, and her back hair tied up in a big knot, flinging her arms about, and--"

"That'll do, Walter," said Sarah. "It is an unusually powerful effort for you. I have no desire to lecture on 'Woman's Rights,' though I think they ought to have them all the same."

"I guess you'll get yours. You'll make your husband stand round, if you ever get one."

Sarah laughed good-naturedly and retorted, "I shall pity your wife, if she has to darn your stockings."

The next day about lunch time Squire Hudson walked up to the front door and knocked. His approach was witnessed, not without trepidation, for he was not an easy creditor.

The squire looked about him searchingly as he entered. He suspected that the interest was not ready, and the farmer's grave face confirmed his suspicions. That he was glad of this of course Mark Nelson did not dream, for he was not aware of his creditor's deep laid plans.

"A fine day!" said the squire, with suavity. "I hope you are well, Mrs. Nelson."

"Pretty well, thank you, sir."

"Have you heard from Tom lately?"

"Yes. He had just reached California."

"Then of course he could not say anything of his prospects?"

"It was too soon."

"You must miss him a good deal--all of you."

"I am thinking of him all the time," said Mrs. Nelson.

"To be sure, that is natural in a mother. But if the boy does well, that will repay you hereafter."

"If I only felt sure he would do well."

"Oh, he is young and industrious. He will be sure to make his way. He'll like it too. Why, my Sinclair envies him the chance of leaving home. He wanted to go with him."

"Sinclair would not like to go in the same way as Tom, with the prospect of having to work hard after he got there," said Mark Nelson.

"To be sure not, neighbor Nelson. My boy has never been brought up to work. My circumstances--ahem!--have not made it necessary."

"Sinclair is fortunate in having a rich father," said the farmer.

"So I tell him," said the squire, complacently. "His fortune is already made."

"What are you going to do with him, squire?"

"Oh, I shall make a professional man of him--a lawyer, most likely," said the rich man, complacently. "I can give him a suitable income till he gets into a paying practice."

"That will be a good many years," thought Sarah, "unless Sinclair works harder than he has lately at school," but the shrewd young lady kept this thought to herself.

One by one wife and children left the room, for it was well understood that the squire came on business and would be likely to desire a private interview with the farmer. They went into the kitchen, closing the door behind them, and awaited anxiously the result of the interview.

"I do hope Squire Hudson will be considerate," said Mrs. Nelson, anxiously.

"I am afraid he won't be, mother," said Sarah. "He is a hard man."

"Sinclair puts on no end of airs," said Walter. "By the way he struts round you would think he owned the whole town. You had better set your cap for him, Sarah, for he will be rich some day."

"I would rather be an old maid than marry him," said Sarah, decidedly.

"Very likely your wish will be gratified," said her brother.

Mrs. Nelson did not smile at this sally, for her mind was too full of anxiety.

CHAPTER XIX

A MODERN SHYLOCK

"I believe your interest falls due today, Mr. Nelson," said the squire, when he found himself alone with his debtor.

"Yes," answered the farmer, slowly. It was not very likely to slip his mind.

"I suppose you have the money ready," continued the squire, who supposed no such thing.

"I have a part of it ready," said Mark Nelson, with an effort.

"A part," repeated his creditor, with a frown.

"Yes. I can give you thirty-six dollars today."

"Only thirty-six dollars! The amount due is sixty-six."

"I know it, Squire Hudson, but this has been a bad year for the farmers, as you probably know. Owing to the drought, my crops fell off at least one quarter."

"I can't help that," said the squire, coldly.

"If you will be a little patient," said Mr. Nelson, uneasily.

"Neighbor Nelson," said his creditor, interrupting him, "I wish to ask you one question. When I lent you money on mortgage was there a stipulation that if there was a drought I was to wait for my just interest?"

"No, Squire Hudson."

"To be sure not. I would not of course lend you money on any such terms. It was understood that my interest was to be paid semi-annually--was it not so?"

"Yes, but--"

"Wait a moment. You must certainly agree that I am entitled to prompt payment. A bargain is a bargain."

"I don't dispute it, Squire Hudson, and I have tried to be ready for you, but in spite of all my efforts I am thirty dollars short."

"Do you expect me to be content with this explanation?"

"I think you are rather hard on me, squire. It isn't as if I had the money and objected to pay. I am a poor man, but no one ever lost a dollar by me, and I don't mean that any one shall while I have my life and strength."

"That's all very well, but it won't make up the thirty dollars in which you are delinquent."

"What would you have me do? I cannot make money."

"I wouldn't give much for an investment when the interest is delayed. It is no longer worth its face. If any of my railroad bonds defer their usual interest they at once drop in value."

"I know very little of railroad bonds, never having any money to invest in them, but I think my farm will be full security for all the money I owe you."

"Suppose I should foreclose--you would consider it an unkind thing and a great hardship, wouldn't you?"

"It would take away my means of supporting my family. I don't think you would go to extremes for the sake of thirty dollars."

"It isn't the amount of money, neighbor Nelson, that is to be considered. It is the principle that is involved."

This is a very common pretext with men who have made up their minds to do a mean thing. Generally speaking it is false, and the money is the first consideration.

"Will you give me two months to pay the balance of interest?" asked Mark Nelson.

"What better prospect have you of being able to pay me then?"

"As soon as Tom has any money to send, he will remit to me. I think it probable that I shall hear from him in the course of two months."

"If that is your reliance," said the squire, shrugging his shoulders, "I am afraid you are leaning upon a broken reed. I know boys pretty well, and I fancy Tom will find a use for all the money he earns."

"You don't know him, Squire Hudson. He is a very conscientious boy, and he understands very well the sacrifice I made in raising money to send him to California. He is not very likely to forget that."

"It seems to me that the sacrifice was mine," said the squire, with a half sneer. "If I remember rightly, I advanced the money which he took away with him."

Mark Nelson flushed, and he answered warmly, "You did advance the money, Squire Hudson, but I gave you security for it."

"And the very first interest that has come due you are not prepared to meet. You can't blame me for feeling a little doubt as to the wisdom of my advance."

"Are you very much in need of the thirty dollars?" asked Mr. Nelson, nettled at the squire's tone.

What do you mean, sir?"

"Is it subjecting you to any great inconvenience to wait a couple of months for it? That is what I mean."

"My circumstances are not such," returned the squire, haughtily, "as to make me feel even the loss of thirty dollars."

"I wish I could say the same, but I cannot. Since, then, it will occasion you no inconvenience, I ask you as a favor that you will let the balance rest for two months."

Squire Hudson saw that he was cornered, but none the less was he disposed to yield the point. He even felt provoked with the farmer for having forced from him an acknowledgment that he did not need the money he so persistently demanded.

"I told you before," he said, "that it was not the amount of money, but the principle, that I care for. You cannot have forgotten this."

"I don't see how any principle is involved, Squire Hudson."

"You look at the matter solely from a debtor's point of view. If you held the mortgage, instead of myself, you would change your view very quickly."

"I don't think I should," said the farmer, slowly. "I would be considerate to a poor neighbor, even if it did inconvenience me a little."

"The poor neighbor should not have borrowed money on which he was unable to pay interest," said Squire Hudson, severely.

"How could I anticipate the drought that has diminished my crops?" said Mark Nelson, with spirit.

"That is neither here nor there. You knew that the interest must be paid, drought or no drought, crop or no crop."

"I cannot argue with you further, since you refuse to consider circumstances over which I have had no control. You refuse to grant me any delay?"

"I do."

"Since I have not the money to pay you, will you tell me what you require?"

"How many cows do you keep?"

"Three."

"You can give me one of these, and I will consider it an equivalent for the thirty dollars."

"Do you require this?" asked the farmer, uneasily.

"Yes, unless you have some other satisfactory arrangement to propose."

"I am afraid I have nothing else which you would regard as satisfactory. The loss of a cow will diminish my income. Instead of three, I ought to have four or five. I shouldn't like to be reduced to two."

"Very likely not, but an honest man is willing to make a sacrifice in order to meet his just liabilities. Besides, you expect to have the money, you say, in a couple of months. When it has come, you may have your cow back, on paying two months' interest on the deferred payment. That is only fair."

"Say no more, Squire Hudson," said the farmer. "I must, of course, consent to this arrangement since you insist upon it. How soon do you wish for the cow?"

"You had better let your son Walter drive it over this afternoon."

"He is losing no time," thought Mark Nelson, bitterly. "He does not even appear to be willing that I should have the benefit of this night's milking."

"You may send me Whiteface," continued Squire Hudson, who knew that this was the most valuable of the three cows.

"That is my best cow," protested the farmer.

"That makes little difference, as you expect to redeem it in two months."

Mark Nelson was silent. He felt indignant with Squire Hudson for his cruel exaction, but he felt that he was in his power, and that he must submit to his exactions.

"You will attend to this matter?" asked the squire, as he rose and prepared to go.

"Yes," answered the farmer, coldly.

When his creditor was gone he went into the kitchen and acquainted the family with what had passed. Great were the grief and indignation of the children, and Walter expressed a desire that Squire Hudson might lose all his property as a fitting reward for his meanness.

"Heaven help me if I can't meet the next interest!" said Mark Nelson, later in the day, to his wife.

"Don't be too much troubled about the future, Mark," said his wife, who was of a more hopeful temperament than her husband. "I am sure that you will get some help from Tom before six months are over."

"I hope so," answered her husband, but for the rest of the day he was very grave.

Walter drove over Whiteface, at his father's request, but he came near crying, stout boy as he was, at the loss of the faithful animal which his father had reared from a calf.

CHAPTER XX

AT SACRAMENTO

After his escape from the grizzly Tom had no further adventures of an exciting character. One afternoon he and his companions arrived at Sacramento. It was but a small settlement, but it was more town-like than any place they had yet seen in California. They drove to a two-story frame building, which was the chief hotel in the town. Taking the precaution to inquire the price of board and lodging, they were dismayed by the extravagance of the charges. Tom saw that his reserve fund of twenty dollars would scarcely last him forty-eight hours.

A bird's eye view of Sacramento in 1857

"I can't stay here, Mr. Ferguson," he said. "I will take my chances and camp out, if necessary."

"I agree with you, lad. I'm not inclined to waste my substance on luxurious living."

"There won't be much luxurious living, I guess," said Ebenezer Onthank, who, with Yankee curiosity, had already visited the kitchen and obtained some idea of the fare to be expected. "I kin get better board at Green Mountain Mills for three dollars a week, and folks are darned glad to accommodate you for that price. These chaps seem to think and act as if we were made of money."

"I wish some of your Green Mountain Mills boarding-houses were here," said Tom. "I could save plenty of money then."

"Well, gentlemen, do you want to stay here?" inquired the landlord.

"We'd like to, squire, but not bein' millionaires I guess we'll have to put it off till times are better."

"Just as you say," said the landlord, indifferently. "There's others waiting for the only room I have empty." Then, noticing for the first time the express wagon which Tom had left outside, he asked, in a tone of interest, "Who owns that team?"

"It belongs to this boy and myself," answered Ferguson.

"Where did it come from?"

"The States."

"You don't want to sell, do you?"

Tom was about to reply in the affirmative, but the Scot, more shrewd, answered indifferently, "We may sell it when we get to San Francisco."

"I need just such a team as that," said the landlord, eagerly. "I'll give you a good price for it. You can go down the river to Frisco."

"I suppose we might," said Ferguson, slowly, "if it was worth our while."

"What'll you take, cash down?" inquired the landlord, earnestly.

"Nay, my friend, I prefer to hear your views as to the price."

"I will give you eight hundred dollars for the wagon."

This was certainly an excellent profit, for but three hundred had been paid for horse and wagon. Tom's heart beat fast with excitement, for he remembered that one-third of the money would come to him. If it had depended upon him he would have clinched the bargain at once, but he wisely left the matter in the hands of his companion and partner.

"That seems a fair offer," said Ferguson, "but I think we may as well wait till we reach San Francisco. Besides, we want to sell the horse, too."

"I will give you a thousand dollars for the two," said the landlord.

A man with his pantaloons tucked in his boots, a coarse woolen shirt, and a wide-brimmed sombrero, which overshadowed a face bearing a beard of a week's growth, was leaning against the door-post.

"Landlord," said he, "I see your price, and I'll go two hundred better."

Tom stared at the speaker in surprise. He looked like a man who would have found it hard to raise twelve dollars, yet he had made an offer of twelve hundred. Our hero did not learn till afterwards that the man had "struck it rich" at the mines, sold out his claim for ten thousand dollars, and for the time being was the lucky possessor of a large bank account.

"Now, Tom Scott," expostulated the landlord, "this ain't fair. I want the wagon more'n you do, and you're a-raisin' the price on me."

"How do you know that?" drawled Scott. "I've got a pile, and I mean to take it easy while it lasts. I'm going back to the mines like a gentleman, with my own team, you bet, if I've got money enough to buy one."

The landlord was satisfied that, if he wanted the team, he must outbid his competitor, and he advanced his offer to thirteen hundred dollars. But Tom Scott was not terrified. His money had come easily, and he would not let two or three hundred dollars stand in the way of his wishes.

"I'll go fifteen," he drawled.

The landlord shrugged his shoulders, and said, in a disappointed tone, "You'll have to take it, Scott. You've gone ahead of my pile."

"Well, stranger, is it a bargain?" asked Scott.

The Scotchman, though inwardly elated as well as astonished at the extraordinary offer he had received, answered quietly, "If my partner agrees."

"I guess we'd better sell," said Tom, trying not to betray his inward satisfaction.

"All right," said Scott, appearing to be well pleased. "You can have your money when you want it. If you are going to Frisco, I'll give you an order on my banker there."

"Tom Scott's a square man, and his order will fetch the money," said the landlord, observing Ferguson's prudent hesitation.

"That is satisfactory," replied Ferguson.

In five minutes more the business was concluded, and Ferguson and Tom, longing to congratulate each other on their good fortune, walked off together.

"We're in luck, Mr. Ferguson," said Tom. "I don't know whether I stand on my head or my heels. I never expected such a price."

"Twelve hundred dollars is a great profit," said Ferguson. "I almost doubt whether we are justified in asking such an extortionate price of the poor man."

"He is pleased with his bargain, and I don't think we need to trouble ourselves about that," answered Tom. "Besides, you know we can't compare prices with those at home."

"No doubt there is reason in what you say, my lad, but it's not easy at first to make allowance for the difference."

"That's so, Mr. Ferguson. When shall we go to San Francisco?"

"We will go tomorrow, if we can. I suppose you will wish to send some money to your father."

"Yes, I am in a hurry to send to him, for I am sure he needs it already. I can hardly realize that I am worth five hundred dollars."

"Five hundred?"

"Yes, I had a third share in the team."

"That isn't my way of looking at it, Tom."

"Is it possible Mr. Ferguson would cheat me out of my fair share?" thought Tom, but he only harbored the suspicion for an instant. He had seen too much of his friend to believe such a thing, and he quietly waited for an explanation.

"I'll tell you how I propose that we divide it, Tom. First we'll take out the money each of us put in, one hundred for you and two hundred for me, and then we'll divide the profit equally."

"But," protested Tom, "you are entitled to two-thirds."

"Then I won't take it," said Ferguson, decidedly. "I only want half of the profit. That will give me eight hundred dollars, and that ought to satisfy me."

"And I shall have seven hundred," said Tom, his eyes sparkling.

"Precisely."

"How kind you are, Mr. Ferguson!" exclaimed Tom, eagerly seizing the Scotchman's hand.

"No, my lad. I am only just. I am glad to help a boy who is working for his father and family."

"I shouldn't deserve to succeed if I didn't," said Tom, earnestly.

"Always bear that in mind, my lad, and God will smile on your efforts and raise you up friends."

In spite of the high price, Tom and his partner felt justified now in stopping over night at the hotel where they had met with such a piece of good luck, and the next day started down the river for San Francisco.

CHAPTER XXI

TOM BUYS A BUSINESS

It was an interesting moment for our two friends when they landed in San Francisco. The future Western metropolis was only a town of scattered wooden and adobe houses, with irregular streets and a general lack of uniformity in its buildings, but everybody seemed on the alert. The number of drones was wonderfully small; even the constitutionally lazy could not resist the golden incentives to labor. Money was looked upon with very different eyes there than in the East. No one took the trouble to dispute prices, and a man who landed with an article rare or desirable could often obtain twenty times its value. Within ten minutes of his arrival Tom witnessed a case of this kind.

Just as he was entering Montgomery street he noticed a man-- evidently a new-comer--with a fine bunch of pineapples in his hand. He had just arrived in the steamer Columbus, then anchored out in the stream.

"I shouldn't mind having one of those pineapples," said Tom to Ferguson.

"Doubtless they are high-priced, being a rarity," said the Scotchman.

Just then a passer-by, attracted like Tom, and feeling a similar longing, stepped up to the new-comer.

"Are those pineapples for sale?" he asked.

"Yes, if you'll pay enough," was the half-jocular reply.

"Name your price."

"Ten dollars."

"Here is your money," and he put a gold piece into the hand of the astounded passenger, which represented ten times the sum he had paid for the fruit at San Blas.

"That's a pretty steep price," said Tom, "for six pineapples."

"It is very wasteful to spend such a sight of money to pamper the appetite," said the canny Scot. "Truly, a fool and his money are soon parted."

He was destined to be still more surprised. The purchaser within five minutes transferred half his purchase to another for fifteen dollars.

"Gold seems to be plenty here," said Tom.

"I hope all provisions are not as high," said Ferguson, "or we shall soon have a chance to spend all we have."

"Where shall we go first?" asked Tom.

"We had better go to a public house and secure a lodging," said Ferguson.

"I wish I knew someone here to direct me."

Scarcely had Tom uttered these words than he cried out in surprise, "Why, there's John Miles!"

They were passing a little, unpainted, wooden building, of one and a half stories, used as a grocery. A German name was on the sign, but behind the rough counter stood the familiar form of John Miles.

Tom dashed into the store, followed by his more dignified companion.

"How are you, John?" he exclaimed.

"Why, if it isn't Tom," returned Miles, his face showing the joy he felt. "And here's Mr. Ferguson, too."

Then there ensued a hearty shaking of hands, followed by the question, "When did you get here?"

"About twenty minutes ago."

"And you came straight to me. That's good."

"So it is, but it's an accident. We had no idea where you were. So you are a grocer, John. Is the place yours?"

"If it is, then I've changed my name," said Miles, pointing to the sign bearing the name:

JOHN SCHINKELWITZ.

"The first name's right, at any rate," said Tom, laughing. "I suppose you are the clerk, then."

"Yes."

"How long have you been here?"

"Four weeks."

"Is it a good business?"

"Very good. My Dutch friend pays me five dollars a day, and I sleep here."

"Among the groceries?"

"Yes. It saves me the expense of a bed outside, and that is a good deal. I haven't saved quite enough to pay you yet, Tom, but I can soon."

"No hurry, John. I have been lucky since I saw you."

"I am glad to hear it, Tom. Did the claim prove more productive?"

"No, but I have been speculating. Guess how much money I have with me."

"A hundred and fifty dollars."

"More."

"Two hundred."

"More yet."

"Not three hundred, Tom?"

"I won't make you guess any more. I have seven hundred dollars. No wonder you look surprised. I'll tell you how I made it," and Tom repeated the story of his purchase and its profitable sale.

"I am not so much surprised now," said Miles, "for in this country a man will have what he takes a fancy to, no matter what it costs. I am glad the good luck came to you and Mr. Ferguson. I shouldn't mind having that amount of money myself."

"What would you do with it?"

"I would buy out my employer, and then I could make money fast."

"Does he want to sell?"

"Yes, he wants to go to the mines."

"Would he sell for such a small sum?"

"Yes. There isn't much of a stock, but we are constantly replenishing. I tell you what, Tom, you buy him out, and I'll manage the business."

"Are you in earnest, John?"

"Certainly I am."

"But I want to send some money home," objected Tom.

"How much?"

"A hundred dollars at least."

"I'll lend you the hundred, my lad," said Ferguson, "and fifty more, and you can take your own money and buy the business. I don't favor acting hastily, in general, but I have faith in our friend here, and I am led to believe that the enterprise will be a profitable one."

"You'll be my partner, Tom, and I'll give you a third of the profits without your doing a thing. If you work with me, you shall have as much more as will be satisfactory."

"I would rather go back to the mines, John, and leave you to manage this business by yourself. A quarter of the profits will satisfy me."

"No, it shall be a third. As you furnish the capital, that is only fair."

"We may be counting our chickens too soon. Perhaps your Dutch friend, whose name I can't pronounce, won't sell."

"Here he is to speak for himself."

A short German, with a ponderous frame, and a broad, good-humored face, here entered the grocery, panting with the exertion of walking, and looked inquiringly at Tom and the Scotchman.

"Herr Schinkelwitz, this is my friend, Tom Nelson," said Miles.

"Glad to see you, mine vriend," said the German, addressing Ferguson.

"No, that is Mr. Ferguson," said Miles, smiling. "I should have introduced him first."

"Wie gehts, Herr Ferguson?" said the grocer. "You have one strange name."

"Your name seems strange to me," said the Scotchman.

"Oh, no. Schinkelwitz is a very common name. Most peoples admire my name."

Tom was considerably amused, but Herr Schinkelwitz did not observe the smile which he could not repress.

"I have told my friends you would like to sell out the business," said Miles.

"Oh, ja, it is a good business, but my health is not good. I think it will be much better at the mines. You will do well to buy it yourself."

"I would if I had money enough."

"Ja, I must have the money, for I shall need it."

"My friend here has money, and may buy of you," said Miles, indicating Tom.

"What, the boy?"

"Yes."

"Where did he get so much money?"

"At the mines."

"Oh, ja, that is a good place to get gold. Well, my young vriend, I will sell cheap."

It will not be necessary to enter into a detailed account of the negotiation. It is enough to say that for the sum of seven hundred dollars Herr Schinkelwitz made over the business to Herr Tom, as he called him, and our hero found himself penniless, but the owner of a grocery. In half an hour it was all completed.

"Now, Tom, you are my boss," said Miles. "Shall I put your name outside?"

"No, John, put your own. I am only a silent partner, you know."

"I congratulate you, Tom," said Ferguson. "Here are two hundred dollars, for which you can give me your note."

"Two hundred?"

"Yes. You will need some yourself, besides what you send to your father."

"Suppose I can't pay you back?"

"Then I will levy on the grocery, my lad," said Ferguson.

CHAPTER XXII

A GAMBLING HOUSE

Having completed this important business arrangement, the two friends went out to explore the town. The limits were narrow compared with those of the flourishing city of the present day. Where the Palace and Grand hotels now stand was a sand-hill, and the bay encroached upon the business part of the city far more than now.

Scarcely a stone's throw from the grocery, on Montgomery street, between California and Sacramento, was the office of Adams' Express, which advertised to forward gold dust and packages by every steamer.

"I will go in here, Mr. Ferguson," said Tom. "I shall not feel comfortable till I have started this money homeward. I am sure it will be wanted."

"Right, my lad. We will attend to it, by all means."

They entered the building--a very humble one it would now be considered--but they found other customers before them and had to wait for their turn.

"What can I do for you?" asked the clerk, in a quick, business-like tone.

"I want to send home a hundred dollars," said Tom.

"Give me the address."

This was done, the money paid over, and a receipt returned in two minutes.

"How long before my father will receive the money?" asked Tom.

"The steamer starts in three days. About a month will be needed."

Then Tom moved aside, and the next man took his place.

"I am glad that is attended to," said Tom, relieved. "Now, Mr. Ferguson, I will go wherever you wish."

"We had better secure a lodging," said the Scotchman. "When we are sure of a bed we can walk about at our leisure."

Lodgings were to be had, but they were generally very dear. The first room looked at was five dollars per day, without board--a price our friends were unwilling to pay. Finally they found a decent, though small room, with rather a narrow bed, which could be had for three fifths of that sum, and they took it.

"We will have to go back to the mines soon," said Tom. "San Francisco is too expensive for us to live in."

"You can afford it better than I, Tom," said his friend.

"Why?"

"Because you have a business that brings you an income."

"Oh, I forgot that," said our hero, smiling. "Things happen so fast here that I haven't got used to my new position. Do you think I invested my money wisely, Mr. Ferguson?"

"Yes, my lad, since your agent is a trustworthy, honest man."

"I am sure I can trust John Miles."

"If I were not confident of it, also, I would not have encouraged you to take so important a step."

"I think I won't write to father about it," said Tom, after a pause. "He might think I had acted foolishl and become anxious. If I succeed, then I shall be glad to surprise him. I think I shall make money, but I don't want to count on it too much. I shall be ready to go back with you to the mines whenever you say the word."

As they sauntered about, gazing curiously at the motley sights around them, they heard strains of music. It appeared to proceed from a large wooden building, with a jutting roof, under which, on benches, lounged a number of persons, some of them Mexicans, in their native costumes, smoking cigarettes. A large American flag was displayed over the door, and a crowd was constantly passing in and out.

"Let us go in," said Tom.

His companion made no objection, and they entered. The first sight of the interior made clear the character of the place. There were numerous tables, spread with games--faro, monte, and roulette--each surrounded by an absorbed and interested group. "Easy come, easy go," was the rule with the early California pioneers, and the gaming-table enlisted in its service many men who would not have dreamed at home that they could ever be brought to tolerate such an instrument of evil.

Tom was a country boy, and unsophisticated, but he could not help understanding the nature of the business which brought so many to the place.

"I suppose they are gambling," he said.

"Yes, poor, deluded creatures!" said the Scotchman, who had been brought up to an abhorrence of games of chance. "They are wasting their time and their substance and foolishly laying up for themselves future misery."

Had this remark been heard it would have excited indignation, and perhaps subjected the speaker to insult, but the players were too intent upon their varying chances to pay any attention to the remarks of by-standers.

"I hope, Tom, you will never yield to the seductive lures of the gaming-table," continued Ferguson.

"I don't think there is much danger," said Tom. "I have always been taught that gambling is wicked."

"May you long feel so, my lad!"

Tom did, however, watch the players with interest. He saw money lost and won, without understanding exactly how it was decided. From the game his attention was drawn to the gamesters. He was led to notice, particularly, a young man of prepossessing countenance, who was evidently profoundly excited. From time to time he drew out a roll of gold pieces, which he placed on a card and invariably lost. He must have had a considerable sum, but, small or large, he was in ill-luck, and he constantly lost. As he neared the end of his resources the feverish blush upon his handsome features was succeeded by a deep pallor, and there was no mistaking the expression of deep anguish and despair which announced that he had reached the end.

A man loses his last cent in a gambling house, 1849

Tom became painfully interested in the young man and silently drew the attention of his companion to him. When the end came, and the victim, thoroughly "cleaned out," turned to go out, Tom said, in a low voice, "Let us follow him."

Ferguson acquiesced. He, too, had become interested, and the young man's expression as he passed our two friends was so despairing that Ferguson felt some alarm as to the effect of his disappointment upon his mind.

Once in the street, Ferguson and Tom followed the unfortunate young man into an obscure street, keeping up with difficulty, for his pace was rapid and excited. It proved to be a fortunate thing, for when he supposed himself free from observation the young man drew a pistol, and, with an incoherent exclamation, placed it in contact with his temple.

Tom sprang forward, and so did the Scotchman, but Tom was the quicker and more agile, and he dashed the pistol aside just in time to prevent a suicide.

"Why did you do that?" asked the baffled would-be-suicide, gloomily, turning his gaze upon Tom.

"I was afraid you were going to kill yourself."

"So I was."

"What could induce you to take such a rash step?" asked Ferguson.

"I have been a reckless fool. I have lost all my money at the accursed gambling-table, and my life is not worth retaining."

"It appears to me," said the Scotchman, quietly, "that you set too high a value upon money. You have certainly been very foolish to risk it at the gaming-table, and the loss will no doubt inconvenience you, but was your money all you had to live for?"

The young man regarded Ferguson with some surprise, but his excitement was evidently abated. The quiet tone of the speaker had a favorable effect upon him.

"I didn't think of it in that light," he admitted.

"Have you no relatives to whom your life is of value?"

"Yes," answered the young man. "I have a mother and sister."

"Would not your death affect them more than the loss of money?"

"Yes."

"It seems to me that to take your life would be to treat them cruelly."

The young man was evidently agitated by contending thoughts.

"I suppose you are right," he said, slowly, "but let me tell you all, and you can judge me better. I arrived in California six months ago. My home is in Ohio, not far from Cincinnati. I was fortunate enough to commence mining at a point on the western slope of the Sierra Nevada Mountains where I was almost alone. I 'struck it rich,' and two days since arrived in San Francisco with over two thousand dollars in gold dust."

"You were certainly in luck," said Ferguson, surprised.

"I turned it into money, and, in strolling about the city, was lured into that accursed den. I looked on and was fascinated. I thought I would try my luck. I began with a small stake and kept on till I had lost every dollar. In one hour the fruits of six months' labor are gone. Do you wonder that I am reduced to despair?"

CHAPTER XXIII

A NEW SCHEME

"I see no cause for despair," replied Ferguson, in the same calm tone.

"I have not a penny left out of the two thousand dollars I had only an hour ago."

"I understand all that."

"I am a ruined man," said the young man, despondently.

"I don't admit that. How old are you?"

"Twenty-one."

"You are well and strong, are you not?"

"Oh, yes, I have nothing to complain of on that score."

"Then it appears to me that your loss is not serious. Your capital still remains."

"My capital?" repeated the young man.

"Yes, your strong arms, your education, your capacity to labor."

"But I shall have to begin over again."

"Beginning over again at your age, when, possibly, fifty years of life lie before you, is not such a serious matter. Were I in your situation--and I am twice as old as you--I should not think of despairing. Don't you think it would be rather foolish for two thousand dollars, which you have been only six months in accumulating, to throw away fifty years, and all that you can make in that time, thereby bringing a lifelong grief to your mother and sister?"

The calm, logical tone of the Scotchman had its effect.

"I see that I was about to add to one piece of folly another far greater," said the young man. "I don't know who you are, sir, but I heartily thank you and your son for saving my life."

"This is not my son, but my young friend, Thomas Nelson," said Ferguson. "I am not so fortunate as to have a son."

"Well, God bless you both, and good night!"

"Excuse my persistency, but may I ask where you are going?"

"I am not going to repeat my folly of just now, if that is what you mean."

"I did not suspect you of that, but are you sure of a bed anywhere?"

"No, I have no money to pay for one. I shall walk the streets or possibly lie down in some quiet place. I was accustomed to roughing it at the mines and can do it again if necessary."

"Tom and I have a room in which you are welcome to find a shelter. I am sorry that our bed is too narrow to hold another."

"Thank you. That will be better than to sleep in the streets. But are you not afraid to make me this offer?"

"Why should I be?"

"I might rob you during the night."

"You might, but you don't look like one who would so reward confidence."

"You are right. If you had fifty thousand dollars I would not touch a dollar of it. I will accept your offer. How can I repay you for your kindness?"

"There may be a way. We will talk of that this evening."

Nine o'clock found the three collected in the small room which had been hired by Ferguson for himself and Tom.

"My friend," said Ferguson, "you told us that you found a favorable place for mining up in the Sierras."

"Yes, I 'struck it rich.'"

"I take it for granted that you did not exhaust the wealth of the place?"

"Far from it. I only dipped into it. There is abundance left."

"Is this place known to many?"

"To only one, so far as I know. He and I worked independently but were company for each other."

"But what induced you to leave so rich a claim?"

"I was tired of working and wanted to come to the city for a change. You know what a change I have experienced here."

"Why don't you go back and start anew in the place where you met with your former good fortune?" asked Ferguson.

"Because I am penniless. I must find something to do here for a while. When I have got together a little fund, sufficient for the purpose, I will go back."

"Would you go back now, if you had the chance?"

"Would I? Certainly I would, for I could make money faster there than here."

"Would you have any objection to let Tom and myself accompany you?"

"Not the least. I should be glad of your company. There is gold enough for us all."

"Then we will start tomorrow, that is, if you and Tom are willing."

"I am ready," said Tom, promptly.

"But I have nothing. I don't like to be an expense to you," objected the young man.

"We will pay your expenses. We shall be more than recompensed by the richness of the mines. We might find something to do here, but both Tom and myself prefer the freedom of the mining camp, and, if the spot is as rich as you have led us to suspect, we shall make more money there."

"Agreed!" said the young man, promptly. "Name the hour of starting, and rely upon me to be ready."

Ferguson was evidently well pleased with this response. He felt that his new acquaintance would be so far away from the city and would sooner retrieve his fortunes at the mines. He hoped, too, to find opportunity to strengthen his principles and guard him against the temptations of the city when he should again visit it. Again, he had reason to think that the arrangement would benefit Tom and himself in a pecuniary way, and the Scotchman was by no means indifferent to that consideration, though, as we have seen, he did not unduly exalt the power or value of money.

Tom, too, was pleased with the prospect. He was grateful and attached to Ferguson, whom he felt to be a true friend, but he was glad to have another companion nearer his own age. The young man was of a prepossessing exterior, and, when he had shaken off his present disquietude, looked as if he might be a cheerful and agreeable companion.

"Since we are to live together, for a time at least, and become fellow workers," said Ferguson, "we ought to know each other better. I will introduce myself first."

Hereupon Ferguson gave a brief account of himself, which need not be repeated, and then called upon Tom, who followed his example.

"Now it is my turn," said their new acquaintance. "You don't even know my name yet, though you have done me such an important service. I have already told you that I am from Ohio. My

255

name is Richard Russell, though my friends generally call me Dick. My father, whom I had the misfortune to lose several years ago, was at one time a member of Congress. He left a small property, the income of which is barely sufficient to provide my mother and sister with the comforts of life. I had a fair education, including enough Latin and Greek to fit me for entering college. My mother desired me to enter, but I knew that she could not keep me there without practicing pinching economy, and I secured a place with a small salary in a business house in Cincinnati. A year since, when the papers were full of the gold discoveries on this coast, I was seized, like so many others, with the golden fever, and I arranged to start overland. It would have proved a wise step had I not been so rash a fool as to squander my earnings, for two thousand dollars in six months compare very favorably with twelve dollars a week, which I was earning at home. I might have gone home by the next steamer, and I had money enough to carry me through a course of legal study, had I desired. I am out of patience with myself when I think of how I have thrown away my good fortune."

"Don't think too much of the past, which cannot be recalled. Resolve not to repeat your folly, and all may yet be well."

"I have fully resolved upon that," said Russell, earnestly.

"Do you think you shall study law, if you are again fortunate, Mr. Russell?" asked Tom.

"If you please don't call me Mr. Russell, unless you want me to call you Mr. Nelson. Call me Dick."

"I will," said Tom, smiling, "for I am not ready to be called Mr. Nelson yet."

"Now, to answer your question. If I can get two thousand dollars together again, I shall probably study law. Of course I don't mean to be a miner all my life any more than you. Now, Tom, what are your plans?"

"I think I should like to be a lawyer, too, but I must earn more than two thousand dollars first."

"Two thousand ought to be sufficient to educate you if you are economical."

"It would be, but I want to pay off a mortgage on my father's farm before I begin to lay up money for myself."

"You are a good fellow, Tom, and I wish you success."

"Thank you, Dick. I will succeed if hard work can bring success."

"Good night to you both," said Ferguson. "I want to sleep well to prepare myself for starting tomorrow."

In half an hour all three were sleeping soundly.

CHAPTER XXIV

PREPARING FOR A NEW START

When Tom opened his eyes he did not at first remember where he was, but a glance at Dick Russell, his new acquaintance, stretched out on the floor and still sleeping, quickly recalled the important events of the day previous. Mr. Ferguson was already dressed.

"Well, Tom, are you rested?" he asked.

"Yes, Mr. Ferguson. I slept like a top. What time is it?"

"It is seven o'clock. Our new friend is still asleep."

"I suppose he was on his feet all day yesterday."

"I don't know whether I ought to hurry you away from San Francisco so soon, Tom," said his Scotch friend. "We only arrived yesterday, and you have not had time to see the place and enjoy yourself after your hard work at the mines."

"I don't care for that, Mr. Ferguson. I am anxious to be at work again. I didn't come out here to enjoy myself but to make money for my father."

"You have succeeded pretty well thus far, Tom."

"Yes, but I have made more by the sale of the team than by work at the mines."

Seeking gold in California: Tom and Mr. Ferguson reflect back on River Bend and on the new start that awaits them.

"True, but that is a legitimate transaction. If our friend here has reported correctly, we shall find mining more profitable in the place he mentions than at River Bend."

"I have no objection to that, though I was satisfied with River Bend. Wouldn't it be splendid, Mr. Ferguson, if we could do as well in the next six months as he did?"

"Making two thousand dollars each?"

"Yes."

"We may accomplish it, but it is best not to calculate upon it."

"If I could only free the farm from that troublesome mortgage I should be proud and happy. It has worn upon father, as I could see, and he has been compelled to toil early and late to pay the interest, besides supporting us all."

"How much is the mortgage, Tom?"

"Twenty-two hundred dollars."

"You have made a good beginning towards it already, Tom. You have seven hundred dollars invested in business."

"But out of that I owe you a hundred and fifty, Mr. Ferguson."

"Don't trouble yourself about that, Tom. Unless I should stand in great need of it, I will wait till you have paid off the mortgage before asking to have it repaid."

"You are very kind, Mr. Ferguson," said Tom, gratefully. "A part of my seven hundred dollars rightfully belongs to you, for you owned two-thirds of the horse and wagon."

"I couldn't have bought them without your help, Tom. So you see that you enabled me to make money. I am quite satisfied with an equal partnership."

"And I am very well satisfied with my partner," said Tom, smiling. "Shall we wake up Russell?"

"Yes, for we have much to do today."

"John Miles will be surprised at my leaving the city so quick."

"By the way, Tom, as he is to remain here, while you are out of the reach of post-offices, it may be well to ask your father to direct future letters to his care, and he can forward them as he has opportunity."

"That is a good idea. I will write today so as to catch the next steamer, and I will also speak to John."

Tom had to shake Dick Russell energetically before that young man opened his eyes.

"What's the matter?" he cried, drowsily.

"Don't you want some breakfast?" asked Tom.

"Oh, it's you, Tom! Yes, you have touched the right chord. I have a first-class appetite--and no money," he added, his face clouding.

"Mr. Ferguson is treasurer," said Tom, lightly, wishing to divert Russell from the thoughts of his heavy loss and the folly to which he owed it, "but we know very little of the city. Can you guide us to a good restaurant?"

"To a good one, but not a cheap one. Everything is high here."

"Then it is fortunate we are going to leave so soon."

In a small restaurant on Montgomery street, our three friends partook of a hearty breakfast. It might not have attracted an epicure, but neither of the three was fastidious, and, though the charge was five dollars, Ferguson, economical as he was, paid the bill cheerfully. It was the first "civilized" breakfast he had eaten for months, and it might be months before he would be able to partake of another as good.

"I wish we could breakfast like this at the mines," said Tom.

"So say I," chimed in Dick Russell, "but you know that the gold-hunter must sacrifice home comforts."

"I shan't complain of that, if I can do as well as you did," said Tom.

"I see no reason why you can't. There is plenty of gold there, and all that is needed is work and perseverance."

"I am willing to contribute them," said Tom. "I mean to do my best to succeed."

"None of us can do more, my lad," said Ferguson. "Let us hope that God will prosper our undertakings."

"I say, I am glad I have met with you two," said Dick Russell. "You'll keep me on the right track, and, in spite of my past folly, I hope in time to win success."

"I am glad to hear you speak so sensibly, my young friend," said the Scotchman, kindly. "It's a great deal better to put your back to the wheel once more than to take the life God gave you."

"Don't speak of that again, Mr. Ferguson," said Russell, shuddering. "I don't like to think of it."

"He'll do," thought Ferguson, with satisfaction. "His mind is now in a healthy condition, and I have great hopes for him."

The rest of the day was devoted to the purchase of supplies. Ferguson also bought a mule, on behalf of the party, which was of service in carrying a part of their burdens. It was not until afternoon that Tom found an opportunity to call on John Miles and acquaint him with his almost immediate departure.

"I am sorry you are going away so soon, Tom," said Miles. "I thought you would stay at least a week."

"So I would if I were not so anxious to be at work once more. You know how my father is situated, John, for I have told you more than once."

"Yes, Tom, but I see no reason why you should feel uneasy. With the help you are to send him, there will be no trouble about his paying his interest regularly."

"I know that, John, but I shall feel uneasy until the mortgage is paid off and he is out of Squire Hudson's power."

"For how long a time has the farm your father owns been encumbered with this mortgage?"

"For ten years, at least."

"Is the mortgage for any specified term of years?"

"I don't think so."

"It merely runs from year to year then?"

"I suppose so."

"In that case this Squire Hudson could foreclose at any time, could he not?"

"Yes," answered Tom, soberly.

"Don't make yourself uneasy about it, however," said Miles, observing that Tom seemed apprehensive. "As your father's farm is not particularly valuable, there can be no danger of foreclosure. By the way, wouldn't you like to have me remit your father something next month out of the profits of the business? I can charge it to your account."

"I am glad you mentioned it, John. You may send him fifty or seventy-five dollars, if my share should amount to so much."

"I will."

"And I am going to have my home letters directed to your care. You can forward them to me whenever you have an opportunity."

"I won't fail, Tom. If there is anything you need sent out to you, you have only to write me, and I will attend to your commissions."

"It is very convenient to have an agent in the city," said Tom, smiling. "I shall feel much more comfortable out at the mines."

"I wish you good luck, Tom, but remember, even if you don't succeed in your search for gold, I shall be making money for you here."

"You make me feel quite like a capitalist, John."

"I hope you may be one some day. Good bye!"

They shook hands and parted. Before nightfall Tom had started on his new journey in quest of gold.

CHAPTER XXV

WHITEFACE

Mark Nelson missed sorely the cow which he had been compelled to yield to the squire on account of default of interest. Whiteface was his best cow and a great favorite with all the children. She gave nearly as much milk as the other two and had been one of the main dependences of the family. It was worth considerably more than the thirty dollars for which the squire took it, but he insisted upon that and no other, and Whiteface had to go.

Six months had passed, and there seemed to be very little chance of redeeming the lost cow. Squire Hudson had agreed to give her back on payment of the balance due, with accrued interest, but neither he nor Mark Nelson expected that such an offer would be made.

"I was passing Squire Hudson's today and saw poor Whiteface," said Walter one evening. "I think she knew me, for when I called her she lowed back."

"I wish we had her back," said Sarah. "It was heartless of the squire to take her. He has a dozen cows of his own."

"He hasn't any heart," said Walter, "or, if he has, it must be pretty small."

"We must not forget that he was entitled to some security for the balance of interest I owe him," said the farmer.

"The cow was worth a good deal more than thirty dollars," said Sarah.

"Yes, she was, but I am not sure whether I could have got any more money for her at a forced sale. Then you know the squire is pledged to give her back whenever I can pay him the thirty dollars, with interest."

"I wish you could pay it now, father," said Walter.

"So do I, my boy, but I cannot, unless your brother sends me some money."

"It is three weeks since we have heard from Tom," said Mrs. Nelson, anxiously. "I am afraid he is sick."

"Don't worry yourself with imaginary fears, Mary," said her husband. "Tom may be sick, of course, but he is strong and healthy, and we won't fear such a thing without some ground. Probably a letter is on the way from him now."

"I hope he is making money," said Walter. "I wish I were with him."

"I would never consent to have you go too," said Mrs. Nelson, hastily.

"I don't think Walter seriously thinks of leaving," said Mr. Nelson, smiling. "As he is only thirteen years old, I should be inclined to object myself. I must have him at home to help me with the farm."

"I should be perfectly contented to stay at home if we had Whiteface back," said Walter. "I've a great mind to steal her out of the squire's yard. I bet she'd be glad to come."

"Don't speak in that way, Walter," said his father. "I dislike to have you speak of stealing, even in fun."

At this moment there was a knock at the front door. Farmer Nelson's house was an old-fashioned one, and it was not provided with a bell.

"Go to the door, Sarah," said her father.

Sarah obeyed.

"Good evening, Nahum," she said to the village expressman.

"I've got a small package for your folks," said Nahum. "It's marked all over. Guess it came from Californy."

"It must be from Tom," exclaimed Sarah, in delight.

"That's what I thought," said the expressman, who knew everybody in the village and could probably give a fairly correct list of their sisters, cousins, and aunts, with a fair guess at their worldly circumstances.

"Is there anything to pay, Nahum?"

"Only fifty cents--the expressage from Boston. Never mind about it now, for I'm in a hurry. Your father can hand it to me next time he sees me."

"Oh father, here's a package from Tom," said Sarah, hurrying into the room where they were all sitting.

"Open it quick," said Walter. "See if there's any money in it."

The cord was cut, and a small box was disclosed containing a hundred dollars in gold pieces and a line from Tom, stating that he was doing well and that he hoped soon to send some more money.

"A hundred dollars! What a lot of money!" exclaimed Walter, gazing on the little pile of coins as if fascinated.

"I am so glad the dear boy is doing well," said Mrs. Nelson.

"Now we can have Whiteface back, can't we, father?" asked Walter, joyfully.

"Yes, Walter," said Mark Nelson, almost as excited as his son. "I will go over the first thing in the morning."

"Can't we go over this evening?" asked Walter, impatiently.

"No, it is dark, and Whiteface is stalled for the night."

"You'll have seventy dollars left over, father, won't you?"

"Yes, and that will provide for my next interest. I feel grateful and happy at Tom's success and his thoughtfulness."

Could Tom have seen the effect of his remittance it would have made his heart glad, and he would have felt abundantly repaid for his labor and self-denial.

CHAPTER XXVI

SQUIRE HUDSON'S DISAPPOINTMENT

If Whiteface was missed at her old home, she was scarcely less appreciated by her new possessor. On the very morning succeeding the day when Tom's remittance was received, the squire remarked to his head workman, "Whiteface is an excellent cow, Abner."

"Yes, squire, I calculate she's the best you've got."

"I don't know but she is, Abner," said the squire, complacently. "I consider her worth at least fifty dollars."

"So she is, every cent of it."

"And she cost me only thirty," thought Squire Hudson, with a smile of content.

He was a rich man and abundantly able to pay his poor neighbor the full value of the cow, but somehow it never occurred to him to do it. He was not above taking an unfair advantage of a man who was unluckily in his power. Of course the squire knew that Farmer Nelson had a right to redeem the cow at the price agreed upon with interest, but he felt pretty safe on this point. The farmer was not very likely to have thirty dollars to spare, and as for a remittance from Tom the squire was pretty sure none would be received.

"It'll be all the boy can do to take care of himself out there," he reflected, "let alone sending money home. He may send ten dollars or so some time, but it's very doubtful, very doubtful!"

Squire Hudson turned to go back to the house when he saw the man of whom he had been thinking coming up the road. He stopped short, thinking the farmer might wish to speak to him.

"Good morning, Mr. Nelson," he said, pleasantly, for he was in good-humor.

"Good morning, squire."

"Your Whiteface has got to feel quite at home in my barnyard."

"She is a good cow, Squire Hudson."

"Yes, tolerable, tolerable."

"She is worth more than the thirty dollars for which you took her."

"Well, I don't know about that. Cows are pretty cheap nowadays."

"I see how it is," thought the squire. "Nelson wants me to allow him more for the cow, but a bargain is a bargain, and I shan't do it."

"I always valued her at a considerably higher price."

"No doubt, no doubt. You raised her yourself, didn't you?"

"Yes."

"That makes a difference, of course. You attach a sentimental value to her, but that doesn't affect her real value. I really can't allow you any more for her."

"I don't want you to, Squire Hudson."

The squire looked astonished.

"What is the man driving at?" he thought.

"She may not be worth any more to you, and so you won't mind my taking her back."

"Taking her back!" exclaimed the squire.

"Certainly, it was agreed that I could redeem her at any time by paying you the thirty dollars and interest."

"Not after two months," said the squire, hastily.

"It is not two months. It was only six weeks yesterday. The fact is, squire, I've come for Whiteface, and I've got the money for you."

"Have you heard from Tom?" asked the squire, with a blank look of disappointment.

"Yes, I heard from him yesterday."

"And he sent you some money?"

"Yes, he reports that he is doing well."

"Did he send you thirty dollars?"

"Rather more than that," said Mark Nelson, not caring to gratify the curiosity of his creditor.

"I think you had better keep your money and leave Whiteface with me," said Squire Hudson, after a pause.

"I would rather not, squire. The fact is, Whiteface is a sort of pet at home, and we all want her back."

Squire Hudson was disconcerted. He had not expected that Mr. Nelson would be able to redeem the cow, and he was reluctant to give her up. But there was no excuse for retaining her. His agreement stood in the way.

"Neighbor Nelson," he said, after a pause, "I don't mind giving you five dollars over and above what you owe me for Whiteface. Come, that's a good offer."

Mark Nelson shook his head.

"She's worth more than that," he said. "But that's neither here nor there. I raised the animal, and it was sorely against my will that I parted with her six weeks ago. Now that I have the money to pay you, I want her back."

"I think you are standing in your own light, Mr. Nelson," said the squire. "I have taken a fancy to the cow and am willing to pay more for her than she is worth. I will say ten dollars."

Mark Nelson shook his head.

"I'd rather have Whiteface than the money," he said.

"If she comes into my possession again," said Squire Hudson, "I shall not be willing to grant you the privilege of redeeming her. It won't be many months before another payment becomes due."

"I hope to be ready to meet it, squire," said the farmer, not appearing at all anxious.

Mark Nelson's favorite cow, Whiteface

"He seems very independent," thought the squire, watching, moodily, the cow driven away by her former owner. "He may sing another tune on interest day. I wonder how much the boy sent home."

Had he known that Mr. Nelson had in his pocket enough money to pay the whole of the next accruing interest, he would have felt more doubtful about recovering the cow which he now coveted more than ever.

"Well, Abner, I've lost her," said the squire, hurrying to his assistant, "but she'll be back here some day, mark my words!"

"I thought you bought her, squire," said Abner, in surprise.

"Well, not exactly. I took her for a debt, but Nelson had the right of redeeming her, and he has done it. His boy sent him the money."

"That Tom Nelson is a smart boy," said Abner, who, though in the squire's employ, was friendly to our hero.

"Well, so-so," remarked the squire, indifferently. "I helped him to go to California, but I am not sure whether it was a wise step. I let my feelings get the better of my judgment."

"Then it is the first time," was Abner's unspoken comment.

"It may turn out for the best," he said aloud.

"I doubt if I shall ever see my money again," said the squire, but he did not seem to take it to heart, judging from his manner and tone.

"Didn't you have security for the loan?" asked Abner.

"Well, ye-es," answered the squire, slowly, "but not very good. The farm was already mortgaged for its full value."

"The squire is getting benevolent," thought Abner, "or he wants me to think so, but I'm inclined to think he has some object under it all. What is it?"

A few weeks later Farmer Nelson's heart was gladdened by the receipt of another remittance, this time sent by John Miles, out of the profit of the business in which Tom was his partner. The amount this time was seventy-five dollars. It made him feel quite rich.

"Mary," he said, "we all need some new clothes, and I propose to use this money for that purpose. Now I want you to consider how we can spend it to the best advantage. To begin with, you must buy a new dress. You have long needed one."

Mrs. Nelson demurred a little but was forced to admit that the dress was needed. So the purchases were made at once. It is wonderful how far seventy-five dollars will go in an economical family of plain tastes. It was soon apparent to the neighbors that the Nelsons were exhibiting signs of prosperity.

"It must be Tom," they decided.

Efforts were made to ascertain just how much our hero had sent home, but on this point the Nelsons would not speak definitely. They reported in general terms that Tom was doing well.

Of course Squire Hudson was not ignorant of the apparent improvement in the fortunes of his debtor. Strange to say, he seemed rather annoyed. He was pleased, however, by the outlay for dress.

"They're getting extravagant, Abner," he said, cheerfully. "I thought Mark Nelson was a man of more sense. Because his son has sent home a little money, he must rig out the whole family in new clothes. 'A fool and his money are soon parted.'"

"Mark Nelson is no fool," said Abner, stoutly.

"He is in this instance," said the squire, sharply. "However, I don't object to it, if he likes to violate the rules of prudence. It strikes me, however, that it would be well for him to pay up the money I advanced for Tom's expenses, before buying new clothes wholesale."

Abner repeated this to Mr. Nelson.

The farmer answered quietly, "The squire is not wholly wrong. It is good doctrine to pay your debts before you spend money for what you don't need. In this case, however, we did need the clothes we bought. Now that we are provided, I hope, before very long, if Tom is prospered, to pay back the two hundred dollars the squire advanced for him."

"I hope you will, I'm sure," said Abner. "That's a smart boy of yours, and I always said so."

"He is a good boy, and I am sure he will do what is right."

"He's a blamed sight better than the squire's boy. Sinclair is a stuck-up jackanapes, and it would do me good to kick him."

"It might not do him any good."

"I am not sure about that. I think he needs it."

CHAPTER XXVII

THE NEW DIGGINGS

Meanwhile Tom and his party, pursuing their journey by easy stages, for they sensibly determined not to overtask their strength, reached at last the spot of which Russell had spoken. Ferguson and Tom soon found that he had not exaggerated. The new diggings were certainly far richer than those at River Bend. It was, in fact, the bed of a dead river upon which Russell had stumbled without knowing it. My readers are probably aware that in the beds of rivers or creeks the early miners found their first harvest of gold, and, that, where practicable, these were mined by turning the stream in the dry season, when the water was low. As it may not be so well understood what is meant by a dead river, I quote a passage from an article in the "Overland Monthly," as found in the pages of the "Pacific Coast Mining Review," for the year 1878-79:

"A dead river is one which formerly existed, but exists no longer. In volcanic regions it sometimes happens that the liquid lava, seeking the lowest ground, fills up the beds of the rivers which die and are replaced by water-courses running in other channels and in different directions. These dead streams are so few, and of so little importance elsewhere, that, as yet, I believe, no class name has been given to them; but in California they are among the chief source of its mineral wealth, and among the most remarkable features of its geological formation. They take us back to a remote era, before the time of Rome, of Greece, or of Egypt; far back beyond the origin of history or tradition, before our coast had taken its present shapes; before Shasta, and Lassen, and Castle Peaks had poured out their lava floods; before the Sacramento river had its birth; and while, if not before, the mastodon, the elephant, the rhinoceros, the horse, the mammoth bull, the tapir, and the bison lived in the land. They are indeed among the most remarkable discoveries of the age, and among the greatest wonders of geology. They deserve some common name, and we have to choose between 'extinct' and 'dead.' We speak of 'extinct volcanoes,' and of 'dead languages,' and, as the latter is Saxon and short, we prefer it. They have been called 'old channels;' but this name does not convey the proper idea, since a channel is not necessarily a river, and an old channel is not necessarily a dead one. A dead river is a channel formerly occupied by a running stream, but now filled up with earthy or rocky matter, and is not to be confounded with a channel that is open and remains dry during the greater part of the year because of a lack of water, or that has been abandoned by the stream for a deeper channel elsewhere. A dry river-bed is not a dead river.

"The dead rivers of California, so far as are known, are on the western slope of the Sierra Nevada, from five hundred to seven thousand feet above the level of the sea. They are all gold-yielding, and therefore they have been sought and examined. They have yielded probably three hundred millions in all; they now produce perhaps eight million dollars annually. They are not less interesting to the miner than to the geologist, not less important to the statesman than to the antiquarian."

At the risk of being considered tedious by some of my readers, I will transcribe the writer's explanation of the existence of these dead rivers. For this reason we must go back to a remote geological epoch: "The main cause must have been the subsequent rise of the Sierra Nevada. Suppose that a range of mountains, seven thousand feet high, were upheaved thirty miles east of the Mississippi; that the bed of that stream were on the mountain side, three thousand feet above the sea, and that thirty miles west the country maintained its present level; the result would be that the present Mississippi would soon be a dead river; it would be cut across by streams running down the mountain side, and flowing into a new Mississippi, thirty miles or more west of the present one. We know that the Sierra Nevada has been upheaved; that a large stream ran on what is now the mountain side, and that it has been succeeded by a new river farther west, and we must infer that the death of the old and the birth of the new river were caused by the upheaval."

Reference is here made to the Big Blue Lead, the largest dead river known in California, which has been traced for a distance of sixty-five miles, from Little Grizzly, in Sierra County, to Forest Hill, in Placer County. The original river, however, is thought to have run for many hundreds of miles. Eventually traces of its existence may be found elsewhere.

It is not to be supposed that Tom and his friends knew anything about dead rivers, or troubled themselves as to how the rich deposits had been made, or how long they had been waiting discovery. They were chiefly engaged with more practical considerations. They found a rich harvest in the ravines, and they went to work energetically.

The work was monotonous, and a detailed account of their progress would be tiresome. What we chiefly care about is results, and these may be gathered from a conversation which took place some five months later.

Under a tent, at nightfall, reclined the three friends. They looked contented and on good terms with the world, but, though prosperous, they certainly did not look it. In fact, they were all three exceedingly, almost disreputably, shabby. They looked more like tramps than respectable gold miners.

"Tom, you are looking very ragged," said Dick Russell, surveying our hero critically.

"I know it, Dick. I feel as though I had just come out of a rag-bag. I can't say that you look much better, nor Ferguson either."

"This rough work is hard on clothing," said Russell. "I wish there were a ready-made clothing store near by."

"So do I. I would pay a high price for a good suit."

"If our friends at home could see us, what would they think, eh, Tom?"

"That we were candidates for the poorhouse."

"That's so. I've been into several poorhouses in the course of my life, but I never saw any of the inmates quite so poorly clad as we are."

"You are right," said Ferguson, "but there are generally compensations. I was taking account of stock, and I estimate that I have from sixteen to eighteen hundred dollars' worth of gold dust."

"I have nearly as much," said Tom.

"My pile won't vary far from Tom's," said Russell.

"That is a pretty good showing for five months, my friend," said the Scotchman.

"It will make up for the old clothes," said Tom.

"I have been thinking," said Ferguson, "that we need a vacation. What do you say to starting next week for San Francisco?"

"I agree," said Russell, promptly.

"And I," said Tom. "I should like to see John Miles."

"Very well. We will continue our work about a week longer and then start."

CHAPTER XXVIII

A RICH DEPOSIT

About the middle of the next morning Tom suddenly stopped work.

"What's the matter, Tom? Are you tired?"

"No, but I feel like exploring a little. Who goes with me?"

"Not I," answered Ferguson. "Let well enough alone."

"I'll go with you," said Russell. "I should like a holiday. Besides, we may discover something."

"'A rolling stone gathers no moss,'" said Ferguson.

"True, but there's another proverb: 'All work and no play makes Jack a dull boy.' Tom and I will try a little play."

The two friends sauntered away in an idle mood, yet, combining business with pleasure, they watched carefully the surface indications, ready to avail themselves of any that were favorable.

"It's a strange life we are leading, Tom," said Russell. "It is free, and independent, and healthful, but I shouldn't like to live so all my life."

"Nor I," answered Tom. "No amount of gold would repay me."

"Because gold is only valuable for what it will bring. Here it brings nothing."

"Except the hope of future ease and comfort," suggested Tom.

"Of course, that is what we are working for. We have made a good beginning."

"Yes, Dick. I have almost accomplished what I have had in view ever since I left home."

"I know. You mean paying off your father's mortgage."

"That's it. It amounts to twenty-two hundred dollars, and I have but a few hundred dollars more to earn. I would stay here a month or two longer, if my clothes would hold together, but I can't risk it."

"You need rest, at any rate, Tom, leaving clothes out of the question."

As he spoke, Tom, without special thought, drove his pick into the ground. It was a lucky inspiration. Some shining particles attracted the attention of Russell.

"Tom," he exclaimed, in excitement, "do you see that, and that? I believe you've struck a bonanza."

Upon that both set to work in earnest. A further investigation showed that Russell was right. Tom, by good luck, had chanced upon a deposit of far greater richness than any they had yet encountered.

"If it holds out, our fortunes are made, Tom," said Russell. "Go and call Ferguson, and I will remain on guard till you come back."

Tom stood not on the order of his going but went at once.

"What's the matter, Tom?" asked the Scotchman, as, panting and breathless, Tom stood before him. "Has anything happened to Russell?"

"No, it's good news--splendid news, Mr. Ferguson. We've found a place ten times as rich as this. Come at once, and see."

Ferguson made preparations to accompany Tom with what seemed to our hero to be provoking deliberation. In truth the Scotchman, with his national caution, was rather skeptical as to Tom's news and did not suffer himself to become enthusiastic or excited. Tom had hard work to accommodate his impatient steps to the measured pace of his more sedate companion. When at length they reached the spot they found Russell no less impatient.

"I thought you would never come," he said.

"Tom wanted to fly," said Ferguson, "but I am too old for that. Now, what is it you have found?"

When he was shown what had been discovered he admitted that it was very promising.

"If it holds out, we shall be lucky," he said.

"It will hold out," said Russell, enthusiastically.

"It isn't well to be too confident," said Ferguson, cautiously.

"You are very cold-blooded, Mr. Ferguson," said Russell, impatiently. "Won't anything excite you?"

"What good would it do to become excited?" returned the Scotchman. "I am as ready to test the matter as you are, and I shall rejoice if your sanguine expectations are realized. Do not expect too much, however, and you will guard against possible disappointment."

But there was no disappointment awaiting them. They worked steadily for two weeks, with marvelous results. In this time they unearthed six thousand dollars' worth of gold, which by arrangement they divided equally between them, and still the gold deposit was far from being exhausted.

At the end of the fortnight they were visited by a party of capitalists from San Francisco, who were out on an exploring expedition. They recognized the richness of the new discoveries, and after some negotiation offered the three friends ten thousand dollars for their claims. One consideration decided them to accept. It was absolutely necessary for them to go to the city for clothing and other articles, of which they stood in imperative need. They closed the bargain and started on their return.

California Gold Diggers

CHAPTER XXIX

BAD NEWS FROM HOME

Arriving in the city late in the afternoon, Tom went at once to see John Miles. When the latter caught sight of Tom, in his ragged attire, he came to the natural conclusion that our hero had met with hard luck.

"Why, Tom, where did you spring from?" he exclaimed, grasping the hand of his young partner.

"I am just in from the mines."

"I suppose you are in want of money," said Miles, his voice betraying sympathy.

Tom laughed.

"How do you like my appearance, John?" he asked.

"Never mind that, Tom. I see you have had a rough time, but I have been earning money for you."

"Did you send money regularly to father?"

"Yes. I have sent him three hundred dollars in all."

"That's good," said Tom, in a tone of satisfaction. "That has made him easy. I suppose that took up about all I was entitled to?"

"No. I have as much more to your credit. I am ready to pay it to you at once."

"I see, John, you think I have not been doing well."

"You don't look very prosperous, Tom, I must acknowledge."

"Well, John, appearances are deceitful. I have been wonderfully lucky."

"I am delighted to hear it, Tom," said Miles, cordially. "How much is it now?"

"What do you say to a thousand dollars?"

"Excellent."

"Two thousand?"

"You don't mean it!"

"I won't keep you in suspense, John. I don't know exactly how much I've got, but it's over six thousand dollars!"

John Miles stared at our hero in undisguised astonishment.

"Are you sure you're quite right here?" he said, touching his forehead. "You haven't been sunstruck, have you?"

"No, John, it's all as I tell you. Let me explain how my luck came."

In a few sentences Tom made it clear to his partner that his luck was real.

"As to the three hundred dollars due me from you, John," concluded Tom, "I make you a present of it."

"But, Tom--" protested Miles.

"Let it be so, and for the future you shall pay me my share. Have you any letters for me?"

"I have three."

"Give them to me, quick. I am hungry for news from home."

Tom sat down on a keg and fairly devoured the letters, two of which were from his father. One of these gave him much to think of. I will transcribe the passages which gave Tom most concern:

"Yesterday I paid Squire Hudson his regular semi-annual interest, amounting to sixty-six dollars. Thanks to your generous remittances, I had no difficulty in making the payment. Indeed, I had two hundred dollars left over. Imagine my dismay when the squire told me he had made up his mind to call in the mortgage, having another use for the money.

"'But I can't pay it up,' said I.

"'You ought to be able to obtain the money somewhere,' he returned.

"'You are the only capitalist with whom I am acquainted,' said I. 'Since I have paid you the interest promptly, what more can you desire?'

"He insisted that he needed the money. I offered to pay him the two hundred dollars which he had advanced for your journey. He seemed surprised but repeated that he must have the whole. The upshot of it was that he gave me a formal notice of three months, as stipulated in the mortgage. At the end of that time, unless I am ready to pay the twenty-two hundred dollars, he will foreclose, and the old farm must be sold. Of course it will be sold much below its real value. Probably the squire will get it for the amount of the mortgage, and we shall be thrown upon the world, without a home. It seems hard, Tom, and very selfish, but might makes right, and Squire Hudson has the power on his side."

In a postscript Mark Nelson added, "I understand that Squire Hudson has a connection, his wife's brother, for whom he wants the farm. That explains his resolute refusal to give me time to redeem it. Of course it is too early to decide upon any plans. I must hire some tenement to move into when I have to leave here. It will be hard upon us all to give up the old farm. Walter, who has a taste for farming, and whom I look to be my successor, feels very sad. Don't let this news depress you too much, Tom. We shall not suffer. Thanks to you, I have some money ahead, and we shall not lack for comfort."

Tom looked up when he had finished reading the letter.

"John," he said, quickly, "when does the next steamer start for New York?"

"Day after tomorrow."

"Where can I engage passage?"

"Are you going home?"

"Yes, John, it is absolutely necessary. Squire Hudson is about to foreclose the mortgage on my father's farm. I must be there to stop it."

"Have you money enough?"

"Three times over. He shall be defeated in his wicked purpose, or my name isn't Tom Nelson."

Tom spoke in a quick, indignant tone, and his voice had a manly ring.

"Wait, John, let me read you the letter."

"The man's a mean rascal!" said Miles. "A rich man who will take advantage of a poor man's necessity to deprive him of his home deserves to be horsewhipped."

"I shan't attempt that," said Tom, smiling, "but I will disappoint him. He little thinks I have it in my power to defeat his plans."

That very evening Tom engaged passage to New York, and two days later he sailed out of the Golden Gate.

"I don't know how long I shall be gone, John," he said. "You need send me no remittances, for I have money enough with me. You will hear from me as soon as I have reached home and transacted my business with Squire Hudson."

"You will come out here again, Tom, won't you?"

"Yes, and before long. I have been so busily occupied making money that I have seen almost nothing of San Francisco."

Tom did not journey alone. Ferguson, having thriven beyond his expectations, decided to sail to New York, and thence to Scotland, on a visit to his relatives, though he thought it probable he should come back within a year. Dick Russell also was now in a position to study law at home and gave up the business of gold-mining forever.

"I owe all my present prosperity to you two," he said. "But for you I should have blown my brains out five months ago."

"We owe our prosperity to you also," said Tom. "You guided us to the mines from which we gathered a golden harvest."

"We have worked together, and been mutual helpers," said Ferguson. "God has favored us all, and to Him be the thanks!"

CHAPTER XXX

THE NIGHT BEFORE THE AUCTION

It was a sad household, that of Mark Nelson, on the day preceding the departure from the farm. There was to be an auction the next day, at which the farm-stock and farm-implements were to be sold. It was well understood that Squire Hudson was to be the buyer of the farm, and as he was not likely to have any competitor there was little hope that it would fetch more than the amount of the mortgage.

During the afternoon Mr. Nelson called on Squire Hudson to make the best terms he could at private sale.

"The farm is worth at least a thousand dollars more than the mortgage, Squire Hudson," said the farmer.

"It is worth what it will fetch, Mr. Nelson," said the squire.

"Do you mean that an article always commands its full value at auction, Squire Hudson?"

"Ahem! It brings its market value, Mr. Nelson."

"Which may be far below its intrinsic value. Suppose a diamond worth ten thousand dollars were put up at auction in our village, do you consider that it would bring a fair price?"

"Ahem! You are wandering from the subject. We are talking of farms, not diamonds."

"As to the farm, then, you are likely to be the only bidder, unless you allow the mortgage to remain."

"If I were inclined to do that I would not disturb you as long as you paid the interest promptly."

"Then you decline to buy the farm at private sale?"

"I do."

"I don't think you will be any better off in the end, Squire Hudson, for oppressing a poor man and robbing him of his little all," said Mark Nelson, bitterly.

"You don't look at the matter from a business point of view," said the squire, coldly. "I am acting as any business man would under the circumstances."

"I cannot believe you, sir. All business men are not so hard-hearted."

"I really don't think there is any use in prolonging this interview," said Squire Hudson, stiffly. "I have resolved upon my course, in which I am perfectly justified, however you may choose to regard it."

This removed the farmer's last hope, and he had only to look about for another home for his family. There was small choice of houses in the little farming town. In fact there was but one house--a shabby, dilapidated building, a mile from the church and store. This, Mr. Nelson, having no choice, engaged for a period of three months.

"It makes me homesick to think of going to live in that barn," said Sarah, as they were sitting together after supper.

"It may not be so bad as you think, Sarah," said her mother, but she secretly sympathized with her daughter.

"I wish Squire Hudson had to live there himself," said Walter, in an angry outburst.

Usually Walter was checked by his father when uttering such speeches, but tonight Mark Nelson took no notice of his son's angry remark. He felt that it would only be a righteous retribution upon the squire for his cold selfishness.

While they were sitting in the plain room endeared to them by the association of years, a sound of wheels was heard, and the village stage stopped before the door.

"Who can it be?" said Sarah, wonderingly.

The whole family hurried to the window. What youthful, yet manly figure, was that actively descending from his perch beside the driver?

"It's Tom!" exclaimed Mrs. Nelson. "Heaven be praised! It is my dear boy."

Tom was almost suffocated by the embraces which he received on entering the house.

"How you have grown, Tom!" said Sarah. "And how well you look!"

"Thank you for the compliment," said Tom, laughing. "But I don't feel well."

"What is the matter?" asked his mother, with maternal solicitude.

"I am as hungry as a bear. Have you got anything to eat in the house?"

This hint was enough. Fresh tea was made, and the wanderer was soon sitting before a bountiful supply of food, cooked in his mother's best style.

"It seems good to be at home," said Tom, looking around him, his face beaming with happiness.

"Did you get my letter, Tom, announcing the squire's intention to foreclose the mortgage?" asked his father, gravely.

"Yes, father. Is it really true?"

"Yes, he will listen to no persuasions."

"When does the sale take place?"

"Tomorrow."

"I shall be present. Have you thought of any other house, father?"

"The old Belcher house is the only one I can hire."

"That is a poor place."

"It must do for lack of a better."

"I didn't think the squire would act so meanly. At any rate, father, I will see that you don't any of you suffer for lack of money."

"Have you been doing well, Tom?" asked Walter.

"Ask me tomorrow, Walter. Tonight I want to hear all the news, and everything that has happened since I went away."

CHAPTER XXXI

BIDDING FOR THE FARM

"I apprehend," said the squire to his brother-in-law the next morning, "that we shall get the farm at our own price."

"I hope we shall, squire," said the poor relative, deferentially. "I suppose this man Nelson is sorry to part with it."

"Of course. He charges me with meanness, oppressing the poor, and so on, but of course I don't mind that. It's a matter of business, as I told him."

"To be sure."

"I am not to be moved by sentimental considerations. Business is business, but he won't see it in that light."

"You consider the farm worth considerable more than the amount of the mortgage, of course?"

"It is worth four thousand dollars, in my opinion," said the squire, complacently.

"If you get it for twenty-two hundred, it will be an excellent bargain."

"Father," exclaimed Sinclair, entering the breakfast room, rather hurriedly, "Tom Nelson has got home."

"Where did you hear this, my son?" asked Squire Hudson, in surprise.

"At the store. He got home by coach last evening."

"Got discontented, I suppose," said the squire, in a tone of triumph. "I thought that was how it would turn out. He can't expect me to advance money to take him out there again."

"I wish you would let me go," said Sinclair.

"Some day I may take a trip out there with you, my son. Have you seen Thomas?"

"No, he keeps mighty close. He hasn't even been round at the store."

"He is ashamed to show himself, I suppose. He will have to work on the farm--on a farm again."

"I suppose that will be a hard pill for him to swallow," said Sinclair.

"No doubt. He is poor and proud, like his father before him. I am glad of one thing--that I am sure of getting back the two hundred dollars I advanced for his journey. I wonder where he raised money to get back."

*****

Though there were not likely to be any competitors for the farm, a considerable number gathered at the sale. There was a general feeling of sympathy for the Nelsons, but no one was able to express that sympathy in a tangible form. Squire Hudson cared little for the opinion of his neighbors. Some of them were in debt to him, and he looked down upon them with the arrogance of wealth.

Tom received many friendly greetings. He was plainly dressed, quiet in his manner and seemed to take matters very coolly.

At length the farm was put up, the auctioneer naturally turning towards the squire, who responded pompously, "I bid twenty-two hundred dollars, the amount of the mortgage I hold upon the property."

"Is there any other bid?" asked the auctioneer.

"I bid twenty-five hundred dollars," said a clear, boyish voice.

All were startled, and all eyes were turned upon Tom Nelson, who came slightly forward.

"Twenty-five hundred!" repeated the auctioneer, hesitating whether he should receive the bid.

"I protest against this outrage," exclaimed Squire Hudson, angrily. "The bid is ridiculous."

"Why is my bid ridiculous, Squire Hudson?" asked Tom, calmly.

"Because you haven't got the money. It is a transparent attempt to run up the price of the farm."

"You know nothing of my circumstances, Squire Hudson," said Tom, independently. "I stand ready to pay the sum I bid, and, should you outbid me, I am ready to prove to any committee you may appoint, that I possess the money, or all my bids shall go for nothing, and you can have the farm at your first offer."

"That is fair!" cried all.

"This is all nonsense," said the squire. "Those of you who choose may believe this boy, I don't."

"Going at twenty-five hundred!" said the auctioneer.

"Twenty-five hundred and fifty!" said the squire, adding, "I make the bid on the terms proposed by the boy."

285

"Twenty-eight hundred!" said Tom.

"And fifty!" bid the squire.

"Three thousand!" instantly came from Tom.

No one was more surprised than Tom's own family at this unexpected scene. He had not dropped a hint as to his intentions, choosing to take all by surprise. Mark Nelson was perplexed. Though he had great confidence in Tom, he feared that he could not make good his bold bids.

At length the farm was knocked down to our hero at three thousand five hundred dollars.

"Now," said the squire, angrily, "I demand that this farce come to an end. I believe the bidding of this boy to be a premeditated swindle. If so, I will do my best to have him punished."

"And I," said Tom, boldly, "have an equal right to demand that Squire Hudson submit proof that he is responsible for the amount of his offers."

"Curse your impudence!" exclaimed the squire, foaming with rage.

"But I waive that right," continued Tom, "and will ask Squire Hudson to name two gentlemen present to examine the proofs which I have to offer of my ability to back my bids."

"I name Mr. Jones and Mr. Howe," said the squire, quickly, "and request them to act at once."

"That is my desire," said Tom.

In five minutes the committee reported that Tom had shown them bank-books, of two Boston banks, certifying that he held two thousand dollars on deposit in one, and four thousand in the other.

"Is that satisfactory?" asked Tom, coolly.

"No," shouted the squire, "I believe that the books are bogus."

But the rest of those present entertained no doubts, and our hero was at once surrounded by admiring friends, who shook his hand till it fairly ached.

"Squire Hudson, your mortgage shall be paid whenever you desire," said Tom.

"Three cheers for Tom Nelson!" proposed someone, and the cheers were given with a will. During the confusion the squire and his brother-in-law slipped out of the house, thoroughly discomfited.

CHAPTER XXXII

MANHOOD

If Squire Hudson was surprised at Tom's suddenly revealed wealth, Mr. Nelson was no less so. When Tom first commenced bidding, his father feared that he was only trying to annoy the squire or, perhaps, seeking to force him to pay a higher price for the farm. But when investigation revealed the fact of Tom's riches, and he saw the mountain of debt lifted from his little property, he was overjoyed and grateful.

"I can't understand it, Tom," he said, "how could you possibly get possession of so much money?"

"I have worked hard, father, but that won't explain it. I have been very lucky, and my good luck has enabled me to save the farm."

"I think you will be easier with me than the squire, Tom," said his father, smiling. "I will make out a mortgage to you, since your money has been used to redeem the farm."

"I shall have no claim on the farm," said Tom, "or if I have I give it to you. I have money enough for myself and hope to earn a good deal more besides."

"If that is the case, Tom, I will gladly accept your gift. It will be a great relief to think that I have no interest to pay. Now I shall be able to get along easily. I have over two hundred dollars on hand."

"I want to make your life easier, hereafter, father. I think you need a larger income than the farm will yield you, and I will therefore send you a hundred dollars every quarter."

"You are very generous, Tom, but I fear you will soon get rid of all your money at this rate."

"I will explain my circumstances, father, and then you will think differently. I have a business in San Francisco which will yield me at least a thousand dollars a year, without my personal attention, and after paying the squire what is due him I shall have about four thousand dollars left. This I mean to invest securely in Boston."

"I can hardly realize that you are so rich, Tom."

"I can scarcely realize it myself, father. When I think of the change that fifteen months have made in my circumstances I consider myself the luckiest boy in the world and have great cause for gratitude."

It will be understood that, though Tom had bid thirty-five hundred dollars for the farm, all he was required to pay was the amount of the mortgage, the bid having been made in his father's interest. In a few days the business was completed, and Mr. Nelson found himself the owner of an unencumbered property.

Tom remained a week longer in the village and then started once more for California. His mother urged him to remain at home, now that he had so much money, but Tom reminded her that he was partner in a business in San Francisco and that he needed to look after his interests there. John Miles might be sick, or die, and in that case he might meet with serious losses.

Returning to San Francisco Tom became an active instead of a silent partner. The business was considerably enlarged and became much more profitable. At the end of two years Tom sold out to his partner for several thousand dollars, and, entering an office, studied law, devoting a portion of his time to general study. At a comparatively early age he was admitted to the bar of his adopted city and, by degrees, got into lucrative practice. He had become so much attached to California that he decided to make it his permanent home.

Up among the New Hampshire hills his father still tills his little farm, but he no longer depends upon it for his entire living. Tom regularly sends the allowance he promised, and in addition his brothers are often the recipients of handsome gifts. Harry, developing a taste for study, was sent to Exeter Academy, from which in due course he was transferred to Harvard. He, too, was destined for the law, and when he had taken his legal degree, he joined Tom in California and is now his partner.

Other changes there are in the little village. Squire Hudson is dead, and Sinclair, making haste to sell the homestead, moved to New York, engaged in speculation, and lost everything. One day, shabbily dressed, he entered Tom's office in San Francisco and asked for the loan of fifty dollars to enable him to reach the mines. Tom gave it, for old acquaintance' sake. It was not the last request for money made by Sinclair. Nothing has been heard of him for some years, and it is probable that a life which was of no service to any one is finished. He had the best start in life but misused his advantages. Tom has worthily employed the talents committed to his charge and is happy, honored, and prosperous.

THE END

TEACHERS GUIDE QUESTIONS FOR THE YOUNG MINER

1. In Chapter I, Tom, Mr. Ferguson, Captain Fletcher and Mr. Peabody talk about how much they would like to earn from the mines. Tom says that he would be very satisfied with $5,000. How much is this today? How much does Mr. Peabody want to make? Does his work ethic match this goal? How do you predict Mr. Peabody will succeed?

2. In Chapter IV, before John Miles departs for San Francisco, he and Mr. Ferguson compare instances of hard work to chances of mere luck. What examples does John Miles provide to prove his point, and what does Mr. Ferguson argue? Who do you agree with and why? Do you have a different opinion of luck?

3. Chapter VII is titled "The Heathen Chinee." What does the way that Alger describes Chinese men tell you about how they were perceived during this time period? How has language and representation of groups of people changed over time? In this same chapter, Alger mentions Bret Harte twice. Who is Bret?

4. John Miles and Bill Crane both happen upon the same lonely house in the woods. How does each man approach Mrs. Brown in his first moments of acquaintance? How does each man react to the marriage proposal? What does this tell you about each man's character? Give specific examples.

5. Ebenezer Onthank makes several assumptions about Tom and Mr. Ferguson in Chapters XV and XVI relating first to nut-cakes, then their sleeping habits and finally about Tom's marksmanship. Describe these assumptions in detail, and what Mr. Onthank concludes. Was Mr. Onthank correct in making them?

6. Describe Mark Nelson and Squire Hudson's meeting in Chapter XIX. Who do you believe is correct?

7. At the end of Chapter XX, Mr. Ferguson takes less than his share of the profits he and Tom make from the sale of the wagon. What reason does Mr. Ferguson give to Tom for doing so? How has this reason motivated Tom throughout his journey and during his work?

8. In Chapter XXII, Mr. Ferguson and Tom save Richard Russell's life. Name three ways Mr. Ferguson and Tom are rewarded for saving his life.

9. At the auction for Mr. Nelson's farm, why does Squire Hudson disbelieve that Tom has enough money to counter his offer? What beliefs prevent him from accepting that Tom can pay for the mortgage?

10. After his family is able to stay on their farm, what does Tom do? What qualities does he have that you think will help him succeed? Name three and explain why you chose those three.

TEACHERS GUIDE ANSWERS FOR THE YOUNG MINER

1. Five thousand dollars in 1849 is worth roughly $151,500 today. Mr. Peabody would like to earn $50,000, but his work ethic does not match his goal. He expects gold very easy to come by.

2. John Miles argues that when "when two men work side by side with equal industry and one finds a nugget worth thousands of dollars while the other plods along at a few dollars a day," there is some luck in the former finding a large nugget of gold. He also argues that it is luck when one man is born to a wealthy family and one born to a poor family and hard work.

3. Mr. Ferguson does not so readily attribute success to luck. He argues that, "what we call good luck, generally comes from greater industry, good judgment, and, above all, the prompt use of opportunities." When Miles gives the example of a man born to wealth and a man born to poverty, Ferguson purports that in this case the one born to poverty is luckier because he is removed from temptation. Thus he believes in some types of luck, but holds true that hard work is what brings success.

4. Alger portrays Chinese men as sly, cunning and heathen, and this was how many people perceived them. Language and representation of language has changed over time because today we are more conscious to not group people together and draw broad conclusions about them. We also try to avoid generalizations that are negative. Bret Harte was an American author and poet who depicted and described the American West and pioneering life in California in the mid- to late 1800s.

5. John Miles is polite to Mrs. Brown and honestly confesses that he has no money to give her in exchange for food. He concludes that she is a strong, determined woman who can fend for herself, and when she proposes marriage to him, Miles gracefully declines. Bill Crane, on the other hand, tries to avoid paying for a meal though Mrs. Brown later offers it for free. He becomes so excited at the thought of her fortune that he agrees to marry her even though he knows little about her. These two encounters further reveal that John Miles is a level-headed, honest and thoughtful man and that Bill Crane is a bit sneaky, overly concerned with money reactionary.

6.   Ebenezer Onthank is astonished that Mr. Ferguson is not familiar with nut-cakes, and he implies that Mr. Ferguson is peculiar. Only after his shock do they realize that nut-cakes go by a different name where Mr. Ferguson comes from. When Tom and Mr. Ferguson sleep later than Onthank, he assumes that the former two are naturally lazy, though the reader understands this not to be the case. Lastly, Onthank urges Tom to give him the gun because he believes Tom to be too young and inexperienced to have accurate aim. In all three assumptions, Onthank is incorrect.

7.   During Mark Nelson and Squire Hudson's meeting, the squire continuously points to the business aspects of the loan. He has no sympathy for Mark Nelson's pleas for understanding – the squire refuses to take the drought, or the fact that they are neighbors and should be friendly, into consideration.

8.   Mr. Ferguson explains that he never could have bought the wagon if Tom did not contribute his share. Ferguson also says he is glad to help a boy who is helping and working for his family. The thought of his family and their financial needs motivates Tom to work hard and to succeed.

9.   Mr. Ferguson and Tom are rewarded for saving Richard Russell's life by making a new friend, by discovering a new, rich mining camp and by later selling the camp to new miners.

10. Squire Hudson does not believe Tom has enough money to counter his offer because Tom is so young and he cannot fathom Tom having the sufficient funds. The squire assumes it is a blatant trick to raise the bidding price and make the squire pay more. After his family is able to stay on their farm, Tom returns to California to attend to his business. He works on it for several years before selling his share, studying law and becoming an attorney.

VOCABULARY WORDS FOR
THE YOUNG MINER

bonanza: a situation or event that creates a sudden increase in wealth, good fortune, or profits

"'Tom,' he exclaimed, in excitement, 'do you see that, and that? I believe you've struck a bonanza.'"

cupidity: a greed for money or possessions

Miles confessed to himself with sadness that he had been imprudent to leave the bag where it would naturally excite the cupidity of any passing adventurer.

deign: to do something that one considers to be beneath one's dignity

Bruin deigned no reply, but continued to survey him with steady, unwinking eyes.

epicure: a person who takes considerable pleasure in fine food and drink

It might not have attracted an epicure, but neither of the three was fastidious...

espied: to catch sight of

Presently he espied the two Chinamen.

expostulate: to express strong disapproval or disagreement

"Now, Tom Scott," expostulated the landlord, "this ain't fair. I want the wagon more'n you do, and you're a-raisin' the price on me."

goluptious: splendid, delightful or magnificent

"If you ever come to Green Mountain Mills, I'll get marm to fry a batch of nut-cakes, and you'll say they're goluptious."

guileless: free of deceit; artless

But, guileless as they seemed, they had proved more than a match for Bill Crane and his victim.

lugubrious: looking or sounding sad or dismal

Crane stared at the deceptive bag in the most lugubrious astonishment.

ocular: relating to the eyes or vision

Bill Crane took another look at the contents of the bag, hoping that he had been deceived by some ocular delusion, but the second examination brought him no comfort.

pecuniary: of, relating to, or consisting of money.

Again, he had reason to think that the arrangement would benefit Tom and himself in a pecuniary way, and the Scotchman was by no means indifferent to that consideration, though, as we have seen, he did not unduly exalt the power or value of money.

prudential: involving or showing care and forethought, typically in business

Bill Crane had not filled the bag with sand and thrown it away from prudential considerations,

sward: an expanse of short grass

He selected as his breakfast table the green sward beside a sparkling mountain streamlet.

vaquero: (in Spanish-speaking parts of the US) a cowboy or a cattle driver

A shout caused Tom suddenly to turn his head, and to his joy he saw a mounted Mexican vaquero, who had brought him timely relief.

victual: food or provisions as prepared for consumption

"If you'll wait long enough for me to make some hot tea and warm the victuals, you shall have a chance to judge of my cookin'."

wanton: (of a cruel or violent action) deliberate and unprovoked

Miles decided that for some unknown reason the thief had transferred its contents to some other bag--perhaps his own--and then had discarded the original one, in wanton humor filling it instead with sand.

COMMENTARY FOR
THE YOUNG ADVENTURER AND
THE YOUNG MINER

by Rick Newcombe

While the early Horatio Alger stories took place in New York City, some of the later stories were set on the West Coast or they focused on traveling from New York to San Francisco in the 1870s. The Young Adventurer is mainly about the journey, while The Young Miner shows us what happens after they arrive.

Thomas Nelson is the hero of both books. We follow his exploits as he travels more than 3,000 miles by train, steamboat and horseback, all when he is barely 16 years old. This was an era before planes and automobiles had even been invented.

Tom's "Stories of Success" are absolutely amazing, and they are pure Horatio Alger.

We first meet Tom when he is with his father, mother, brothers and sisters on their dirt-poor farm in New Hampshire. We learn that the richest man in town, Squire Hudson, is cruel and heartless, while Tom's struggling father, Mark Nelson, is warm and loving. These are not unusual characterizations -- of nasty rich people and kind poor people -- in Horatio Alger stories.

Despite the widespread misconception that Horatio Alger was an advocate for the rich, Alger's view of money was far more nuanced. Wealth can be great, he said, and it can be awful. It can be used for good: to feed the hungry, for instance; and it can be used for evil: to force a family out of their home.

Mark Nelson's heart is filled with love and happiness, particularly since his wife, who was known as Mary Dale when they met, is so beautiful and cheerful. We learn that Squire Hudson still harbors a grudge because he wanted to marry her, but she said no and chose Mark Nelson instead. Hudson secretly vows to get even by plotting to drive the Nelsons off their farm and into the poorhouse. "When she and her children are paupers, she may regret the slight she put upon me," he says to himself.

Alger's writing style is witty, his plots are ingenious and his dialogue is clear, easy to understand and, at times, brilliant. For instance, when he wants to tell the reader that Squire Hudson's wife is not beautiful compared with Mary Nelson, he does so by allowing us to hear the squire's thoughts. His wife is talking about Mrs. Nelson, and says she is with Mark Nelson only because she did not have any other proposals of marriage, not knowing that her own husband had proposed to Mary.

The squire replied:

"'Probably she did (have other proposals), for she was a very pretty girl.'

"'Then she's faded,' said Mrs. Hudson, tossing her head.

"Squire Hudson did not reply; but as his eyes rested on the sharp, querulous face of his helpmate, and he compared it mentally with the pleasant face of Mrs. Nelson, he said to himself that, faded or not, the latter was still better looking than his wife had been in the days of her youth. Of course it would not do to say so, for Mrs. Hudson was not amiable."

Tom senses danger for his family during their discussion about finances, and he wants to do something about it. His sister and father comment about the unequal distribution of wealth. It doesn't seem fair that one family would have so much and another so little. But Horatio Alger was no socialist, and Americans in the 1870s looked to their own initiative -- not government handouts -- for creating wealth.

Publisher's Weekly magazine asserts that Horatio Alger helped form the American character, and in the 21st century, we still strive for material success through hard work, rather than taking it from others. As the columnist Charles Krauthammer said, "Americans, generally speaking, don't envy the rich. They want to be rich."

There was little chance for Tom to get rich or help his family financially if he stayed on the New Hampshire farm. It appears that the family had already moved once, from New Jersey. But this time Tom knew he would have to travel west to find his fortune. The California gold rush was in the newspapers, and Tom set a goal to join the thousands of other prospectors.

He had no money to buy tickets for traveling such a long distance. How could he possibly even begin? Horatio Alger tells us:

"The world was all before him where to choose. His available capital was small, it is true, amounting only to thirty-seven cents and a jack-knife; but he had, besides, a stout heart, a pair of strong hands, an honest face, and plenty of perseverance -- not bad equipment for a young adventurer."

This was Horatio Alger's way of telling us that the intangible virtues of courage, strength, honesty and perseverance are more important than money. If you live your life with these virtues, the money will follow.

The issue of honesty comes up repeatedly in both books, which is not surprising, considering that most Americans view honesty as one of the most important character traits of successful people. For instance, we have all heard the stories about George Washington admitting to chopping down a cherry tree, saying, "I cannot tell a lie," and Abraham Lincoln walking a long distance to return some change after a store clerk had given him too much. True or not, they are part of this nation's mythology.

Tom Nelson's honesty does not always pay off immediately -- in fact, at one point it looks like he might be put in jail -- but in the end, honesty does prove to be the best policy.

Tom has remarkable courage. He takes calculated risks in a series of thrilling adventures in both books, and he succeeds over and over.

Throughout the stories, Horatio Alger creates characters with opposing character traits, which helps the reader see the contrast between right and wrong. For instance, we see Sinclair Hudson, the arrogant son of the squire, who is lazy and envious while Tom is industrious and generous. We see the swindlers and thieves, Milton Graham and his friend Vincent, and Bill Crane in another episode, all of whom keep tripping over themselves and failing in their devious designs.

We see other thieves in The Young Miner, including two Chinese men, who are referred to as "heathens" and "Chinamen," which was typical of the times. Mark Twain wrote a newspaper story defending Chinese workers in Northern California, and he referred to them as "Chinamen," which I'm sure he meant as a term of endearment. Today, that word is considered offensive, but in the 1870s, it was not.

Native Americans don't fare much better. Native Americans were called "savages" and worse in the writings of the time, so it is not surprising to see similar descriptions in Horatio Alger stories.

The last Horatio Alger novel was written years before the passage of Prohibition, and we have no idea what Alger's political views on the subject were, but it is clear that the author was anti-alcohol in his own life. He creates a realistic fight scene in a saloon involving a temperance man from Scotland, Donald Ferguson, and a fall-down drunk American who is totally obnoxious in the Missouri tavern. Alger also was resolutely opposed to tobacco, though an occasional praiseworthy character can be seen enjoying a pipe after dinner. It was mainly the boys and young men who spent their money on cigars while visiting pool halls and saloons that he mocked.

Wearing nice clothes was so important during this time period. If you were poor, you wore rags. If you had some money, you could afford nice clothes. As part of that emphasis on appearance, a pocket watch, or vest watch, was considered a status symbol. When Tom acquires one as a gift, he agrees with his donor, Mr. Waterbury, that on the first day he will check the time every few minutes, just as Mr. Waterbury did when he was a young man with his first watch.

Let me offer two unrelated comments about the vest watch because I believe it carries great significance. First, it is important that Tom had asked his mother to sew in an extra pocket for this watch, although at the time he had neither a watch nor even the slightest prospect of obtaining one. Still, he had faith and optimism. He expected that someday he would indeed have such a watch. By having his mother sew the pocket in his vest, he was using what we today call "visualization" to achieve his goal.

Paul J. Meyer, founder of the company Success Motivation Institute, recorded a powerful speech called "The Power of Goal Setting," in which he talked about the importance of expecting positive results. He cited Charles Kettering's "birdcage theory." Kettering headed up the research department at General Motors for 20 years and was responsible for the electrical starting motor and leaded gasoline. He said that if you were to buy a birdcage and put it in your room, it would be only a matter of time before you succumbed and put a bird in it. Along the same lines, Tom Nelson had asked his mother to sew in a pocket for his vest watch, which created a constant reminder, a forced visualization, of what he wanted, and it was only a matter of time before he got the watch.

Horatio Alger was a century and a half ahead of today's motivational writers, who say the same thing but probably are unaware that they are standing on his shoulders. If you want a contemporary example, look at this passage from Rhonda Byrne's bestselling book, The Secret, which was first published in 2006. She tells the story of a woman who found her "perfect partner" by doing precisely what Tom Nelson's mother did for him by sewing that pocket:

"Then one day as she arrived home and was parking her car in the middle of her garage, she gasped as she realized that her actions were contradicting what she wanted. If her car was in the middle of the garage, there was no room for her perfect partner's car! Her actions were powerfully saying to the Universe that she did not believe she was going to receive what she had asked for. So she immediately cleaned up her garage and parked her car to one side, leaving space for her perfect partner's car on the other side."

The second observation involves the issue of how so many things of the past come back in a different form in the present. Isn't it interesting how, for more than a century after the Horatio Alger stories were first printed, most people checked the time by wearing wristwatches? They would not reach into their pockets to find a timepiece. Yet, in the 21st century, if you ask someone the time, more often than not they will reach into their pockets to check the time on their smart phone.

This is one of the most fascinating aspects of reading Horatio Alger stories -- to see America as it was between 1865 and 1900. This was a time when nearly everyone was consumed with getting rich. Mark Twain called it the "Gilded Age." Reading the Horatio Alger Series gives many details of America at the time, both externally -- the hardships, the crudeness of life without running water or electricity -- and internally, which includes the way they thought. This has been called the "climate of opinion." Money was a constant topic of conversation, and government was hardly mentioned at all. For many years after the Civil War, the federal government in Washington, D.C., was not an important part of the lives of most Americans.

At the end of The Young Miner, we see that Tom is indeed on the path to great riches. He has been able to help his family out, and he is totally independent, becoming a wealthy merchant in San Francisco. (If you want to know the value of his wealth in today's dollars, Google the words "inflation calculator," and you will find a number of websites that will help you calculate the answer.)

He also shows a generous spirit by giving the hapless Sinclair Hudson money as a favor because he is so downtrodden.

Tom Nelson lives his life with an air of "positive expectancy." He is always cheerful and optimistic. He is poised and confident. For instance, when a servant tells him to go to the back door, he politely stands his ground. He embraces hard work. He is courageous when encountering new adventures, even when it looks like the American Indians might kill him.

In other words, he is the original embodiment of the values embraced in what has become, over the years, a multibillion-dollar self-improvement industry. Horatio Alger spelled out the keys to success and happiness, not with a list of rules or principles, but by creating the ideal boy as he becomes a man. He called his central characters "heroes" because they represent the ultimate personification of the ideal young man, as he grows from adolescence, on his exciting and prosperous adventures in these inspiring "Stories of Success."

Rick Newcombe is the founder and CEO of Creators Syndicate, Creators Publishing and Sumner Books.

THE LIFE AND THEMES OF

HORATIO ALGER, JR.

By Stefan Kanfer

The Merriam-Webster Dictionary devotes one sentence to him: "Of, relating to, or resembling the fiction of Horatio Alger in which success is achieved through self-reliance and hard work."

True as far as it goes, but that sentence reveals nothing about the man or his accomplishment. Then again, other contemporary reference books are just as terse. Not one acknowledges that Alger in his day (circa 1880-1920) was a publishing phenomenon. During those decades, when a sale of 10,000 volumes was deemed a triumph, readers bought more than 200 million copies of Alger's works, placing him in a league with J.K. Rowling and Stephen King.

Alas, today most of his novels—and there are more than 100—are out of print. But not for long. Thanks to the resuscitation efforts of Sumner Books, a division of Creators Syndicate, Alger's best literary productions are being furnished with fresh covers, new fonts and energetic promotion.

Seldom has there been a more relevant illustration of the maxim that what goes around comes around. At the turn of the 19th century, Alger was the standard-bearer of a phenomenally successful experiment in social reform and personal improvement. That movement inspired disadvantaged kids to move on up, leading juvenile delinquents into productive, significant lives. Men as different as Groucho Marx and Ernest Hemingway were fans.

"Horatio Alger's books conveyed a powerful message to me," wrote Marx, "and to many of my young friends as well—that if you worked hard at your trade, the big chance would eventually come. As a child I didn't regard it as a myth, and as an old man I think of it as the story of my life."

Hemingway's sister Marcelline recalled that during their childhood, "There was one summer when Ernest couldn't get enough of Horatio Alger." Not that Alger's boys' books influenced Papa's prose style. But there must have been something in the writer's stress on grit and self-reliance that affected young Ernest, as it did so many of his contemporaries.

By the end of the Roaring Twenties, though, Horatio Alger had become as passé as the Ford Model T. During the Depression he fared no better; Nathaniel West's satirical 1934 novel, A Cool Million, sent Alger's plots in reverse, as the naïve protagonist loses limb after limb seeking success among rapacious capitalists. Decades later, the film adaptation of Hunter Thompson's 1971 novel, Fear and Loathing in Las Vegas, presented the antihero as "Horatio Alger gone mad on drugs in Las Vegas."

What lay behind Alger's ability to enchant so many Americans—and to enrage so many others? The author's story furnishes a trove of clues:

The sickly child of a Unitarian minister in Marlborough, Massachusetts, Horatio, born in 1832, was always the smallest in his class and far from an academic star. Still, his report cards were good enough for admission to Harvard. There his academic prowess was in inverse proportion to his size (5 feet 2 inches). He won prizes, published verse and fiction in undergraduate magazines, and labeled the entire four years a period of "unmixed happiness."

Decades would pass before he found such contentment again. Upon graduation, Horatio attempted to make his way as a writer. After five unsuccessful years, he returned to Harvard, this time to study at the Divinity School. In 1860 the Reverend Horatio Alger was named minister of the First Parish Unitarian Church of Brewster on Cape Cod. Salary: $800 per year. To supplement his meager income, he turned once again to writing. This time, his stories were well-received, and he allowed himself to dream of a dual career of preacher and writer. That's when catastrophe struck.

It was of his own making, if one historian is to be believed. According to this claim, a 13-year-old told his parents that the new parson had made advances to him. An investigation began. Another lad made a similar complaint. Faced with charges of behaving inappropriately, the accused was allowed to resign—with the proviso that he leave town at once.

Sometime later, Horatio wrote a poem about one Friar Anselmo, who had committed an unspecified crime. Melancholy and remorseful, he comes across a wounded traveler and gives him aid. Whereupon an angel materializes and offers salvation:

Thy guilty stains shall be washed white again
By noble service done thy fellow man.

The fugitive repaired to New York City in the spring of 1866, resolved to live out the Christian ideal, expiating his sin by saving others. The Manhattan he entered was the epicenter of the Gilded Age, a magnet for millions of ambitious climbers, drawn by the post-Civil War boom. Out of sight of the glittering prosperity, the mansions and carriages, however, was another New York, a squalid night town that travelers compared to Calcutta, India.

In The Good Old Days, They Were Terrible, historian Otto Bettmann reports that there was scarcely a slum that pedestrians could negotiate "without climbing over a heap of trash or, in rain, wading through a bed of slime." Many streets were so dangerous that policemen hesitated to walk them alone. A Gramercy Park resident noted in his diary, "Most of my friends are investing in revolvers and carry them about at night"—and the Park was one of the city's better neighborhoods.

The New York City street urchin entered the national consciousness in those years. More than 60,000 neglected or abandoned kids ran unsupervised in the street, partly because of the fallout from the tidal waves of immigration from Europe and partly because of families broken by the Civil War.

What was to be done about these juveniles likely to die on the streets or to end up behind bars? The Reverend Charles Loring Brace founded the Children's Aid Society, designed to take homeless or abused kids away from their corrosive environments. At the same time, John Hughes, New York's first Roman Catholic archbishop, set up parochial schools and a residential institution called the Catholic Protectory, which brought up abandoned or orphaned children to be useful members of society.

Horatio Alger joined these efforts at reclamation. He, too, asked himself what could be done about homeless children. Seeking answers, he wandered through the city's worst neighborhoods. He interviewed "street arabs" who spoke of broken homes, violent confrontations with parents, doomed futures. He observed how their cocky attitudes masked a profound despair. He advised them to get real jobs instead of hanging about, squandering whatever came their way from shining shoes or picking pockets. A handful nodded in agreement, expressing the desire to change their lives; most were content to take life as they found it.

Why, he pondered, did individuals subjected to the same conditions turn out so differently? One boy might become a thief, a sociopath, even a killer. His neighbor, perhaps his brother, might aim to be an upright citizen. What was the difference between them?

What saved certain boys, he came to believe, was a quality that gave them the strength to resist sloth and temptation. In a word, character. But was this inborn? In that case determinism won the day, and change was out of the question. Or, given the right opportunity and attitude, could a dispossessed youth win his share of the American dream? The latter, Alger believed—but only if the boy stopped regarding himself as a victim.

As Alger meditated upon the worst crime of the slums—the stealing of childhood from children—an idea came to him. He would be Brother Anselmo redivivus. He had sinned against youths; now he would rescue them—and in the process save himself. As the novelist put it, by depicting the situation of city waifs, he would "excite a deeper and more widespread sympathy in the public mind, as well as exert a salutary influence upon the class of whom he is writing, by setting before them inspiring examples of what energy, ambition, and an honest purpose may achieve."

Ragged Dick became the template of the fiction to follow. Subtitled Street Life in New York with the Boot Blacks, it charted the rise of a 14-year-old boy from poverty to prosperity. Dick Hunter is an adolescent with all odds against him. He has no family, he smokes, drinks alcohol when he can afford it—not very often on the small change he gets from shining gentlemen's shoes—and sleeps on gratings in the winter.

Yet something separates him from his fellow waifs. He refuses to pick pockets like the others, won't mock his elders, and yearns to "grow up 'spectable.'" His bearing and his innate decency attract the attention of upright New Yorkers. One introduces him to his church; another presents Dick with a few dollars.

The earnest youth resolves to become literate to save his money and live a clean life. One day on a walk near South Ferry he sees a toddler fall in the water. Without hesitation, Dick jumps in and saves the drowning child. In gratitude, the father, an affluent businessman, offers the rescuer a job in his office. Gainfully employed, the onetime vagabond Dick Hunter becomes Richard Hunter Esq., and shuts the door forever on the "old vagabond life which he hoped never to resume."

Naïve? Simplistic? To the jaded, the cynical and the ignorant, yes. But not to thousands of children trapped in the real world of poverty and early death. They got the message of Ragged Dick and demanded more Horatio Alger novels with more moral lessons for them to absorb. Those books changed—and in many cases saved—lives a century before Dr. Martin Luther King Jr. stated his belief that what mattered was not the color of one's skin but the content of one's character.

Today, if you listen closely you can hear, amid the jeers, the escalating sound of the last laugh. In 1947, the Horatio Alger Association was founded. It attracts more prominent men and women now than it did then. The group is dedicated to recognizing American leaders who rose, like Alger's young heroes, from humble origins "through honesty, hard work, self-reliance and perseverance." With grants to U.S. high-school students who have "faced and overcome great obstacles in their young lives," the association encourages them to emulate such enterprising and disparate members as Oprah Winfrey and Ray Kroc, Tom Brokaw and Maya Angelou, Stan Musial and Colin Powell.

They can all testify to the truths that lie between the covers of this volume. Turn the first few pages, and you'll understand why so many followed Horatio Alger's breathless, cliff-hanging chapters leading the way from skid row to success. And why so many more are about to read that map in a world where everything has changed—except the basic truths of life.

Stefan Kanfer is an award-winning writer for City Journal and the author of numerous best-selling books.

ABOUT HORATIO ALGER, JR.

Horatio Alger was born in 1832 in Chelsea, Massachusetts. He spent his early years in the small town and under the guidance of the church and his father, the town pastor, before the family moved just west of Boston to the town of Marlborough.

As a shy young boy, Alger poured himself into books and soon became a distinguished student. He studied at Harvard and Harvard Divinity School before becoming a minister. He practiced ministry for a few years near Boston and on Cape Cod, but he was distracted by his true passion: writing.

He loved to write, and by 1865 Alger had written a handful of stories, including Frank's Campaign and Paul Prescott's Charge. The latter was the first in a series of stories that would eventually lead to his great success. In 1866, Alger moved to New York to write poetry, newspaper stories and magazine articles. However, he was shocked to find so many homeless and forgotten children among the streets, an unfortunate consequence of the Civil War. He made it his duty to aid the condition of these lost children, both through his stories and by his continuous acts of benevolence.

Horatio Alger became a household name shortly after the Civil War when he began publishing stories in the form of serializations. These serializations were featured in magazines such as Student and Schoolmate and were later compiled as books. Alger's books became enormously popular, especially among teenage boys across the country, and they soon reached millions and millions of readers. Alger continued to produce several stories a year, and, in later years, wrote novels in and of themselves instead of novels from magazine serials.

The years immediately following the Civil War were the same years when the United States emerged as one nation on the road to becoming a worldwide empire. The years between 1865 and 1900 were the years of the empire builders, with the rags-to-riches stories of John D. Rockefeller, Andrew Carnegie, Cornelius Vanderbilt and Thomas Edison. They were the years that laid the foundation for Henry Ford and other business titans and for the spectacular growth of the American economy throughout the 20th century and through today. During these years, Alger published well over 100 stories, poems and novels that spoke to the timeless themes and successes of this era.

The theme of Alger's books is consistent: If you work hard, go the extra mile, are faithful and honest, show kindness and generosity, and maintain a cheerful, positive and optimistic attitude, you will succeed in creating financial security and happiness. On the other hand, if you lie, cheat, steal, are lazy or envious, and try to take advantage of other people, you will be doomed to failure and misery. Despite his background as a preacher, Alger does not make these points in a self-righteous or pontificating way. What he does instead -- just like the parables that Jesus told -- is to create stories that illustrate the virtues that lead to success. And the stories that Alger creates are no ordinary stories. Each one is filled with lively plots and twists and turns, ones that are always unexpected and keep the reader wanting to know what's going to happen next.

As Alger grew older, he continuously strived to write the Great American Novel, little realizing that the rags-to-riches stories he created were more influential than any other novelists'. He travelled out west in early 1877 searching for new material and returned near the end of the year, producing similar stories with a new western backdrop. By 1897, Alger was suffering from asthma, bronchitis and slight short-term memory loss. He moved in with his sister in South Natick, Massachusetts where he spent the last two years of his life.

Most people have never heard of Horatio Alger while some are vaguely familiar with the term "rags-to-riches." In the Alger family, it was the norm to burn correspondence and manuscripts, and this, coupled with Alger's shyness, has greatly kept him from history's limelight. Though too often forgotten today, Alger's works and the themes within them still affect the American psyche. Many assert that there is a lagging spirit in present American culture, that these inspiring stories are irrelevant. Young people are bombarded with external stimuli that make it difficult for them to get to know themselves. Wide-eyed innocence and childlike enthusiasm, once revered as admirable qualities, are sources of mockery and disdain, which makes cynicism and pessimism inevitable. Video games, television shows, movies and music are all aimed at titillating and at seeing who can be the most gritty, violent or shocking. More than a few commentators have used the word "degrading" to describe the assault that children encounter today.

This is unfortunate. Young people need heroes and role models today just as much as they did in the 1870s and '80s, when Alger was creating them at a feverish pace from his New York City apartment, writing as many as four books at a time. Publisher A.K. Loring asserted that Alger's books "captured the spirits of reborn America" for "above all you can hear the cry of triumph of the oppressed over the oppressor ... What Alger has done is to portray the soul – the ambitious soul – of the country." Years later, biographer Edwin P. Hoyt concludes that Alger is "a writer whose influence on the American scene has been so profound that it is hard to measure." Indeed, Alger's works made an overwhelming impression on American culture and society that are still alive with us today. It is for this reason that these classics must be brought to a new generation of readers.

OUR COMMITMENT TO
HORATIO ALGER

By Rick Newcombe

Sumner Books is totally committed to reviving interest in Horatio Alger, one of the best-selling authors of all time yet someone who has been all but forgotten today. I'd like to tell you how this project came about.

Probably the best starting point is to tell you a little about myself. I grew up in suburban Chicago, and my parents were religious and fundamentally optimistic in their outlook on life. They encouraged all eight of their children to be positive in our thinking and hope and pray for the best in all situations. In my adolescence, I discovered many of the self-help authors from the 20th century, including Dale Carnegie, Napoleon Hill and Norman Vincent Peale. I remember reading a small magazine in the 1970s, when I was in my 20s, called Success Unlimited and being inspired each month to work hard and stay positive. The publisher of this magazine was W. Clement Stone, who started his career selling insurance policies door to door and who went on to build Combined Insurance, which became part of Aon, one of the largest insurance companies in the world.

By the time Mr. Stone died in 2002, he was a very successful businessman, an extremely generous philanthropist and totally committed to spreading the gospel of positive thinking. I remember reading one of his books, The Success System That Never Fails, which was both an autobiography and a blueprint for achieving success. Stone told the story of spending a summer on a farm in Michigan when he was 12, getting fresh air, helping on the farm and enjoying picnics, carnivals and camping out.

W. Clement Stone

"But I'll never forget the first day I went upstairs to the attic," he wrote, "for there I met Horatio Alger. At least 50 of his books, dusty and weather-worn, were piled in the corner. I took one down to the hammock in the front yard and started to read."

Stone said he was so enthralled he couldn't stop. "I read through all of them that summer," he wrote.

He said the principle in each book was that "the hero became a success because he was a man of character -- the villain a failure because he deceived and embezzled. How many Alger books were sold? No one knows. Estimates range from 100 million to 300 million. We do know that his books inspired thousands of American boys from poor families to strive to do the right thing because it was right and to acquire wealth."

That was the first time I had heard of Horatio Alger, but it never occurred to me to try to find his books. Over the years, I founded Creators Syndicate, which became one of the most successful newspaper syndication companies in the world. I attribute much of our success to our positive thinking and upbeat attitude. We became a multimillion-dollar international corporation by syndicating a wide variety of journalists, celebrities and award-winning cartoonists.

As we were expanding into new businesses, e-books and audiobooks were a natural starting point because we work with so many talented writers and artists. But we also wanted to try new things. With that in mind, I remembered Mr. Stone's enthusiastic recommendation of Horatio Alger's books, and I decided to read some. Many were available as e-books, and I thoroughly enjoyed them.an

I had a good feeling whenever I was transported back to New York City as it was in 1870, when trains were called "cars" and there were no automobiles. There was a constant risk of crossing the streets without streetlights or walk signs. A number of years later, the Brooklyn Dodgers, now the Los Angeles Dodgers, got their name from the treacherous dodging of horses, wagons and streetcars that was required to cross the street in the city. In those days, plumbing with hot and cold running water was not taken for granted, much less radios, televisions, computers or smartphones. Are you kidding? A smartphone in the 1860s? There wasn't even a telephone.

But what great stories Alger wrote -- one after another. I couldn't get enough of them! And it was impossible not to feel grateful for all the modern conveniences of the 21st century when immersing myself in the world of America as it was in the 1860s and '70s.

As I read book after book, I felt like a teenager all over again, excited about the future and the promise of a brighter tomorrow. It was then that I decided to go full bore into spreading the word of Horatio Alger.

One of the problems with the e-books was the lack of organization; another was the maddening number of typos, over and over and over, or the lack of illustrations or the lack of a table of contents. In fact, what was intended to be a good deed to spread Mr. Alger's message really turned out to be something of a disservice.

So I made it my mission to have professional editors edit the texts so there were no typographical or spelling errors. We found appropriate illustrations. We included detailed tables of contents for each book, and we decided to publish them in groups, when appropriate, which has never been done before. We are including commentaries and teachers guides with each e-book.

We also decided to make audiobooks of as many of these "Stories of Success" as possible. We hired a terrific actor, Ben Gillman, and his initial experience shows you how far we have to go to spread the word. Ben went to the Hollywood public library to find some Horatio Alger books, but there was none. "You'd have to go to the downtown public library, in the historical section, to find those," the librarian told him.

Remember, this is one of the best-selling American authors of all time, yet it is as if he never existed.

Part of the problem is that some of the caricatures of Horatio Alger over the years have been absolutely brutal. Even to this day, the Encyclopedia Britannica, from which we expect objective reporting, calls Alger's dialogue and plots "outrageously bad." Come again? The encyclopedia is supposed to provide broad knowledge on specific subjects, not offer the biased literary criticism of a handful of editors. Talk about being unfair -- and just plain wrong!

How do you answer a cheap shot like that? Really, it is nothing more than an incredibly snooty opinion; in fact, it is an "outrageously bad" opinion. Remember, the Horatio Alger books were intended to be not great literature but rather inspirational stories to motivate young boys to achieve a better life. If the dialogue and plots were not lively and believable, the books would not have sold in the millions. The fact that Horatio Alger helped form the American character shows that an incredible number of boys ate up his books as thrilling and believable.

The brilliant writer Stefan Kanfer wrote an extensive review of Horatio Alger's works in 2000 for City Journal magazine, a publication of the prestigious Manhattan Institute. He started off believing the critics, but when he actually read some of Horatio Alger's books, he drew a totally different conclusion. "I began reading the novels aloud to my children," he wrote. "We found them well-plotted, entertaining, and instructive, not at all the righteous antiquities that I had been led to believe. Almost every chapter ends with a cliff-hanger, and all of us could hardly wait for the next night to find out what happened. The conclusions never failed to produce an emotional satisfaction and a feeling that what the author was selling -- independence, forbearance, square dealing -- was well worth buying."

We can only speculate about why the critics have been so harsh on Horatio Alger, but no doubt some it stems from their being turned off by precisely the character traits that Mr. Kanfer identifies. Like it or not, there is a mindset that scoffs at individual achievement through hard work, a positive attitude and generosity -- living every day with an "attitude of gratitude," which is the essence of Horatio Alger's message.

W. Clement Stone was routinely mocked for starting the day by saying, "I feel healthy! I feel happy! I feel terrific!" He encouraged his employees to do the same. In fact, he encouraged everyone to demonstrate outward enthusiasm and PMA, which stood for a positive mental attitude. His critics thought he was ridiculous, but Mr. Stone got the last laugh, living to age 100, which he had set as his goal, and accumulating hundreds of millions of dollars.

Roswell Crawford is an important character in Ragged Dick and Fame and Fortune because he oozes the world-owes-me-a-living attitude that is so common today. "Roswell was troubled with a large share of pride," Alger writes, "though it might have troubled himself to explain what he had to be proud of."

Roswell never understands the importance of integrity and its relationship to earning one's living. In fact, he once says that he would be happy to be paid $10 a week for nothing. "Well, if I get it, I don't care if I don't earn it," he says. In fact, Roswell is ashamed to be seen in the streets carrying a large bundle as part of a delivery for his job. Before being fired, his boss tells him, "You appear to think yourself of too great consequence to discharge properly the duties of your position."

Contrast that with Richard Hunter's attitude toward his entry-level job when he first starts working at the firm. "I'm ready to do anything that is required of me. I want to make myself useful," he says.

I have the impression that was the same attitude that Horatio Alger had as he approached his goal of becoming a successful writer who could change the world -- or at least the world of the thousands of homeless street urchins in the big city. It is difficult to imagine how bad their plight was. For instance, in 1874, which was seven years after Ragged Dick was first published, there was a little girl named Mary Ellen Wilson, who was beaten unmercifully by her stepmother. She was sent out into the streets ill-clothed in winter. There were other abuses, and they were horrible.

So a social worker named Etta Angel Wheeler wanted to intervene, to help get the child out of that environment. But there were no laws to protect children in such situations. Etta was desperate -- and clever. She enlisted the help of the American Society for the Prevention of Cruelty to Animals because animals were protected by law. Her attorneys argued that Mary Ellen, "as a member of the animal kingdom, deserved the same protection as abused animals." This led to new legislation and various child protective services.

Horatio Alger was at the forefront of this movement. He wanted to help the poor kids in the inner city, and he wound up not only helping them but inspiring millions of other young readers across the country. Many of them transformed their lives as a direct result of the inspiration of the "Stories of Success" that Horatio Alger managed to tell in one exciting setting after another.

It is not surprising that Ernest Hemingway's sister said that her brother could not get enough of Horatio Alger or that Walter Brennan, a famous actor for much of the 20th century, devoured his books. As the legendary Groucho Marx said: "Horatio Alger's books conveyed a powerful message to me and to many of my young friends -- that if you worked hard at your trade, the big chance would eventually come. As a child, I didn't regard it as a myth, and as an old man, I think of it as the story of my life."

Groucho was speaking for millions of Americans in the past and, we hope, millions more in the future.

Rick Newcombe is the founder and CEO of Creators Syndicate, Creators Publishing and Sumner Books.

PREVIEW OF ANOTHER ADVENTURE IN THE HORATIO ALGER "STORIES OF SUCCESS" SERIES

BOUND TO RISE

By Horatio Alger, Jr.

"Sit up to the table, children, breakfast's ready."

The speaker was a woman of middle age, not good-looking in the ordinary acceptation of the term, but nevertheless she looked good. She was dressed with extreme plainness, in a cheap calico; but though cheap, the dress was neat. The children she addressed were six in number, varying in age from twelve to four. The oldest, Harry, the hero of the present story, was a broad-shouldered, sturdy boy, with a frank, open face, resolute, though good-natured.

"Father isn't here," said Fanny, the second child.

"He'll be in directly. He went to the store, and he may stop as he comes back to milk."

The table was set in the center of the room, covered with a coarse tablecloth. The breakfast provided was hardly of a kind to tempt an epicure. There was a loaf of bread cut into slices, and a dish of boiled potatoes. There was no butter and no meat, for the family was very poor.

The children sat up to the table and began to eat. They were blessed with good appetites, and did not grumble, as the majority of my readers would have done, at the scanty fare. They had not been accustomed to anything better, and their appetites were not pampered by indulgence.

They had scarcely commenced the meal when the father entered. Like his wife, he was coarsely dressed. In personal appearance he resembled his oldest boy. His wife looking up as he entered perceived that he looked troubled.

Boiled potatoes: the modest meal we see the Walton family eating at the beginning of the story.

"What is the matter, Hiram?" she asked. "You look as if something had happened."

"Nothing has happened yet," he answered; "but I am afraid we are going to lose the cow."

"Going to lose the cow!" repeated Mrs. Walton in dismay.

"She is sick. I don't know what's the matter with her."

"Perhaps it is only a trifle. She may get over it during the day."

"She may, but I'm afraid she won't. Farmer Henderson's cow was taken just that way last fall, and he couldn't save her."

"What are you going to do?"

"I have been to Elihu Perkins, and he's coming over to see what he can do for her. He can save her if anybody can."

The children listened to this conversation, and, young as they were, the elder ones understood the calamity involved in the possible loss of the cow. They had but one, and that was relied upon to furnish milk for the family, and, besides a small amount of butter and cheese, not for home consumption, but for sale at the store in exchange for necessary groceries. The Waltons were too poor to indulge in these luxuries.

The father was a farmer on a small scale; that is, he cultivated ten acres of poor land, out of which he extorted a living for his family, or rather a partial living. Besides this he worked for his neighbors by the day, sometimes as a farm laborer, sometimes at odd jobs of different kinds, for he was a sort of a Jack at all trades. But his income, all told, was miserably small, and required the utmost economy and good management on the part of his wife to make it equal to the necessity of a growing family of children.

Hiram Walton was a man of good natural abilities, though of not much education, and after half an hour's conversation with him one would say, unhesitatingly, that he deserved a better fate than his hand-to-hand struggle with poverty. But he was one of those men who, for some unaccountable reason, never get on in the world. They can do a great many things creditably, but do not have the knack of conquering fortune. So Hiram had always been a poor man, and probably always would be poor. He was discontented at times, and often felt the disadvantages of his lot, but he was lacking in energy and ambition, and perhaps this was the chief reason why he did not succeed better.

After breakfast Elihu Perkins, the "cow doctor," came to the door. He was an old man with iron-gray hair, and always wore steel-bowed spectacles; at least for twenty years nobody in the town could remember ever having seen him without them. It was the general opinion that he wore them during the night. Once when questioned on the subject, he laughingly said that he "couldn't see to go to sleep without his specs".

"Well, neighbor Walton, so the cow's sick?" he said, opening the outer door without ceremony.

"Yes, Elihu, she looks down in the mouth. I hope you can save her."

"I kin tell better when I've seen the critter. When you've got through breakfast, we'll go out to the barn."

"I've got through now," said Mr. Walton, whose anxiety for the cow had diminished his appetite.

"May I go, too, father?" asked Harry, rising from the table.

"Yes, if you want to."

The three went out to the small, weather-beaten building which served as a barn for the want of a better. It was small, but still large enough to contain all the crops, which Mr. Walton could raise. Probably he could have got more out of the land if he had had means to develop its resources; but it was naturally barren, and needed much more manure than he was able to spread over it.

So the yield to an acre was correspondingly small, and likely, from year to year, to grow smaller rather than larger.

They opened the small barn door, which led to the part occupied by the cow's stall. The cow was lying down, breathing with difficulty. Elihu Perkins looked at her sharply through his specs.

"What do you think of her, neighbor Perkins?" asked the owner, anxiously.

The cow doctor shifted a piece of tobacco from one cheek to the other, and looked wise.

"I think the critter's nigh her end," he said, at last.

"Is she so bad as that?"

"Pears like it. She looks like Farmer Henderson's that died a while ago. I couldn't save her."

"Save my cow, if you can. I don't know what I should do without her."

"I'll do my best, but you mustn't blame me if I can't bring her round. You see there's this about dumb critters that makes 'em harder to cure than human bein's. They can't tell their symptoms, nor how they feel; and that's why it's harder to be a cow doctor than a doctor for humans. You've got to go by the looks, and looks is deceivin'. If I could only ask the critter how she feels, and where she feels worst, I might have some guide to go by. Not but I've had my luck. There's more'n one of 'em I've saved, if I do say it myself."

"I know you can save her if anyone can, Elihu," said Mr. Walton, who appreciated the danger of the cow, and was anxious to have the doctor begin.

"Yes, I guess I know about as much about them critters as anybody," said the garrulous old man, who had a proper appreciation of his dignity and attainments as a cow doctor. "I've had as good success as anyone I know on. If I can't cure her, you may call her a gone case. Have you got any hot water in the house?"

"I'll go in and see."

"I'll go, father," said Harry.

"Well, come right back. We have no time to lose."

Harry appreciated the need of haste as well as his father, and speedily reappeared with a pail of hot water.

"That's right, Harry," said his father. "Now you'd better go into the house and do your chores, so as not to be late for school."

Harry would have liked to remain and watch the steps, which were being taken for the recovery of the cow; but he knew he had barely time to do the "chores" referred to before school, and he was far from wishing to be late there. He had an ardent thirst for learning, and, young as he was, ranked first in the district school, which he attended. I am not about to present my young hero as a marvel of learning, for he was not so. He had improved what opportunities he had enjoyed, but these were very limited. Since he was nine years of age, his schooling had been for the most part limited to eleven weeks in the year. There was a summer as well as a winter school; but in the summer he only attended irregularly, being needed to work at home. His father could not afford to hire help, and there were many ways in which Harry, though young, could help him. So it happened that Harry, though a tolerably good scholar, was deficient in many respects, on account of the limited nature of his opportunities.

He set to work at once at the chores. First he went to the woodpile and sawed and split a quantity of wood, enough to keep the kitchen stove supplied till he came home again from school in the afternoon. This duty was regularly required of him. His father never touched the saw or the ax, but placed upon Harry the general charge of the fuel department.

After sawing and splitting what he thought to be sufficient, he carried it into the house by armfuls, and piled it up near the kitchen stove. He next drew several buckets of water from the well, for it was washing day, brought up some vegetables from the cellar to boil for lunch, and then got ready for school.

BE SURE TO LISTEN TO THE
AUDIOBOOK "STORIES OF SUCCESS"
SERIES BY HORATIO ALGER,
AVAILABLE ON AUDIBLE.COM AND
ITUNES. GO TO
WWW.SUMNERBOOKS.COM.

www.ingramcontent.com/pod-product-compliance
Lightning Source LLC
Chambersburg PA
CBHW071058250626
47159CB00002B/512